THE HIGH ROMANCE

THE MACMILLAN COMPANY
NEW YORK · BOSTON · CHICAGO · DALLAS
ATLANTA · SAN FRANCISCO

MACMILLAN & CO., LIMITED
LONDON · BOMBAY · CALCUTTA
MELBOURNE

THE MACMILLAN CO. OF CANADA, LTD.
TORONTO

THE BOOK OF
THE HIGH ROMANCE

A SPIRITUAL AUTOBIOGRAPHY

BY
MICHAEL WILLIAMS

New York
THE MACMILLAN COMPANY
1918

TO
MARGARET

There is a story inside the story written in this book, my dear Peggy; a secret story, written within and beneath and through the other one, as in a code understandable only by you and me. It is the story I could not write as it deserves to be written even though my skill were all that as a young man I used to think it was. Moreover, it ought not to be written even if I could do it; because books belong to the world but our love does not. Yet the book comes from our love, it is ours, like our children; but if we sent our children out into the world, to do some piece of work, or to carry a message, still would we know that no matter how well they might acquit themselves, their best and their loveliest belonged to us, belonged to the fireside—that fine flame of odorous pine and oak and sea-drift which has illuminated so many of the best pages of the inside-story. If, however, I were to have attempted to relate that never-ending romance which is all our own: the story that simply refuses to slacken in interest; you know, I am sure, the paragraph in the written story, the outside-story, where the other, the secret, the inside-story, would begin. Exactly how you would start it, I of course cannot tell; but for me it begins with a lonely, wild-hearted young poet staring in strange astonishment at a gypsy-faced girl— (born and bred in New England, where did she get that impetuous energy of life?), in a cream coloured waist, and a ra-a-ather short skirt, with the most bewitching little feet, curled up on a couch in a Boston boarding house (imagine it, romance, the high romance, in a Boston boarding house; but so it was). It would continue in a wizardry of moonlight, in a park where tall, dusky trees under a violet-purple sky laughed and whispered together in the warm, perfumed summer breezes, and it would be starred with mystical, musical words—like Norumbega, and Franklin. The first makes me dream of the music of wood-wind and violins—like those in Tristen and Isolde, do you remember? The second is like the chime of silver bells and cymbals, and suggests players moving in wood-land masques upon a forest bank. Are they names of places, I wonder, or magical words, part of an enchanter's spell? And there would be chapters containing other strange words and names; Nemonie, for example, and why it stands for love-in-friendship; and Marnie, and Tippyann; and why Manchester and Manchester Green bring back the thought of deep things, of things belonging only to the secret book, the inside-story. And, also, it would have to explain why in the very greatest chapters of all the true books of the high romance it is written that the love and the union of husband and wife are types and figures of the love of God for the soul, and their union; but this is like unto the story that Paul brought back from the third heaven: equally as true and equally as untellable. But this I know, and this I may say, namely, that if there has been granted to me so great a thing as even to suggest, even to hint at, the reality and the beauty of the high romance, I owe, next only to God, the thanks to my wife.

PART I
THE OUTWARD WAY

THE BOOK OF
THE HIGH ROMANCE

CHAPTER I

THE CRYSTAL HOUSE

1. My Father

MY father was a sailor who had worked his way from before the mast to the captaincy and ownership of a brigantine plying in the West Indian trade from Halifax, Nova Scotia. I do not know much about his family origin, or his early life; but it runs in my mind that his father had been a Welshman, an officer in the British Navy, who for some unknown reason retired from the service and settled in Cape Breton, where he married, and died not long afterwards. My father began his sea-faring life when he was a boy of sixteen; at first going out with the fishing fleet, and then to deeper waters, and the far places; acquiring sufficient education, at last, through his own unaided efforts to gain first a mate's, and then his captain's papers. He was a very tall, dark-featured, handsome man; who looked much more like a military officer than a sailor, so erect did he carry himself. His fellow sailors called him "The Gentleman." He was in the prime of life, and going with the fair tide of his fortunes, when he sailed away upon his last voyage, from which he never returned, and which was the beginning of my own adventures in the high romance of life.

I was then fourteen years old, and the eldest of six children; five boys and one girl. We lived in a comfortable wooden house standing in a quiet street that ran from the foot of Citadel Hill—the fortress that dominates the city—southward for a few miles, ending not far from the military graveyard.

Some distance beyond the graveyard began the forest of spruce, hemlock, and maples which covered Point Pleasant, the extremity of the peninsula on which the city lay, dividing the great harbour into two unequal portions. From the upper windows of the house there was a far glimpse of the harbour mouth and the sea. The sound of the surf could be heard at tidal hours, and the air of the street was surcharged with seasmell. The shutting down of thick fog was frequent; causing a chill and melancholy obscurity, accentuated by the dismal sound of horns and bells. I would feel an instant depression of spirit as the air darkened and dampened and the horn on Devil's Island began to groan from its hoarsened throat. I hated foggy weather, not because of darkness, for I loved the night, so long as there were stars, or the moon; but the tenebrous vagueness of the fog—the sense also of its menace to those upon the sea, obscurely offended me.

Hundreds of schooners and brigantines in those days made Halifax their home port, plying to and from the West Indies, exchanging the salt codfish,

lumber, and ice of that northland country for the rum
and molasses, sugar and fruits, of the tropics. The
vast harbour, the shores of which up to the very streets
of the city were covered with sombre forests of spruce
and hemlock, was enlivened by puffing, fussy tug-
boats and scores of white sails furling or unfurling,
and by the rattling of anchor chains, and the hearty
voices of sailors and fishermen tramping round their
capstans, or working about the wharves, singing old
chanteys or swearing in the strange dialects of Cape
Breton and Nova Scotian Scotch, French, or Irish.
Water Street and the quarter adjacent were crowded
with West Indian warehouses, marine store deal-
ers, grog-shops, and the children-stuffed tenements of families humbly dependent in one way
or another upon the moody and capricious
sea.

Morning, noon and night I heard with constant
pleasure the clear, brisk bugle calls ringing out from
the barracks near Citadel Hill. Troops frequently
marched through the city. The scarlet uniforms of
infantrymen dotted the grey of the streets with bright
spots.

Halifax in my time was the headquarters for the
British-Atlantic squadron as well as a garrison town.
It was made lively with sailors and fishermen seeking
compensation for the toil and danger of the sea.
There was the fluttering of flags, the throbbing of band
music, the blare of bugles and drumming, from the
war-ships and from a score of forts and barracks.
Strong and contagious currents of vital passions, and
the intangible yet potent sorceries wrought by the
spirits of the world, the flesh, and the devil, circulated

in its sea-freshened atmosphere. Men there came
together who knew all the ends of the earth and the
sins and joys and sufferings thereof; men of the world-
encircling army of England who had protected or
fought for its flag in Burmah, Afghanistan, or the
Indies east or west; and sailors who knew the ports
and islands of all the seas.

Twice I went with my father long voyages, when I
was very young, visiting Trinidad, Jamaica, and other
West Indian islands. But my memories of my father
especially concern themselves with his returns from
the sea. Then what fun, excitement, wonder, and romance! For when he came home from a voyage,
life in our home—as in so many other homes of
that city of the sea on such occasions—became exalted, vividly coloured, swift of movement. If it was
summer, he would drive from the wharf in an open
carriage; if it was winter, in a sleigh, with the bells
all a-jangling, the carriage or sleigh stuffed full of
gifts. There would be fragrant crates or baskets of
strange, tropical fruits: pineapples, cocoanuts, alli-
gator pears, mangoes, Jamaica oranges, sugar-cane
from Trinidad; curious shells, which we children put
to our ears in order to hear the sound of far away
waters; branches of coral; pieces of silk; and Spanish
shawls.

Fellow captains began the next day to come to this
house where during its master's long absences no men
save the priest or the doctor would be seen; only
women: the wives or the widows of seamen. These
big, rough men shook the house with their tread and
their voices; they made it suddenly seem very small.
They drank French wine from Martinique, or rum

from Barbadoes, and smoked richly odorous cigars smuggled out of Cuba or Puerto Rico.

. . . Then my father would go away again, and life slackened, and drooped and paled.

2. My Father's Last Voyage

When I was about thirteen years old, my father bought a ship of his own, mortgaging the house in Queen Street to pay for it, and took my mother and the two younger children with him on a long voyage. Two other children were placed with relatives, while Ernest and I, the two eldest, were sent to the boarding school conducted by the Jesuit Fathers in New Brunswick.

One day, some three months after entering the school, while on a high swing in the college recreation grounds, I fell, and broke my leg. I was placed in the infirmary and word of the accident was sent to my father's agents in New York—the port he was expected to call at on his homeward voyage from Jamaica.

When my mother heard of the accident nothing would satisfy her but to leave the ship at New York, hurry to me by railway and take me home; there to be coddled while my leg mended. My father was opposed to the plan. I was receiving the best of care at the infirmary of the college. I would be all right just where I was.

He wanted my mother to stay on the brigantine and go back with him to Jamaica. He had been offered a contract to take a cargo to a Central American port. It would be more profitable than the Jamaica voyage, but yellow fever was then prevalent along the Central American coast.

So my father said that if my mother remained with him he would take the Kingston offer; if she returned to Halifax, he would take the Central American freight. He had no fear of fever for himself, but, of course, he would not expose his wife and children to Yellow Jack.

My mother tried to win on both points—to return, and at the same time to get my father to consent to go to Kingston and not to Central America. He could not be moved, however, and at last my mother decided that she must go back to me. She really felt little fear for her husband. The wives of sailors are like the wives of city firemen or railway engineers—they get used, after a while, to the dangers their husbands run and take small account of matters that would appal the wives of other men.

So my mother took the train for New Brunswick, and not many days later my father sailed for Colon. On board, acting as one of the crew in order to learn seamanship, was my half-brother Matthew, my father's son by his first marriage.

My mother duly reached the college and took me home to Halifax, where I completed my period of convalescence, and then hopped around on crutches, rejoicing over my brothers, who had to go to school, while I did not.

3. How My Mother Dreamed Strange Dreams

Dreams had at one time played a large part in my mother's life. She was at this time very young, hardly more than a girl, and beautiful; a loving mother. She was a Welshwoman—of the strange, Celtic blood that has produced seers and visionaries since the dawn of history. As a girl, she had been subject to dreams of flying. She would seem to make strange and awful flights through the air, visiting countries she had never heard or read of. From these dreams she would wake exhausted, frightened, and trembling. As she grew older, however, the dreams ceased and for many years her sleep had been untroubled; until this night.

Our house, as I have said, was not far from Citadel Hill, which holds—or did hold, twenty-five years ago —a quite peculiar place in the lives of the wives and children of sailors, because it was the custom to hoist on the flagstaff surmounting the ramparts the signals of arriving ships. They would be sighted from Sambro Light, thirty miles beyond the harbour, to the south, and their coming announced by telegraph.

It was now drawing nigh the time when my father might be expected, and every day we ran into the street a dozen times to see if "his flag" was flying.

. . . .

. . . And many were the women in that seaport town who watched day after day, until their hearts sickened, for signals that never were displayed—the signals of vessels which had sailed to the Port of Missing Ships. And sometimes it happened that a signal would be shown, and yet the ship would never arrive.

. . . I remember how once we were gladdened by the appearance of a signal which denoted the approach of a vessel on which the elder of my two half-brothers was second mate. On his next voyage, he was to go with my father as first mate. His ship came so near the harbour as to take a pilot aboard. Yet she never came into port.

It was near sundown when she had been sighted. That night, there came on a blinding storm of snow and wind. The ship disappeared with more than twenty men. Her wreckage never came ashore. She must have struck a rock and sunk into the depths; or else was run down by one of several large steamers which left or entered port that night. . . .

. . . .

But now, to tell the dreams my mother dreamed, dreams which have so deeply puzzled me. . . .

She dreamed, on the first occasion, that she was awake and sitting in her room at night, where there came a fluttering and tapping of something against the window glass. Inexplicably startled, she hesitated for a long time, but at last slowly approached the window.

There, through the glass, she saw by the dim light of the lamp, a small, black bird with a cross vaguely marked in white on its breast. It was a bird strange to that northern land, but similar ones my mother had seen in sub-tropical countries.

She felt an anxiety to observe it closer. She tried to open the window to let it into the room. At this moment, however, it turned, and winged its way into the darkness.

My mother was deeply perturbed. It seemed to her that the appearance of the bird was ominous—but ominous of what, she could not tell. And even while she stood there, brooding on its coming and its meaning to her—for that it meant something to her she felt sure—the room faded before her eyes, and she was far from it, and far from the city.

As she looked, she recognized the new scene. She was before the door of my school in New Brunswick. She had come to take me home to recover from the effects of my accident. As she entered the hallway, a group of priests came forward, dressed in their long, black cassocks. They were whispering together, and were seemingly very much disturbed. From the depths of the college there came the sound of low, mournful singing and muttered prayers; all most inexpressibly dreary.

I was carried out to her in the arms of two of the bigger students, and my mother ran forward to embrace me. Just then a messenger came rushing into the hall, calling loudly on my mother's name. He was shouting:

"You are to go home at once! The Captain is very ill! He wants you!"

A priest came to my mother and told her a cab was at the door. Into this my mother and I were hurried. We were driven swiftly to a wharf.

This was a highly incongruous detail, for the college was situated in an inland town.

It seemed to my mother that the ship rushed on at a high rate of speed through a stormy sea, under a black, cloud-filled sky. But of time she had no idea. She could not tell whether it took years or seconds to make the voyage. It ended at a wharf in the harbour of Halifax. There was a cab waiting, and into this she and I were hustled by waiting men, and then the cab was driven in wild haste through a bewildering maze of streets.

As we drew near our house, a bell began to toll dismally. The street was filled with a throng of people. They pressed about the cab, stopping it, and crying out:

"You are too late! You are too late! The Captain is dead!"

The shock of the announcement awoke her, with a cry on her lips that rang through the still house, and tears streaming down her face. Even the realization of the fact that it was only a dream did not suffice to shake off her terror and grief. The next day, she told her dream to several of her friends, and said she feared it foreboded trouble.

Her friends sensibly laughed at such superstitious ideas, and when, a few days later, my mother received a letter written by my father from Colon, saying all was well, she was poignantly relieved. . . . She did not stop to think that this letter had been a long time coming from Colon, and that much might have happened since it was written.

Some weeks afterward, we children were playing in the street before our house, when one of the priests attached to the cathedral called on our mother.

A few minutes later a flustered neighbour gathered us together and took us into the kitchen, bidding us to be "very good, and not make a noise," because our mother was not well. The door of the kitchen was locked, and from behind the locked door came the sound of a woman crying. . . .

I still remember how I huddled, with two of my

brothers, close against that locked door, little children all of us, and how we wailed in our uncomprehending fear, and cried out for our mother, and beat upon the barrier between us.

. . . .

. . . The priest had brought the news of my father's death.

At the first definite words he uttered, my mother arose from her seat with a cry that rang through the house: "I know he is dead—my dream told me that!"

Yes, he was dead—and, so far as later investigation could show, allowing for the difference in time between Halifax and the point where the vessel was when death came to my father, he had died at the hour when my mother had dreamed her weird dream.

He had caught yellow fever in Colon, but struggled against the disease, until he was many days out at sea. Bad weather obliged him to expose himself, for it unfortunately chanced that the first mate was an incompetent sailor. The day he died, however, the weather was fine.

My father was in his berth when, realizing, no doubt, that his hour was at hand, he arose, walked unassisted to the deck, and laid himself down.

In plain sight of my half-brother Matthew, and of the mates and the sailors, all of whom afterwards told of the occurrence, a small, black bird with a white cross marked on its breast suddenly appeared and perched on my father's bosom, some stray bird blown off from the shore that alighted on the ship.

The awed sailors watched it. They afterward declared that the dying man's lips moved as though he spoke to the bird. Death came to him soon afterward, and then the bird, frightened by the approach of the seamen, arose and fluttered away from the ship, and winged its course toward the unseen shore.

A lock of hair was cut from the dead man's head, for his widow. They put him in the canvas coffin of the sea and launched him into the deep. He first went to sea as a boy; the most of his life was passed on blue water, and I think it well that he should still be rocked by the waves and know the deep peace of the ocean depths.

.   .   .   .

Such was my mother's dream. So far, although strange, there is nothing that cannot be explained by telepathy—by saying that perhaps my father's thoughts, reaching out strongly toward my mother as he died, influenced her thoughts, even in her sleep, and caused her dream.

This may be so—but how shall we explain the following?

Six months later, my mother dreamed another dream.

It seemed to her that she was sitting in a room in her house, with my brother Ernest in her arms, and that Ernest was a baby—although he was in fact a boy of ten.

Then it seemed to her that she saw through a nearby window a cloud coming down out of the sky and approaching the house at a speed which terrified her. But she could not cry out or move. The cloud came to the open window; it streamed through like smoke or fog; then approaching her it formed again into a denser mass, and then opened, and she saw the figure of her dead husband, dressed as she had often seen him dressed in hot weather on ship-board in the tropics—in trousers, and shirt, in his stockinged feet, collarless and bareheaded.

He said nothing, but looked at her sorrowfully, and, coming near, reached down to take the boy from her arms.

She shrank back and attempted to cling to the child—frightened, yet she knew not why, although even in her dream she knew her husband was dead. But he gently, yet irresistibly, loosened her hold on the boy and took him into his own arms.

Then the cloud closed about him and the child, and moved away, and my mother awoke with a cry.

This dream came to her on a Thursday.

The next Sunday was Easter Sunday, and on that day, while playing on the rotten ice covering a disused quarry hole in Point Pleasant Park, my brother fell through and was drowned.

4. Questions Which No Boy Can Answer

So the presence of death made itself felt very early in my life.

I remember, with special vividness, a day when I was playing with a group of boys before our house, before my father's death. We were very noisy, for the game was "Devil Steal the Sheep," and every one was engaged in thumping the adversary of mankind —an old and favourite game among the Canadian boys, in my time, but I have never seen it played by American children. We were screaming in laughter, yelling and running about; but save for our activities the street was still and empty. It was a hot, summer afternoon. The place was one remote from traffic. There was a grocery store on the corner, but no business was going forward. If we children had been still, there would have been profound silence . . . and then the silence came, we grew still.

A man appeared, walking briskly round the corner into our street. He suddenly slumped and fell upon the ground. He dropped as an old coat might slip loosely from a peg. He lay upon the ground like a garment sprawled out.

A man ran out of the grocery, other men hastily following, and we children deserted our game and scurried at their heels.

"Stand back—give him air—loosen his collar—get some water! Who's got a flask?—get away from here, you children! One of you run for the doctor!"

But one man twisted his head over his shoulder, looked up and said, "Never mind the doctor; send for the priest!"

What a queer thing! The man was dead!

And I remember how the children, an eddy of excited life, shrank back in sudden terror of this limp, disheveled heap on the ground.

The silence, I say, had come. It had come for the man on the ground; and for me. I backed away from the group, still gazing fixedly at the dead man. There was a queer feeling in the flesh of my cheeks, as though the skin had crawled tightly together.

What did this thing mean?

The man walked round the corner of the street on a sunny afternoon; a man who was going home to his

family, or to his work, or perhaps on his way to see
the cricket game on the Common. He walked round
the corner—round the corner into a sunny street, and
. . . there was no sun, no cricket, no street, no
family.

But there was death!

And what is death?

"What does it mean when you die?" I asked somebody, our housemaid, I think.

I had run into the house to tell the news.

"Oh, if you die and are a good boy, you go to
heaven!"

"Did the poor man go to heaven?"

"If he was a good man, dear. I hope to gracious
he was—poor soul—what a terrible thing! . . .
You must not ask any more questions. . . ."

Was she right?"

Must we not ask questions about death?

Is it folly to ask questions?

But I could not escape such questions. They were
constantly suggested by the many soldiers' funerals
which passed through our street.

There would come, all at once, the sound of the
music from far away, borne on the wind. There
would be the slow, dull boom of a drum. I would
hasten into the street.

The procession passed very slowly, as if reluctantly, the men bearing their rifles in unnatural positions behind their backs, with the muzzles pointing
to the ground. The dragging shuffle of their heavy
boots was even more lugubrious than the rumbling of
the muffled drums, and the mournful music that made
me feel a sad, feverish excitement. The coffin went

by on a gun carriage, outlined starkly beneath a flag. If the dead man had been an officer his orderly led his horse behind the coffin, saddled and bridled, but covered even to his head with a black cloth which gave the riderless animal an aspect strange and heraldic. So they would pass.   Men in the street would stop and lift their hats.   Presently, from the distance, would come the sound of three volleys of blank cartridges discharged over the open grave.   Sometimes I would follow the procession to the graveyard, and would draw as near to the scene as I dared, my heart throbbing painfully as the volleys shook the air.   Then the earth rattled on the coffin.   The voice of the clergyman—a strange figure in his black cassock and white surplice among the red-coated soldiers—would be heard reading the burial service.   A singular awe and wonder penetrated me when I heard the words:—

"When this corruptible shall have put on incorruption, and this mortal shall have put on immortality, . . . Oh, death, where is thy sting?   Oh, grave, where is thy victory?"

But when the soldiers returned, their heads were erect and high; their rifles pointed upward; they swung along to the liveliest of quickstep marching tunes, while the tightened drums, stripped of the black crêpe, rattled sharply as the sticks snapped down upon them.

.   .   .   .

. . . One day I remember running out into the street close to the soldiers.   Addressing one of them whose face looked good-natured, although determinedly serious, I timidly asked:

"Mister Soldier, what made the other soldier die?"

Looking at me solemnly (and aware that no officer was observing the episode), the man whispered huskily:

"Because he could not get enough air to breathe, sonny—so mind you don't run short yourself!"

Then he winked. But I had not yet been initiated into the occult significance of a blinking eyelid, and I retreated to the sidewalk, pondering upon this singular item of new knowledge, namely, that men die because they cannot get enough air to breathe!

I was profoundly puzzled. This was most strange and mysterious! Gazing upward, where, suspended beneath a blue dome, brightened by brilliant clouds a number of gulls were tracing slow, wide curves of gliding flight, it was impossible to imagine, still less to see, an end to the air. The sky, I knew, was not a solid roof enclosing the world; for this I had learned in school, along with other valuable things intended to help me through life, such as that Washington was the capital of the United States, and that two and two made four. There was air on all sides, up and down and from side to side; miles and millions of miles of air. Why then could not men get all the air they needed? Why should they die? What was it, really and truly, to die? What did the clergyman mean when he said that "This corruptible shall put on incorruptibility? . . ."

.   .   .   .

. . . Fascinating and impenetrable mysteries! For years they brooded over my mind. But I at last gave up my attempts to ask questions concerning them.

For I learned that either grown-up people were as ignorant as myself or else it was wrong to seek such knowledge.

"You're too young to ask silly questions."

"Little boys should be seen and not heard."

"Run away and don't bother me!"

"What a queer child you are, to be sure! Leave those matters alone and you'll be better off."

So I was told, and, by and by, my curiosity, retreating abashed from futile efforts to appease its hunger, remained voiceless, awaiting a more favourable time. I read more and more. I spoke less and less of the things which went on within my heart and mind and soul.

5. I Begin to Face the World

The death of my father left us in absolute poverty; and my mother opened her home (it was heavily mortgaged) to lodgers and boarders, beginning her long fight to rear her children.   Not long afterwards, I was taken from the public school and put to work in a wholesale dry goods warehouse, and began my long fight to rear *my* children,—my brood of dreams; dreams that unrestingly struggled for birth as shapes of art.

My first memory is of a dream, of a dream-idea for a story concerning a crystal house in which music played and beautiful people walked amid crepuscular corridors and gardens.   There was a sound of water; there was the stir of wind in the bushes. I did not talk of it as other children talk of their fancies—I brooded; and as soon as I could hold a pen, I built the first wavering sketch of my house, on paper, with

ink, in words. I learned to read and write at an
early age, and my conscious memories begin with this
act of literary creation.

. . . One day in school my teacher asked the boys
to repeat any verse they knew in which the word
cherubim was used. Several of them repeated lines
from hymns. I remember stumbling through a quotation from Paradise Lost. The teacher stared, and
bade me remain after school was dismissed. I wondered what mischief, unknown or unremembered, I
was to be punished for. But the teacher wished to
talk with, not at me. The raw-boned, Scotch-Irish
enthusiast walked up and down the deserted school-
room reciting his own rhymed version of Pyramus
and Thisbe. He discussed literature with me, the
hobbledehoy. He lent me a copy of Spenser's Faerie
Queen. He wished to see my writings. I walked
home slowly, luxuriously; and was too excited with
my silent happiness to eat my supper.

The teacher raged heatedly against the decision
when he learned, a few weeks later, at a time when
his pupil was being specially prepared by him for the
High School, that I was leaving him—a kind friend
of my widowed mother had obtained work for the
orphan in a wholesale dry-goods warehouse.

I made no outcry. I did not rebel. I did not
understand. I would earn enough to clothe and help
to feed me; the "opening was a splendid one"; I
would become "a drummer," a travelling salesman no
less, by and by, if I proved a good boy, faithful and
industrious; some time (who should say nay?), I
might be a member of the firm. The kind friend
of the family, reassuring my doubting and sorrowing

mother, hastened to qualify this optimistic view by pointing out the exalted splendour of such a destiny.

6. The Shadow

So I left school and went to work in the warehouse. On the day I started my new life, while walking through a small, public park that had once been a burial ground, I was brooding over a poem. It was to be about a captain, who, trying to steer his ship through a storm, amid dangerous reefs, is thrust from the helm by a stranger who appears on the deck. My idea was that the stranger was a stowaway, hiding in the hold; a man who knew the perilous waters through which the craft went staggering, and who came to the aid of the captain. But suddenly my idea changed. I seemed to see the figure on the tilted deck, pushing the captain aside. How I thrilled when I observed that beneath the sou'wester worn by the stranger there was visible no face. The apparition was no man! Who then, could he be? Who but death?

It was as though from the earth of the little park, under the shade of the tall trees nourished by the bones of the dead, there emanated a subtle and compelling suggestion of mortality that insensibly entered my mind as the morning air entered my lungs. In the grove of cool, murmuring elms—their heads warmed by the sun—beneath the brooding earth, the dead lay thick; and in the whispering leaves, in the blades of green, sweet grass, moving to the wind, the dead re-entered life, were again made part of it—life that is not complete without death. And if dead

flesh may suspire into new life through the mysterious
veins of the soil, of the trees, the grass, the atmosphere, a volatile yet essential element of the eternal
chemistry of creation, may not perished hopes and
dreams, forgotten in the depths of the soul, mystically
influence the birth of new aspirations and quicken the
womb of the spirit?   I had dreamed, almost unconsciously, of what the life of the schools, of culture,
might mean to me; and my hopes had died; and perhaps their phantoms mingled with the aura of mortality that on this morning of spring sunshine so
strangely affected me in the transformed graveyard;
bringing to me for the first time what I was never to
forget: the feeling of the part played by death in the
affairs of life.

There was no sadness, far less fear, in the new
idea.   No thoughts are sad to an artist in the act
of creating; only joy accompanies that function of
quint-essential life.   Joy is the will to live.   And my
boy's heart thrilled with the delight of the fresh
incentive, of the new thought, the powerful idea, the
element that gave my work (my work-to-be!) strength
and dignity; a necessary shadow, an essential colour
—a something that I had hitherto lacked.   There
must be rain in the air for the glorious bow to shine
forth its splendour.   Against the shadow of death,
the colours of life would more vividly glow. . . .

Slowly I passed on through the grove—ever afterward to be remembered with the tenacious faculty that
records the images of those places where our deepest
thoughts and most enduring impressions come to us
—on to the warehouse.   To start me aright in the
career that should lead me to a drummer's sample

case, they gave me a broom and a watering pot and bade me sweep the floor of the second-story stock room—a huge place, seventy yards long by forty wide.

That night my pen chafed the broken blisters on my fingers.

7. Years Of Bondage

In this warehouse, I worked for five years, from my thirteenth to my eighteenth year. It was, however, captivity with compensations. In that sleepy sea-port town—not even characteristic of Canadian commercial activities, but, as a military and naval station, dominated by British traditions and customs—commercial life was not the maelstrom in which lives swirl jostling, sinking, and rising, yet all imprisoned, as in the cities of the States. The head of the firm was a kindly Irish-Canadian member of Parliament whose father, the founder of the house, was a baronet; his eldest son was a partner; he supported pensioners; he trained what were virtually apprentices; he was very good to his employés and his example was followed by his chiefs of departments. There was one —Eduard Ryan was his name—whom I wondered at because always he was singing as he went about his work: the work which to me was so distasteful. He was very kind, and to kindness I was sensitive as a plant is to sunshine; but I avoided him, because he was an ardent Catholic, and he kept urging me toward religious duties and practices for which I had no slightest inclination.

I was stock-clerk of one entire floor of the vast four-storied building. I had to sweep the department once a week; dust the goods daily; open and empty the cases and bales; maintain my counters in neat array; and from the stock pick out the goods ordered by the drummers on the road. A great deal of my time I was alone; and I lived a singular life among the thousands of boxed neck-ties, the corsets, collars, soaps,—the "dress-goods," the "linings," the "embroideries," and the rest. Hardly a day passed that I did not bring into my place of work books borrowed from the Public Library, concealed under my coat. I secreted them in various places. I also kept manuscript volumes hidden away—made from old sample books discarded by the drummers; and on the leaves blotched with dried mucilage and patches of fabrics torn out to make room for words, I pencilled my naïve little tales and poems. . . . The artist will make use of anything.

My favourite reading, writing, and dreaming place was by a window at the rear of the building. The window opened on a court at the bottom of which I could watch craftsmen bent over their benches and tables. One was a jeweller; and sometimes there would flash in that dingy well amid the brick stores the scintillant fires of gems, or the gleam of gold. There was also a metal worker, whose hammer chinked musically; and in the autumn and winter evenings the glare of the fire from his little forge would flicker luridly upward, reddening the walls, and swaying on the ceilings of the room, causing me to thrill strangely, and vaguely to dream of stories of mystery and adventurous romance.

I made no friends. I was as solitary as a pigeon in a flight of crows. None knew of my secret dreams

—until a fat-headed drummer came across my book
of poems, told the others, and made a joke of the
matter, a joke that affected me like some shameful
indignity—my soul was bared before grossly laughing men; and I felt as a young girl might when
affronted by some immodest act.

The bell in my department rang my signal; I went
to the manager's desk and was solemnly rebuked for
wasting my time. Nevertheless, small fault was
found with my work. I earned my wage—five
dollars a month. Each year my salary increased
until I was finally receiving five dollars a week! and
I came one degree nearer the end of my career—
the drummer's room upstairs where sample trunks
are packed, and the brisk commercial travellers foregathered, gossiping and exchanging pornographic
stories.

But I never reached that end. Perhaps it was
mere chance that intervened. Or could it have been
that the architect of the house of crystal—that force
beyond the child that had breathed into the forming
brain its mystic plans—reaching out for a new
builder, another maker of things, felt that its apprentice had served years enough of bondage in this
place? . . .

8. Adolescence

For a period of more than a year, I ceased to write,
and read little. Life was subtly, powerfully asserting
its claim upon my body, as well as upon that peculiar
use it demanded of my spirit. There were times
when I felt choked to the point of suffocation within
the four granite walls of the warehouse, into which

the sunshine and air came only through the few opened windows.

Every day at noon a cannon was fired from the ramparts of Fort St. George, on Citadel Hill. While its explosion was shaking the air, hundreds upon hundreds of pigeons would mount from the streets in swirling, interweaving, rising and falling intricacies of flight, the sunshine gleaming on their feathers of white, of pale purple, of softly iridescent blues and greys and mauves. Then they would mass, and sweep in long, looping curves to and fro—an arabesque of life traced upon the sky, a thrilling rhythm made visible. At last, reaching the roof of the Post Office in the market square, they would separate, and settle with fluttering wings and pink, reaching claws, while their soft, liquid cooings came distinctly to my ears as I stood, fascinated, at a window. At these moments, the sense of my captivity would well up behind the starting tears, like a wave that carries spray on its crest.

Or from this upper window I would watch the sailing ships and steamers going to and fro in the harbour; schooners from the fog-held banks of Newfoundland, laden with fish; vessels from Europe and the United States; brigantines from the warm islands of the Caribbean Sea; craft from all the ends of the earth. I felt beneath my feet the heave of the sea, as I had known it in my childhood voyages with my father; I remembered the wondrous islands, where palm trees waved and I plucked tropical fruit; the coolies of Trinidad; the negroes of Barbadoes; the leap and flash of flying fish; the spouting of a whale; the hurricane off Cape Hatteras; the rum my father smuggled from Jamaica which the sailors stole and, drinking, fought through a sudden storm blaspheming, each man-Jack of them drunk most gloriously, —all this I recalled in vivid recurrence of the original sensations, picture after picture flitting before my eyes.

Most clearly of all would I remember a naked youth in Jamaica who came riding at dawn to the beach with six spirited horses that went rearing and plunging into the water of the bay, their manes blowing out above them, their hoofs threshing, while the youth, his bronze body gleaming, strong and lithe and swift, dived from their backs, swam beneath the bellies of the horses, climbed upon their necks; sure, confident, masterful. That boy did not work amid corsets and soaps and dress-goods, cooped up in a warehouse—not he!

A drummer appeared; or a customer; or the elevator rumbled upwards with goods; and from my brooding reveries I would be called to work—

But no! I was called from work!

—In the summer mornings I often rose at daybreak, and went to a wharf in the harbour to plunge into the water, into the cool, fresh morning flood. This wharf was near the spruce forest beyond the city. The air was surcharged with sea-salt and fir-balsam. The vast mouth of the harbour yawned sleepily, still veiled in morning mist, upon the Atlantic;—the Atlantic; that great sea whose name always stirred me like the master-word of a necromancer's spell. The water lipped and lapped on the beach, murmuring and whispering— Oh, of what? There were forts and batteries in the forest;

red-coated soldiers appeared, to fish from the rocks for flounders, smoking their clay pipes and laughing. I was sure that if I could only stay and talk with them I should hear rare stories of warfare and wanderings in far lands.

Or vagabonds from the town walked slouchingly along the roads; they lit fires on the sand and dug clams; gathered periwinkles and mussels, and dulse, that edible sea-weed, and concocted for themselves wonderful breakfasts. There was one lame drunkard who would steal a bottle of milk on his way to the shore for the day, and his fish or clam-chowder was famous.

Curlews and kingfishers skimmed the level reaches by the brackish pond; the gulls began their foraging; the fishermen from Herring Cove were putting out to the banks; anchored ships got under way; brassy bugles blared drill calls from the forts; a detachment of Royal Engineers marched at ease along the road, the young officer in command, smiling to himself and thinking of the dance at Government House the night before. . . .

But time will not linger for dreamers; I had to go home, eat breakfast, get to the warehouse at eight o'clock, and sweep my department, amid the muddy smell made by the water sprinkled on a dusty floor.

9. The Words That Would Not Come

. . . Saturday afternoons and Sundays were my own, all my own; and they were devoted to rambles in the woods, and along the shore. I carried a book but read little. Sometimes, in the midst of a fit of

brooding, I would start into intense physical activity
and race at top speed, leaping from rock to rock; or
climb a tree and swing to the ground again from a
bending bough.   Or in a secluded place I engaged
in some mysterious play of make-believe such as
might have pleased a boy of ten—my lost childhood
living on in my elder blood, struggling to attain the
joys of which it had been deprived.   Or, my mood
modulating to the key of mystic dreams, suddenly
as I was walking, or stretched on the grass, in the
sun, my open book neglected, in the summer air there
would come the wavering semblance of the house of
crystal, and through its shadowy though not gloomy
corridors, through the gardens of dim colours, the
sounds of music, and the influences of perfumes, there
would pass vague and mysterious figures.   Some
were Queens or pale Princesses of romance, followed
by their maidens.   How unlike was their walk, undu-
lant, soft and light, to the tramplings of the Royal
Engineers, the slouching step of the envied vagabonds,
the rolling gait of sailors!   What was in their eyes
that troubled me, that hinted at stories such as sailors
and tramps and soldiers did not know?   Why did my
heart beat hurriedly, why did my breath come faster,
why did my blood become warmer, so that I felt it
running through my veins?

And often the day passed, and the stars appeared,
and night was upon me before I turned homeward.
Stars, or the moon, shedding pale light on the wide
harbour; a white thread of tinkling foam on the black
sand; the trees sighing strangely; the water soughing
amid the shoal-rocks off shore—and I would fuse into
one vast flood of feeling all things that affected me.

The house of crystal would waveringly change to new shapes and receive new guests. The sailors, fishers, vagabonds and business men would mingle with the fair women, amid the music; and invariably while some revel was going on, and the windows shone with lights, while vague love-scenes were enacted in the misty gardens, and wine flowed at the board within—invariably the shadow would appear, he whose face could not be seen, he who on the tilted deck of the dream ship had thrust the Captain from the tiller. . . .

One night just as I thus thought of death interrupting the revels in the house of crystal, I emerged from a clump of trees, and my shadow appeared, bobbed for a breath on the glimmering dust of the roadway, and then suddenly was absorbed in the darkness by the hedge. I stood still, stricken by a thought. Even as all men had shadows of their bodies, so also had they shadows of their souls, of their essence, projected from their bodily forms into space; and these shadows were their deaths! . . .

But upon the writing paper I could not ensnare my thought; I could not build, only dream. The magic words would not come. In despair, I threw aside the pen and crept into bed, crying like a girl-child, convinced that something had happened to me, and that never again would I write.

10. Music Consoled Me

And more and more I plunged myself into all life that I could enter.

One real, potent pleasure I received through membership in the band of one of the local regiments of volunteers. The acme of my pleasure came when the regiment went route marching.

In the big parade ground the long line would break into company formation, then into fours, marking time; the proud colonel would nod, and an important major shout: " Quick march!"

"Rub-adub-adub-adub-adub! Rub-adub-adub-adub-adub!"

Twice the drums roll loudly, inspiringly; the big drum booming, the kettle drums snarling, followed by the full-voiced crash of brass and wood-wind as the band, fifty strong, step forth, leading the line. The gates of the parade ground open; the expectant crowd in the street is parted; the volunteers dimly see the faces of their admiring or envying friends, sisters, sweethearts. . . . The moment is tense; I thrill, as, with small boys holding oil-torches that smoke and flare ruddily to light the music cards of the bandsmen, the regiment pours out from the armoury, the trampling of their steady feet sounding like unto huger and hollower drums than those that pound before them. Above, there is the high, purple, starry vault of the summer sky. The sea-wind is blowing, full of smells of the sea; it bends the flame and smoke of the torches backward. I march in one of the ranks of the clarinets; but I rarely play the instrument, although I hold it to my mouth. I am listening to the others, entranced by the sound; fascinated and stirred to my heart by the romance of this nocturnal expedition; and although I keep step sturdily, I walk as one in a dream. The tossing crimson of the torch-light; the gleams of brass and

German silver, of pipe-clayed helmets and scarlet
tunics; the rhythmic thud of the feet behind me, the
sense of the irresistible onwardness of the regiment
holding me and compelling me forward; the dim
thoughts of war; thoughts that this battalion had
marched into battle, and that again it might do so,
I with it—all this got into my blood like fever.

Twice a week I went to the bandroom for practice.
I was a music-lover, but not a musician; for a long
time I did not advance beyond the stand of the third
clarinets; but I was quite content to be there blowing
monotonous notes of accompaniments! "tul-lul-lul-lul-
la! Tul-lul-lul-lul-la!" over and over again, among
the fifty players, mostly young men of the city, clerks,
mechanics, small business men, but all musicians on
these nights, and smokers and beer drinkers to a man.
And with real love, deep earnestness, they would blow
into the rumbling or cracking brass, the sweet or shrill
sounding wood or reed, tunking the stretched sheep-
skin, clashing upon the cymbals, standing in a circle
at their wooden music stands beneath the malodorous
oil-lamps around which clung and eddied blue-grey
wisps of tobacco-smoke, producing a semblance at
least of the magical sounds of music; and at times
as I stood there with the clarinet held silently at
my mouth, my senses would seem to swim, to bathe,
to dive, to immerse themselves in the torrent of tone
that issued from this assemblage of puffed-cheeked,
sweating men.

11. The Stock Boy Turns Editor

So this year, my nineteenth, passed, and still I
was lonely, still I lived the life of a solitary. I had

family affections; family cares, duties, ties; I even had a few acquaintances that might be termed friends. But what a man wants; what a man will travel the wide world over to find, is sympathy, and appreciation of his work—whatever the work may be. Two plumbers meet—and they can commingle in sympathy as they can solder a joint together. So with a statesman, a singer, a hunter,—what not. I, like most artists, could become interested in any man, and in any man's work; I could understand the peculiar problem of the drummer, of the band-master, of my mother, my sister, my brothers, my friends; but none could understand mine; I lived, so far as all my associates were concerned, in the fourth dimension.

At the end of this year my eagerness to read and write returned as insensibly as it had left me; and I became acquainted with a book-seller interested in literature who wished to start a little magazine. The book-seller engaged to find advertisers enough to pay the printing bills; I undertook the editorship—which meant that I tried to fill the pages of the pamphlet with my own work and some matter clipped from English periodicals. I was not to receive any pay; by and by, we agreed, the magazine would be profitable; then I would have a salary; I would be a free man.

I prepared the matter for the printer; some of my verses; an essay on Robert Louis Stevenson, the ruling literary god of my firmament at that time (R. L. S. had just died); and a sheaf of clippings. Leaving the stock-room at odd times during the day, with cap hidden under jacket, I would steal out the back door where the goods were handled and run at the top of my speed to the printer. My first proofs were won-

derful to me as treasures from the cave where Ali
Baba spake the magic word of fortune. I corrected
them by means of the page on proof-reading which I
tore from the back of the old dictionary at home.

And one day while I was patiently following the
foot-steps of a drummer about the warehouse, dragging a huge wheeled basket in which I was placing
the goods selected to fill the drummer's order, I suddenly heard from the street without the shrill voices
of newsboys calling out the name of my magazine.

What a moment! Something thrilled within me to
the very core of my being; in the depths of my nature
something stirred, erecting itself. It seemed to stand
amid all the darkness, all the doubts, all the uncertainties, upright and indestructible, the centre of all
things; something that dominated—like the figure
I in a medley of letters, around which the others may
be grouped or after which they may be marshalled—
like I prefixed to the letters c-a-n d-o; or the letters
w-i-l-l;—I will; I can do! I had accomplished something—a deed akin to what I desired to do; I had
planted a seed of will, and a flower had sprung from
the soil of circumstances; and, this being so, on this
highway I would travel; and the future opened in a
flash before me like a landscape seen by lightning at
night. . . .

But the drummer said: "For God's sake, kid, get a
move on! What's the matter, anyhow?" And in
words of the same sense my employers spoke to me
soon afterwards. I could not "serve two masters"; I
could not expect to edit a magazine in the time which
they, my employers, hired from me; they had noticed
that my usefulness had been steadily decreasing; in

short, would I take four weeks' notice, or leave at the end of the present month with an extra month's salary?

I accepted the latter alternative. I left the ware-house without emotion, save a faint regret in that never again would I loaf and dream, read and write, in the corner by the corset counter; even my sense of freedom did not reach elation; perhaps because my poor mother took the dismissal so much to heart. It meant more work and worry for her; but I am afraid I did not think of that. I plunged into the work of the magazine; but it lived for only three numbers. The book-seller found that the advertisements did not pay the printer. And he was newly married; his wife did not care for me; indeed, I readily divined— as, without thought or effort I divined the moods of others—that she was jealous. She was a pretty girl, tall and almost stately, and the bookseller was a little man, dyspeptic and be-pimpled; nevertheless she wanted him all the time, jealous even of his thoughts. I remember smiling and marvelling; then I sighed and wondered if ever a woman, entering life from my house of crystal, would desire me as the pretty girl desired the little book-seller.

.   .   .   .

So the magazine died, and went the way of other dreams.

It had gained for me, however, several precious things.

From faraway England came a letter from a real Author: a world-renowned writer, to whom I had sent a copy of my magazine containing my first published story; telling me that I must persevere. "You are an untrained writer, but unquestionably you have power. Keep on," wrote the great English writer. I carried that letter in my pocket for many years. I still treasure it in my heart. It was signed, Israel Zangwill. (It was twenty-five years ago when you sent me that letter, my dear Mr. Zangwill; and no doubt you long ago forgot it—but kind deeds never die.)

Also, I gained a friend; and discovered an author, at one stroke. For in the same street where I had lived all my lonely boyhood years, there had been living a fellow writer, and we had not known each other; another dreamer, and we had dreamed apart. But now I met him! I published his first story. And from the United States, from the editor of a magazine celebrated for its literary quality, came a letter to my contributor praising his work; asking him for stories. So William Holloway's career began; and in time his work was well known in many magazines. And our friendship has endured through all the years since we met, and in a little room, the two of us only, formed the Pine Tree Club—devoted to the discussion and promulgation of Literature: our own in especial.

But, alas, this did not last long, and soon we separated, and I did not see or hear from my new friend for nearly ten years.

For now we left Halifax, for Boston; where we had relatives, and where, we believed, there would be better paid work for all in a great city with room for all who came, with theatres, concert-halls, schools, books, magazines: the *Atlantic Monthly!*—a city where I was to become a famous writer, with life made rich with work, with liberty to create my dreams; with the pursuit of happiness at last begun under favouring auspices.

CHAPTER II

THE HOUSE OF IRON

1. Boston

O UR romantic illusions in regard to Boston soon were dispelled.

Instead of our spacious, airy house in its own big yard near the harbour beach, we lived in a five-roomed tenement, among the crowded tenements of Roxbury.

The wages we boys earned as errand lads, or the like, were larger, indeed, than we earned in Canada—but the purchasing power was so much less. Our mother was obliged to leave the home each day, and work over a sewing machine down-town; returning at night to take up the house-work for the large family.

For several bitter years I lived in Boston in wretchedness, in humiliation, in swinking bodily toil, in grinding poverty.

Utterly without business education, or business faculties, with a heart full of dreams, but with a mind almost wholly untrained, and destitute of friendship or influence, I was quickly submerged in the depths of unskilled labour.

I could not even secure a clerkship in a department store; the best I could do was to tie up bundles in the packing-room.

Afterwards I got employment above ground as a

clerk in a tea store, but my lovable and picturesque employer drank himself into bankruptcy, and again economic necessity hailed me to labour underground as a porter in the filthy, rat-ridden, dank sub-cellar of a five-and-ten-cent store.

I had no leaning toward any craft or trade—save that of writing, and in that, only instinctively; sans practical ideas, I was totally ignorant of how to enter upon the life of letters in the United States, save by writing, and writing, and then writing; but what I wrote at that time was almost entirely without appeal to the magazines.

. . . .

Do you know what a five-and-ten cent store is? Some Americans have made millions of dollars out of them. They exist by selling the cheapest of cheap and nasty goods to the poor, and to the would-be economical. They do not advertise, but seek a position in all the cities they enter where they can gain the advantage of the advertising done by the great department stores. They employ the cheapest of girl-labour. One of their characteristic tricks is to fill a window with, say agateware sauce-pans that could not possibly be bought elsewhere for less than twenty-five cents, together with a placard stating that this "bargain" will be available on a day several weeks ahead. On the appointed morning there is a string of women sometimes a block long in line before the door is opened, and all day long the store is packed with struggling, jostling, cross-tempered women. Now mark the full beauty of the idea! The saucepans are placed on a small table far up the store, in its centre, where only a few people can get at them at a time—and the rest must willy-nilly flood the store, and await their turns—and buy other goods. The cheapness of the trash tempts the pennies away from the poor. A woman will enter to buy a five-cent corkscrew and come out with it and three crooked saucers for a nickel, a shaving cup for a dime, and so on; perhaps a dollar will go.

My employment as porter in this place was the best I could find. Of business I knew nothing, save how to sweep floors, take care of goods, and wait on customers; but at this latter occupation I had never been proficient, never successful; I could not create with my tones, my words, gestures, and manner, that subtle atmosphere in which a buyer, insensibly yet irresistibly, is led by the real salesman to the purchase of wares. The little suggestions of look and tone; the easy fibs and bigger lies; the tricks of persuasion, the onleading wiles—all these I could not master.

—I was one of a gang of twenty men and boys driven by a foreman of half African blood. The foreman was tall, strong, swarthily handsome. When he doffed his overalls at night and stepped out into the streets the figure of an aristocrat of Abyssinia or of Numidia who should not have been wearing American clothes (well as his fitted him), but who should have been driving slaves with a seven-thonged whip through the torrid sand of some equatorial desert. In the gang there was a drink-broken greybeard who had once preached on predestination from a pulpit in Scotland. There was a lean, saturnine Westerner who at night was a professional poker-player in the cheap hotels of the equivocal West End. He worked by day merely as a blind. The cellar was as a jungle wherein he hid in the hours of the sun. There was an aging, silent, neck-bent man who once had owned a grocery store; and although he was neither strong nor agile, he laboured harder than any of the others for his nine dollars a week. The rest was riff-raff,—the rag-tag and bob-tail of the drifting unemployed. Continually they were coming and going; constantly getting drunk and fighting on the job; sometimes stealing; and being discharged and hired from day to day; sometimes from hour to hour. Recruits never failed this gang of unskilled, the unplaced, the nondescript, the inefficient.

We toiled furiously—because the foreman was there; and well did he select his pace-makers. He had eyes of amused scorn, and a voice like poisoned wine. He would tell you in vibrant, musical accents, and smilingly, what a misshapen, malingering, putty-boned hound of the gutters you were as he handed you your time-slip and sent for another man. And through the cavernous cellar his sweetly sonorous tones would purl in a romantic song. He delighted in telling his love-stories to his favourite hanger-on, his pimp, so that others could hear him; and in low snarling words many of the slaves, angry at the thought of white girls smiling at him, would whisper: "The nigger! The dirty nigger!" He knew this, but lounged among us in confident dominance. He had the same indifferent, cynical scorn for us sweat-dirtied slaves of the sub-cellar, whom he drove to mean tasks, as the non-drinking saloon-keeper has for the alcoholics who line the bar, dribbling foolish maunderings—and supplying him with a living.

From the street, far above, the barrels, crates, bales, and boxes were ever rumbling down on the elevators. We received and opened them, distributing their contents through the maze of departments in the vast store overhead. All day long we ran or walked or shuffled—according to our energy, our temperament, or our degree of proximity to the foreman, floorwalkers, or manager—loaded with dishes, candy, dolls, wash-pans—any of the ten thousand and one things sold in the store. Others laboured with the hammers and nail-pullers, bent above the barrels and boxes under the flaring arc-lights, encircled by hectic halos, that hissed in the dark, dust-laden air that was like unto prismatic scum on the surface of a stagnant pool. There was a smell, acrid and powerful—ammoniacal —of damp straw, of rats, of sweat, of tobacco juice, of whiskey and gin, of steam and gas and coal fumes.

I was one of those who ran to and fro with the loads. That was my job from eight o'clock in the morning until noon; from one until six o'clock. I would much rather have never left the cellar. Down there I toiled among fellow slaves; down there I was alone and unseen—the other slaves did not count. But to come up from the cellar and stagger with a load through the crowds of women, and make my way among them to behind the counters where the shop-girls whisked their skirts to make room for me to pile the goods away—I whose dream was of women moving harmoniously through the corridors and gardens of a house of crystal—I who had not known of women buying and selling, chaffering, steal-

ing, brow-beating, back-biting, shuffling, struggling—
this was what made me dream agonies at night.

2. Gleams From The Palace of Art

And I had come to Boston to read books in
the Public Library, and write songs and tales for
which I was to get enough money to support my
mother and sister! I brought as contents of my war-
chest in the descent upon Boston, a number of poems;
the half of a novel; the sketch of a play; and a round
score of short stories. They were nearly all about
the sea. Unfortunately, they were not concerned
with piracies, melodramatic storms, rescues and adventures; but dealt with what you think and dream
of the ocean; what you suppose the sea hoarsely
whispers to itself, and what the gulls watch as they
soar and dip off-shore. My father had died and
been buried at sea; his father had been a sailor. I
had been born on the shore and lived there for nearly
twenty years. There was salt in my blood; there was
a kelpie in my heart; there were storms and calms,
depths and mysteries, fogs and boundless horizons
in my soul.

Why, then, was I not a sailor instead of a slave
in the cellar of a ten-cent store? But why do not
saints go to Heaven? They stay on earth to show
the way to God; and I was land-bound because I
wished to sing the desire of the sea.

By night I sat up till all hours reading and writing
or went prowling through the more crowded city
streets, taking, in Baudelaire's phrase, baths of multitude, and meeting with curious adventures, singular

acquaintances; and learning much queer lore about life. At this time, remember, I was still a growing boy, and it's a good thing that my physique possessed the stamina, the innate strength that it must. I was always reading; carrying books in my pocket to read in the noon hour among the loafers in Boston Common, the fishermen on Tea Wharf, the teamsters around Fanueil Hall Market, for I can always make myself easy on a curbstone, a doorstep, the stringpiece of a dock. I was a constant patron of the Public Library, and on Sundays would often visit the Art Gallery on the side of Copley Square opposite the Library. There I haunted a corner where hung a number of William Blake's drawings, and Burne Jones' "Chaunt D'Amour." I dreamed curious, vague dreams before Blake's pictures, those pictures in which gods and souls move in unearthly rhythms amid swirling eddies of air, fire and water; and I drank of a morbid, and at that time unanalyzable, pleasure before the "Chaunt D'Amour"; thinking today that the fever of sickness then springing up in my body influenced me to recognize those consumptive dreamers, swooning life away in languid ecstacies by the stagnant moat, as fellows of myself! Whistler's etchings brought a more tangible joy. Here was the beauty of real life, of the actual, of the everyday, transmuted by art; and they made me at once humble and ambitious . . . could not words be wrought in a like spirit? Yes, I would think, but I am so ignorant, I have no skill, and I must spend my time sweeping floors, opening crates, lugging goods. . . . Nevertheless, since it is the case with me that if I should be placed in the electric chair I should certainly spend some of my last minutes in dreaming of how the shock of the lethal current, the twitching of the stricken body, and the thoughts of the doomed soul might be rendered in words, even then I was considering how the fellow helots with whom I sweated and sickened could be utilized as literary material. . . .

   .   .   .   .

I had no friends, I who love friends. An old companion of my boyhood was in Boston, but we drifted apart in the city ways. My most constant companion was my landlord, a queer alcoholic Irishman who lived in one of his own tenements and knew Shakespeare by heart, but nothing else; and he knew the bard only as Poll Parrot knows the human language, with no comprehension of ideas. We struck up an odd kind of convivial comradeship, for he was a kind-hearted man, and my friendships are not dependent on my ideas (thanks for that goodly gift, O Life!). Over liquor-slopped tables in the back room of barrooms we carried on interminable discussions of Shakespeare, and quarrelled; for I am Celtic myself, and relish a ruction.

And my poems and stories, sent to the magazines, returned. The whistle of the postman would peal its signal in the dark, grimy, narrow hall-way of the seven-storied rabbit warren of a tenement house where we lived in five little rooms; and I would run to the door to snatch the big envelopes from the letter-slip before the other should have a chance to see them. They all came back, every one.

There was something wrong with my work; it was

bringing no money, to say nothing about place and
name. And I *must* work—I *must* earn money!
The cost of living in the city was frightful—the rent,
the coal, the gas, the food, the clothes—everything
was expensive; you had even to pay car-fare to get
to and from your job. My brothers were finding
difficulty in securing and keeping employment, though
they, unhampered by my particular ambition, were
succeeding better. Yet they earned little,—at best
they could only get positions as messengers and office
boys. Soon, perhaps, even my sister might have
to go into a store, my little sister, my pretty sister,
and when I thought of this possibility, and of the
girls in the ten-cent store, paid three or four dollars
a week, moiling behind the counters, beneath the
earth, under the glaring arc-lights, in the dust and
fetid, sweat-tainted air, tempted by the lewd men
who haunted the stores, driven by task-masters,
jostling together in an outrageous promiscuity—when
I thought of all this, I suffered bitter pain; and
knew that whatever the cost to myself I must hold on
to my job in the basement; must fight with others
for that job; must follow the pace keyed up by the
foreman unto the last peg—unto the point where my
heart strings would snap as a fiddle string snaps when
drawn too tightly.

3. A Gleam of Joy

And on the stretched strings of my heart singular
tunes were played by that force in life to which I was
an instrument. I sang no longer the desire of the
sea; I related no more naïve little legends of what

I supposed the sea hoarsely whispers to itself and what the gulls watch as they soar and dip off-shore. The salt of my blood savoured no rhyming words, but got into my secret tears; and the kelpie that was in my heart instead of singing, wailed. The feature-less shadow—the apparition glimpsed so many times before, companioned my thoughts now, instead of merely visiting them.

The house of crystal grew faint, withdrew into far-off mists, and in the times when I divined its outlines, their soft shimmer, their opalescent hues were not visible; they were harsh; they darkened; and it seemed to me that it was becoming a house of iron, filled with brazen clangours, in which hurried, writhen phantoms of despair jostled in a drive of the dead. Every night I wrote, slowly, with pain and trouble, sometimes far into the late hours; occasion-ally until the grey dawn-light feebly struggled down the shaft. Grim, mordant, bitter, hopeless themes—hard, bleak, iron words.

I did not try to sell these stories; I had no further hope of that kind. They were written because—because I had to write them, even if I had been the one man in the world who could read.

And while I was in the full swing of my night work, a change came into my life. The manager of the store had been watching me; saw that I worked hard; saw that I was not one of the mob of hopelessly inefficient; and one day, to my amazement I was made floor-walker in one of the smaller departments, where twenty girls (girls from sixteen to sixty years old) sold tinware and kitchen utensils. My wages were increased to twelve dollars a week; the manager told me that if I made good I should be given a better position; that, in time, if I should prove a capable, faithful, and industrious employé, I might be made the manager of one of the firm's many stores.

But I was never so employed. Perhaps it was mere chance that intervened. Or could it have been that the architect of the house of iron; the artist who played upon the stretched strings of my heart—that force beyond me that had breathed into the tormented brain its mystic plans, which had reached out for a new builder, another maker of things—felt now that its apprentice had served enough time in bondage in this place?

One day I went to the Common to eat my lunch, and sat there on the bench on the Park Street Mall— those benches of the unshaven, the benches of the un- employed; where loafed the drifting members of the unplaced, the nondescript, the inefficient, the purely unfortunate,—the anonymous mob from which my fellow helots were recruited and into which they so quickly fell back. After eating my sandwiches, languidly—for of late I had had no appetite; I had been languishing in queer fits of depression, of fever, and of listlessness—I idly picked from the ground a wind-blown newspaper, several days old, and glanced over it absently. Suddenly my eyes light- ened; I read with interest, with growing excitement, at last, absorbedly, the contents of a column on the back page. There were quotations from poets new to me; a short story translated from the French; a number of witty, spirited paragraphs written in a singularly lucid and musical prose.

Philip Hale, in the *Boston Journal,* and his daily column, "Talk of the Day!"

I had been deeply—though for years uncritically, uncomprehendingly, disappointed in American current literature. There was so little artistry in the fiction; so obvious a lack of style, force, originality, beauty. How indifferently the magazines compared with Henley's New Review, for example, to which I was devoted when Wells, and Charles Whibley and Joseph Conrad and Max Beerbohm and W. B. Yeats, and others of that great group of writers were appearing with the first fruits of the modern movements!

Of course, there were exceptions. There was Stephen Crane, for example, among writers, and Frank Norris. There was the *Chap Book* and the *Lark,* among periodicals; a few spirits here and there refusing to yield to the curse of commercialism, the malediction of Mammon, which is the blight of American magazines—of most English ones, too, for that matter. And now I had made this great discovery, in this wind-blown newspaper!

How eagerly I devoured it, this food my nature craved, this food that stimulated and refined my appetite for art, and nourished my soul!

I am not by any means singular in my admiring opinion of Mr. Hale's artistry, my appreciation of his splendidly lucid, colourful and musical prose style, and of his vital, illuminating wit and irony; and those who are competent to judge also speak wonderingly of his vast erudition. I know that he has been of far-reaching and inspiring influence, especially among young writers; and if ever I do good work I shall know who helped me most to do

it. Every day thereafter I bought this newspaper;
and at the end of the week, I sent one of my stories,
anonymously, to the editor of the column.

It was printed the next morning! I read it on
the car while hanging to a strap, amid my fellow-
workers.

What a moment! Something thrilled within me,
to the very core of my being; in the depths of my
nature something stirred, erecting itself. It seemed
to stand firmly amid all the doubts, the darkness, the
uncertainties, upright and indestructible, the centre
of all things; something that dominated—like the
letter I in a medley of letters, around which the others
may be grouped or marshalled; like I prefixed to
the letters c-a-n—d-o; or to the letters W-i-l-l; I can
do! I will! I had accomplished something, a deed
akin to what I desired to do; I had planted a seed of
will, and a flower had sprung from the soil of circumstances. This being so, on this highway I would
travel, and the future opened before me in a flash,
like a landscape seen by lightning at night. . . .

4. The Red Hieroglyphic

But the manager said to me, "I'm sorry; I shall
have to take you from your present position; you are
far too easy with the girls; they are becoming de-
moralized in your room—Oh, yes; you may return
to your old place."

And I returned, at the smaller wage, to toil amid
the slaves of the gang; under the flaring arc-lights encircled by hectic haloes as they hissed in the dark,
dust-laden air, that was like unto prismatic scum on

the surface of a stagnant pool; amid the smell, acrid and powerful, of damp straw, of rats, of sweat, of tobacco juice, of gin and whiskey, of steam, and gas, and coal fumes.

Yet even there joy entered my heart. Twice a week or so throughout the summer months a story of mine was printed in the newspaper.

Once or twice, too, letters appeared, commenting on some particular tale. Also, I sent a poem to the *Transcript*, and one day two copies of that great paper came to my tenement, copies containing my poem! I carried the clippings in my pocket, and oftentimes I would take them out, and read—as a dram-drinker steals to his bottle. . . .

—The weakness that had come upon me in the spring increased.

By night I would sweat and cough.

At last, one night, in the depth of winter, something clicked in my throat; my mouth filled with a peculiar taste; I got up, lighted a lamp,—and the something was red; a scarlet hieroglyphic of ominous portent was scrawled upon my handkerchief—and it dampened, and it spread. . . .

Through the rest of the dark hours I was untroubled by cough or restlessness. Wrapped in singular, imperturbable calm, I lay sleepless; and my room-mate was the Shadow, faceless as ever; but I was sure that if its countenance were visible it would show a smile. . . .

The next day I lost my wages of a dollar and a quarter by not showing up at my job. Instead, I

went to the City Hospital; where, after hours of waiting, I at last found myself stripped to the waist, taking
my turn to be examined between an old negro and
a giant of a Norwegian sailor, both of them coughing
like machines, while two physicians went over us
with a stethoscope, and with their questions and their
eyes.   I did not mind their stethoscope, but their cold,
calm, searching eyes afflicted me with a gnawing fear
I had much difficulty in concealing.

"You may dress," one told me.   I obeyed.   Then
they weighed me.   Nothing more was said until I
mustered courage enough to address the chief of the
two physicians.

"Ah, do you think, doctor—do you think—that
blood—was it—was it—"

"Yes; it was from your lungs," he said—

I felt a shock like a blow struck, ridiculously
enough, as even then it seemed to me, in the pit of
my stomach, instead of my heart (I was not aware
of the existence of one's solar plexus in those days!);
a blow that dizzied me, and for a moment all sounds
seemed far away, and the persons around me dim
and distant; but I gulped at the water held to my
lips, and said, "Thank you, doctor, for your advice,"
when I was told that I must leave my employment and
go somewhere and live in the open air.   I left the
hospital holding a card in my hand, which I did not
look at until I reached the street.   Then I read the
top line, printed in large letters "ADVICE TO CON-
SUMPTIVE PATIENTS"; and suddenly I began to
run—I ran as fast as I could, as though I could thus
escape the Pallid One, the Infector of Crowds, the
White Plague of America.

5. Friendship Again

This happening, at any rate, released me from one captivity, even if it placed me in another form of bondage. They let me go from the sub-cellar; I had grown too weak for that job.

And then, one afternoon, I carried into execution a thought which had long been in my mind, and kept putting off, and playing with day after day. I mustered up courage to call upon the editor of *Talk of the Day*. I had often walked through that block in narrow crooked Washington Street which later I was to know so well, where the newspapers are congregated; and gazed at the windows of the *Journal*, and wondered what it was like, inside there.

But this day I actually ventured inside. It was a place just like most newspaper quarters, from Boston to San Francisco: dingy, dirty, dim, and complicated as to stairs, passages, rooms.

But finally I got to the editorial offices. I enquired for Mr. Hale.

"Who is it wants to see him," asked the Cerberus at the door; the usual supercilious office boy.

"Tell him it is the Quietist," I said.

This was the name I signed to my tales and sketches. Somewhere or other I had read a paragraph about "Molinos the Quietist," and the name and ambiguous title (for I had then not the remotest notion of who Molinos really was, or what Quietism could be) pleased me, and I adopted them as my pseudonym.

A man who seemed to me to be about nine feet high (he actually was no taller than myself), came to the door, and I knew (because he loomed so gigantically) that this was Philip Hale!

"Are you the Quietist?" he demanded.

I nodded. I cannot remember if I spoke.

"Good Lord!" he exclaimed. "And I thought you were an old man, with solemn whiskers, who had been everywhere, and seen everything. Come in! Come in."

So began our acquaintance. He soon extracted my story. And then my stories began to be paid for: out of his own pocket, I afterwards discovered, as the *Journal* did not pay for outside contributions to this column.

Later on, he introduced me to Mr. Edward William Thompson, then connected with the *Youth's Companion;* and Mr. Thompson tried his kindest best to help me shape my peculiar craftsmanship so that I could earn some money through it; and, indeed, I did succeed in writing a number of stories and verses which the *Youth's Companion* bought.

But my health was steadily declining, I had hemorrhage after hemorrhage; and Mr. Thompson and Mr. Hale got up a small subscription fund, and saved my life by enabling me to leave Boston and go to North Carolina. . . .

. . . .

And these good friends did more than that. They gave me something, at least, of what I longed for—that which a man will travel the wild world over to find—appreciation of his work; the fellowship of his peculiar kind, insofar as it might be extended by veterans of the pen to a raw and most crude beginner.

. . . .

—Years later, when I collected my Quietist tales in a volume, and Bliss Carman tried to make a certain firm of publishers live up to a promise to publish them (which they did not) I made a slight sign of my gratitude to Mr. Hale by dedicating the book to him. But the publishers would not publish it: they said it was too morbid and unhappy. So I dedicated, instead, my son to Philip Hale; giving him the name of his father's friend. There is nothing morbid or unhappy about this latter offspring, anyhow!

.   .   .   .

6. I Go South.

I went by boat to Norfolk, Virginia, and thence to North Carolina. That journey was a joyful adventure, in spite of my weakness.

The great sea took me back to its bosom, for a space, and whispered the old, soothing stories; and the brooding pine-wood received me as its neophyte.

Again the stars shone in high, arching domes; once more the sun poured out the wine of life, and the moon distilled the ichor of dreams; the flowers grew for me; the wind talked to me, in the trees, in the grass, in the bush, voices of the vaster life that moves in the forms of men and women.

And all the men and women, the soldiers, the tramps, the floor-walkers, the shop-girls, the business men, now moved as they had not moved before— humanly, individually; not as mere puppets of a sardonic Shadow; and I saw them in the light that

had shone upon me out of the heart of my friends
—the light of human kindness.

Ah, where should I be were it not for the kindness
of men and women upon whom I had no claim save
that I was poor, and they gave me to eat and drink;
and fallen, and they raised me up; and sick, and they
came to my assistance?

Long ago, an impotent failure, I should have
yielded utterly to the waiting Shadow, and the House
of Iron would have shut its door upon me for ever.

Friendship—kindness—mutual aid!

These carried me out of the sub-cellar, away for
ever from the toilers and the moilers; but I knew
they were still my brothers and my sisters. I saw
that they were doing as I had done—toiling for the
use of the life that was in them, as the conditions of
the world imposed; toiling in those ways because
they must, as perhaps they would not if in them
spoke as clearly as in me the call to their real work
—to the work in which there is joy. And upon me,
too, again might come captivity unto bitter, unlovable
tasks. Well, if so I must not moil blindly as
before. Death, the seeming enemy, had proved
my friend—had been my rescuer; had inspired the
necessity of the struggle for life. Whatever happened
to me in the future, I was and should remain,
free, because my soul was free. In the midst of all
the doubts, darkness, and uncertainties that surrounded
me, there was something to which I could
rally—there was myself; and there were others. I
was not alone any longer. And if I had been helped,
so also might I help.

Assured of my function I knew myself to be one of the many builders of the crystal house, which the house of iron vainly tries to hide; the house of life; built of its sorrows and joys; the abode of the dreams of men; and even if death claimed me at my labour, some other builder would make out of my doom something of beauty for the tabernacle of man's far vision—would shape a storied window—or, perhaps, place a column in its court; a memorial appropriate and inspiring—erect and dominating, like the letter I.

CHAPTER III

SHAPES OF DEATH

THIS flight southward was my last encounter with my shadowy adversary—or my Friend (I knew not which) during this first period of my boyhood and my youth; a period which was only the prelude to farther and stranger adventures, and deeper, and higher romance; but during my stay in North Carolina I was placed in a position of intimacy with the Shadowy Watcher.

Not for a long time yet, however, was I to learn anything more than the outer, surface aspects of my ambiguous companion.

I have already spoken of my emotions when the scarlet hieroglyphic announced the coming of the white plague upon me; and so I will merely repeat that to the best of my recollection, my feelings could be summed up in the word "indifference." At least, consciously I was indifferent, although it is obvious that subconsciously I was not; for I made decided efforts to escape the doom that was threatened. What I mean is, that in the face of the actual probability that I might fail in my fight, I seemed unmoved, and uncaring. I have often asked myself why this was so; why I, who vibrate to life deeply and continually in so many directions, should have felt that cold carelessness in the face of death. Perhaps it was because life at that time held little of joy; there was nothing in Boston or my Boston life that gave me abiding satisfaction, or seemed worth while living for. Any one who had to work as I worked, and where I worked, certainly could have little reason for regretting leaving it even by the last door of all.

. . . .

The little town where I lived in the South was a town of death. Nearly every day in the busy season, the winter months, when the hotels and the boarding houses were crowded with victims of tuberculosis, was marked by a death. The train that passed through at midnight for the north was popularly known as "the stiffs' express," since it rarely happened that when it stopped a long box was not lifted into the express car. Men and women would come to this town who were beyond all hope of being saved; having simply been ordered south by some physician who wished to get rid of them. It was pitiable beyond words; and ugly beyond painting. And of those who came, by far the most were utterly ignorant of what to do to be saved. They seemed to consider that there was, or that there ought to be, some miraculous or magical quality in the mere "climate" of the place which would save them, or which ought to save them, without the necessity on their part of doing anything at all. And so they would stay indoors, and the men would haunt the billiard rooms and bowling alleys amid the dust and tobacco smoke, and the women, all those that were able, would exert themselves dancing in airless, dusty rooms at the hotels, or sit up late at card parties, and when the coughing, and the sweating, and the wasting away of tissue and of flesh did not stop, but continued, then the querulous complainings would arise on all sides, "I don't think much of the climate of this place—it's a fake!" To back up the supposed magical quality of the "climate," the only thing the most of these exiles from life would do was to swill enormous quantities of various deadly drugs. The odours of creosote and of whiskey were at all times strong. They dosed themselves, and gargled themselves, and thrust their noses into evil smelling clouds of smoke supposed to be a cure for asthma; but they did not sleep in the open air, they did not live in the open air; and so, of course, they died. And the house and the rooms they died in were haunted; they left their disease behind them; there is no doubt in the world that many a weak person coming to this town from the north was infected with disease from the germs left behind by the dead. The consumptives crawled or stalked through the streets, or sat around the post-office, or the bowling alleys, or on the verandas of the hotels; and constantly they hawked and they spat. Of all the knowledge which modern science and progressive human experience has placed at the disposal of the sufferers from the worst of all American diseases, there was apparent in this place but the merest shadow. Here and there you found a physician or a patient who had some idea of the value of open air; but the rest seemed to fear it as they feared the white plague itself. They talked of "Draughts," and "chills," and "breezes," and "night air," as if they were talking of assassins concealed everywhere about their path awaiting the fitting moment to assault them.   And so, as I say, they died; they died; and the midnight train was "the stiffs' express."   And as this town was, so are hundreds of others of such places throughout the land.   It must not be supposed that the truth which is established to-day, that in the air is life for the consumptive, has by any means been recognized in any widespread fashion.

.   .   .   .

The town was too horrible (and too expensive) and after a while I went to live in a one-roomed shack a mile or so from the town, directly opposite a board-ing house where a number of poor labourers lived. Not far away, on the opposite side of the road, there was a ramshackle box factory.   One morning I was thrown out of my bed by some concussion, or shock, the cause of which I knew not.   Bewildered, I ran to the window, and looking out, saw some people running across a field; and was impressed at once by the strange aspect of the landscape.   Just what lent this air of strangeness to the view, I could not at first determine; until all at once it ran across my mind with a shock, "Why, the tall chimney of the box factory is down!"   I hurried into my clothes, and ran along the road.   The box factory was in ruins.   The boiler had exploded, they had hauled one dead man out of the wreck of splintered and shattered boards and bricks, and now they were digging amid the wreckage to get out another man who was groaning.   These two men were the engineer and his fireman.   If the explosion had occurred half

an hour later, some thirty or forty girls and boys
would have been blown up along with the building.
As I got up to the place they had found the groaning
man, and I helped to carry him to the boarding house,
where he had lived. By and by the doctor came, a
little German Jew, who was a consumptive himself,
and a man of quite extraordinary ability; but of
morals that made him the abhorrence of the community. He and I always got along very well, however, since his "housekeeper" and his brandy
debauches meant little that was abhorrent to me. He
pounced upon me at once to help him; and he had
a tough job on hand, there was no doubt of that.
The injured man had swallowed steam; he was a
tremendously powerful young man, and he was
thrashing about the bed in an agony. The people in
the house were useless with bewilderment and excitement. I had to help the doctor while he examined
the man; but we had to call upon the others to assist
us. It took five or six of us to hold the man down
upon the bed. The doctor said there was no hope
for him, that he would probably die in an hour or
two. As a matter of fact, he lived for twenty hours;
and even the continual administration of morphine
could not keep him quiet. I was with him from the
time he was brought into the house until the time
he died, since I was the only person in the neighbour-
hood who did not have to work, and so I remained,
at my friend the doctor's advice, to be of what service
I could. There was not a clean towel, nor a piece
of decent linen in that poor house; so I brought over
from my shack one of my night shirts to put on the
sufferer and some other articles of the kind. Dur-

ing the day, there was little for me to do, but assist
about the bedside; but through the night that followed,
I was alone most of the time, and that night was
hideous.

The young man's parents had been sent for and
might come at any time. Every time I heard a step
without, or whenever the door was opened, I expected
to see a sorrowful, poor mother, and the father.
The thought of the father did not disturb me very
much; but the notion of meeting the mother of this
tortured creature on the bed made me flinch every
time it came to me. He was a dreadful sight; burned,
and scarred, blackened, and blood-bedabbled.

All night long he tossed in delirium, moaning, and
his lungs rattled every time he breathed; and only
once during the night did he seem to have a gleam
of consciousness; and that time he looked at me and
said my name. The utterance of my name frightened
me. I remembered how I jumped and stared at him,
inwardly trembling. I had never seen a man die;
except that one man who dropped dead in the street
when I was a child; I had never watched or waited
by the bedside of one dying; I had never felt life
go out of a human body. This was now my experience, for shortly after dawn, when a dim, wan light
struggled into the room, making the red glow of the
oil lamp seem sickly and morbid, a strange change
came over the aspect of the boy—he was no more
than a boy in years, for all his huge size and terrible
strength. Although no amount of washing had
availed to remove the black stains etched upon the
flesh of his face by the fire and explosion, yet now
a perceptible pallor spread over it under the veil of

the grime. I saw his hand grope upon his breast, and I took the hand between my own; his eyes opened and shut and his mouth opened and shut, and then I felt him die—the departing life beat and trembled and twitched in all the little nerves and muscles of his hand, although the hand itself no longer moved; but all the nerves vibrated like piano strings when you run your fingers over them; a figure of speech which expresses as closely as I can the actual movement of the tendons of his wrist, but which does not at all depict the singular emotion which this movement communicated to me. For a moment I felt as though through these twitchings and tremblings he was trying to speak to me, to communicate some message; but it soon died away; the eyes and the mouth closed, then the jaw dropped, and he was dead.

Not long afterwards his father came; it seemed that his mother could not. A little, humble, work-bent man, he stood and looked a moment at what was on the bed; and then turned away without a word and without a sign. Then came those who perform the last offices for the dead, and I, too, went away. . . .

I returned to my shack, and tried to get some sleep; but I could not do so, and all day long I moved about in a state of nervous tension. That night I attended a meeting of the local "literary club"—a quaint collection of rustic young men and young women who went in for "studies" of various authors of the day. The little town was of course very much excited by the disaster; and I, as an actual participant in the scene, was greatly in demand. I had to relate my story so many times, that at last I began, almost unconsciously, to embroider it with comments. The fact that the young man had died in my night shirt was a circumstance which added a piquantly macabre touch to my narrative. I can still remember the very young and silly kind of pleasure which I took in astonishing the young women who acted as if they were delightfully shocked, by saying: "Oh, well, the poor fellow was an honest soul, and I am sure he will return that night dress of mine when he is through with it. He cannot need it where he is going, you know, for I don't believe they wear them up above, and down below the climate does not permit of the indulgence." I stayed at the club until the last member left, for I knew by the way I felt that a sleepless night was before me; but by ten o'clock the party had broken up and by eleven o'clock the last loiterer had left the closet in one of the local hotels where, despite the prohibition laws of the county, one could get something to drink. I still lingered talking with the hotel keeper, but by twelve o'clock I was homeward bound. My road lay along the railway track for a mile out of town, and then the shortest way to my shack was to plunge to my right through the grounds where the ruins of the box factory were strewn about. When I reached this place I was suddenly seized upon by one of those unaccountable gusts of atavistic superstition that at times seize upon us all. I simply loathed the notion of passing through the wreckage of that mill. My flesh shrank from the ordeal, as though grimy fingers of spectres were reaching out to touch it. And a grimly whimsical fancy popped into my head, and tormented me as many grave reasons for real fear have not done:

"Suppose he is really waiting for me, somewhere among the shadows, with that night dress?" And I seemed to see the pallor of that piece of linen in every patch of light among the scattered fragments of the factory. To go roundabout the factory grounds would have taken me off my course several hundred yards; and rather than give in to my fit of superstitious trembling, I braced myself and pushed across the grounds.

I reached my shack and unlocked the door, and entered, and struck a match to light my lamp—and the next instant I had started back against the wall, transfixed, and quivering with horror. There before me, in the red flare of the match, I saw—sure enough! I saw my night shirt. It had been returned. It had come back! And I felt certain that the one I loaned it to must also be present. Only by a powerful effort of will was I able to steady myself and refrain from rushing blindly out of the shack.

Once I had lighted my lantern, however, it was certain that to outward vision, at any rate, the dead man was not present. Hanging over the foot of the bed was the night gown, however.

As I afterwards discovered, the poor woman who kept the boarding house had taken the night shirt from the corner where it had been thrown by the undertaker; and had washed and ironed it out, and then had brought it to my shack, reaching in through the window, which was never locked, and placing it upon the bed, to be ready for me when I required it. Her thrifty soul objected to wasting a perfectly good garment. . . .

.   .   .   .

When I went north again with the hole in my lungs temporarily stopped up, I drifted into newspaper work as a reporter; and thereafter I had many dealings with the shadow; indeed, I became, as most newspaper reporters are, one of his busy chroniclers. Suicides . . . murders . . . wrecks . . . fires . . . accidents, of many sorts; how many volumes would my newspaper accounts of these make up, I wonder? A shelf full at least.

At night, in a crowded and mephitic courtroom, watching curiously a handcuffed man while he stands up at the bidding of the clerk of the court: "Look upon the jury! Jury look upon the prisoner! Do you find him guilty or not guilty?"

"Guilty," says the foreman; and a growl of voices rumbles through the room—a man has been condemned to death by his fellowmen for the slaying of another. Everybody feasts morbidly upon the sight of the man who is to be hanged by the neck. . . . Thrice have I witnessed such a scene, in Boston or New York, and once have I heard the voice of a mob of ten thousand cheer a verdict of "not guilty" in a famous case. They were cheering the escape from death, not the proving of innocence.

. . . .

And I remember one horrible night—horrible in the retrospect, for at the time I was callous enough —when I took part in a death watch in Charlestown jail, in Boston. A murderer who was to be the first victim of the electric chair in Massachusetts was dying of consumption; would the doctors succeed in keeping him alive long enough to go to his man-ordained doom, or would the bacilli of tuberculosis cheat the chair of its prize? The time of the electrocution was drawing nigh; and the bacilli were working hard —how would the contest result? It was a pretty problem—wonderful story for the "yellows." Hundreds of thousands of readers were interested; the sheriff's office was thronged with reporters from various papers and news associations; and we sent in bulletins by telephone to our offices, and swapped stories and cigars with the officials, and wondered if the dying man would die after our papers had gone to press and thus throw the story to the evening editions? It would be a shabby trick on his part, to be sure!

—And once, permitted to enter the prison beyond the office, I heard the doleful, beastlike, choking cry of the frenzied, fevered, fear-tortured, ignorant Italian peasant for whom the great Hoe presses stood waiting, and whom managing editors were discussing in a dozen editorial offices—his story was selling papers; he was a circulation booster. . . .

And his horrible cry reverberated through the iron silences of the house of horror; and it tailed off into a groaning cough.

But he lived to be electrocuted; the editors and the business managers being duly grateful.

. . . .

Serving many newspapers, I have known the morgues of cities from New York to San Francisco as intimately as most men know their bedrooms; I have counted the shapeless dead as they were dragged out from railroad wrecks, or carried out from a great city hotel that had burned; I have followed the hunt after murderers; and bent with the coroner, sometimes before the coroner, over the suicidal victims of carbolic acid, pistol, knife, rope, drownings. And always my editor was eager for the story of it; he sought zealously the reason for each murder, suicide, accident, but how seldom were the real reasons even hinted at!

I remember one good story I found of a death under an elevator in a department store. . . .

But I was young at my trade, at the time, and so my error was found excusable when I tried to get my story into print—a story of culpable negligence on the part of the management of the store—*a store that was a big advertiser!*

That story was not told. It was one more of the many needless deaths that occur by the thousands. I have heard coroner's juries solemnly rebuke railway companies, and newspapers shriek for the district attorney to do something after some peculiarly horrible wreck; but nothing is ever done, nothing really essential. . . .

For nothing can be done until the axe shall be laid to the root of the tree that yields this everlasting crop of needless and horrible deaths—the tree of selfish Profit. Men and women are killing each other continually, by murder, disease, suicide, or "accidents," that are more truly crimes, because they will not give up selfish profit-seeking and run trains, and do all business, and print newspapers, not to make money for themselves at the expense of others, but as parts of a loving service of man by man. . . .

But if all these truly unnecessary shapes of death were eliminated, would there still not remain many, many forms of painful and sudden and horrible deaths, cutting lives off from the daylight and the sun, and causing endless grief and pain?

Yes.

Then there is a mystery here which no human solution of the subject appears to reveal?

It does indeed thus seem to be.

Yet I cannot, I do not, nor shall I ever rest, until I find an answer to this mystery of death!

CHAPTER IV

THE YELLOW GOD

1. Grub Street

FOR eighteen months I remained in the south. During the first few months I suffered many breakdowns; but after that my favourable environment, and my youth, and the vigorous constitution which underlay the weakened organism, combined to restore me. I earned my living in a variety of ways. For a time I edited a weekly newspaper for an absentee proprietor. He returned unexpectedly one day, and found the office occupied by a group of jolly loafers who were helping me to dispose of a jug of native wine sent as payment for an advertisement; as other advertisements paid my board, and my barbering, etc. He was properly shocked by this orgy, for he was a devout Presbyterian or Methodist, or something; and we parted company.

Hard times followed, interspersed with joy days when the very occasional checks for successful stories came. I carried the chain of a surveyor's party running the line of a projected railway. I picked blackberries in the harvest season, at a penny a quart; and in other vagabondish modes I managed to get along.

I remember one tough time when credit was refused me at the grocery store. But the milkman was more patient, and continued to deliver a quart of milk each morning. When the embargo began, I had half a loaf of bread in my cupboard, a can of cocoa, a package of cornstarch, and a bag of sugar.

So I boiled a pot of cornstarch, and ate it with milk and sugar and bread, and defied all grocers. The second day it occurred to me to flavour my somewhat savourless pudding with cocoa and sugar. The result was ravishing. Brillat-Savarin himself could not have been prouder of his choicest culinary creation than I of this chocolate pudding!

By the end of five or six days of cornstarch, chocolate pudding and milk, I was not so full of gusto. In fact I was not very full of anything. When night would come, I walked to the postoffice—to see if any relief had arrived. I kept away from the streets by day, ashamed to face my creditors.

Then came a check for fifty dollars!

What a meal I had, at the local hotel!

.   .   .   .

Yet in spite of such hardships, and of even more serious handicaps; my frequent alcoholic excesses, for example—my strength returned; and at last I went back to Boston, and resumed my efforts to gain a footing as a writer.

It was a difficult period for me, a period of transition and unsettled conditions in all ways.

The work which I had done for Philip Hale's column had been produced with an almost complete spontaneity. Ideas, or, more exactly, moods which expressed themselves in the form of very brief sketches or tales—fantastic, ironic, mordant in tone—

came to me from I knew not where; and I wrote them down right away, with few changes or revisions. Unquestionably, they possessed literary, artistic, merit; but only by such an editor as Philip Hale could they find recognition or acceptance.

With the ordinary publications, the magazines and newspapers, I was absolutely out of it with this kind of work. Many editors, it is true, wrote to me praising this or that, approving the literary merit of my work, the power of its style, etc. But my tales and sketches were "unhappy," or "morbid," or "unpleasant"; they were therefore unsalable, and I had not yet learned how to write the commercialized stories which have made our American magazines so mediocre and futile; in fact, I could do very little successful work of any kind at that time, or for years later, if I approached my subject consciously.

In those first years, however, in my Quietest sketches and tales, I was (within my own limitations, which were palpable) quite distinctively an artist; a maker of things of beauty for beauty's sake. I did not dream of writing for money first, or success.

Indeed, I was doubly out of touch with the prevailing notes of American "literature." (God save that word, which now applies to railroad time-tables, political advertising, real-estate pamphlets, as well as to the fine art of poetry or prose.) For if there were then very few writers in our country who thought and lived and worked in the spirit of art, and fewer editors or publishers to encourage or foster them, there were on the other hand plenty of writers—and they grew steadily in numbers and influence—who were strongly possessed by the spirit of social service; writers who considered their writing primarily from the point of view of social criticism and re-construction. And for a long time I was also quite outside this stream of tendency.

So I drifted along, baffled and ignorant, bitterly in revolt against the prevailing conventions; the timid respectability of some periodicals; the crass vulgarity and cheapness of spirit of the greater number.

For a little while I became a literary hack for one of the most crude of the popular magazines; the fantastic "Black Cat"; rewriting short stories, and concocting others; crazy tales of murder and mystery.

Fortunately for my chances in the struggle for existence, I possessed a certain facility which while it often militated against good work, helped me to produce magazine tales that would sometimes sell, though not enough during many years to enable me to live thereby.

So I naturally drifted into newspaper work, for the yellow press; going, in time through the various grades from cub reporter to city editor.

How well I remember my first assignment! It was on a Sunday, and I was sent to a negro church in the South End of Boston, where a sensational preacher was expected to proclaim against the tyranny of the white race.

I met a fellow reporter in the frowsy, malodorous conventicle; a beginner like myself. But how different a one! A Harvard man, fastidious and refined, his head, like mine, stuffed with reading and with literary dreams; but not with unassimilated stuff, and with his faculties trained to utilize and apply his reading and his thoughts and observations. I wonder if

Walter Prichard Eaton ever recalls that meeting in the negro church?

.   .   .   .

I discovered in myself an ability to obtain and write the news; and somewhat rapidly advanced, until I was drawing the munificent wages of fifteen dollars a week, and was signing my stories from time to time. Also I had found congenial associates, and in the Cabot Club, and the Bell-in-Hand, I drank ale (and stronger stuff) and ate mutton pies and talked about books and writing with men of that type which the Press seems always to attract; men, that is to say, of genuine literary gifts, some of whom succeed in realizing their talents, while others, either too superficially armed for the battle, or merely fascinated by the glamour of printer's ink, or else cursed with a weakness for strong drink or drugs, merely sink through circle after circle of illusion to the gutters, and the Mills Hotel, and the morgue. How many of these have I not known and companioned in Boston, New York, San Francisco! How many have I not seen go utterly down and finally out. Some few were true artists, no matter what faults they possessed. Others were nothing but scallawags. But others were victims. They were not equipped to strive with mammon and to contend with their fellows for the rewards of the market place. They were dreamers of the beautiful, searchers after the ideal, lost knights of the grail quest, waifs and estrays from the paths of the high romance—yet better men, brighter souls, warmer hearts, by far, than many of those who go by in their motor cars as in chariots, dressed in the pinchback purple and the imitation fine linen of commercial success.

Is there any branch of human effort which has been more basely prostituted to mammon than modern literature?

Oh, you under dogs of Grub Street, you victims of the press, you with whom I drank deep and held high talk—much futile, foolish talk, I confess, but with moments of splendour—I think that even the tavern door may open nearer to the road of the Quest than does the door of a bank—and I honour you more than I do the skillful writer who sells himself.

$\cdot \qquad \cdot \qquad \cdot \qquad \cdot \qquad \cdot \qquad \cdot \qquad \cdot$

2. A Matter Of Reticence

It was while I was in the midst of Bohemia-in-Boston (imagine the conflict of atmosphere) that something happened which was of palmary consequence, yet something which is impossible for me fully to relate, or even adequately to estimate as to its influence and place in my life.

Which brings me to a frank confession of a failure in my effort to chronicle my spiritual adventures. For, after all, I have discovered that it is out of the question to tell all your life to others. There are things that belong too intimately to you and to those near and dear to you to be given publicity, no matter how delicately, how discreetly. There are heights which are too high and depths too deep, to visit in company with others, when you travel, in retrospect, in the country of the soul.

Yet when I began this book, and in many versions of

it which were written before this one, my plan was to tell "all," "everything," "my life just as I lived it, gloomy or sad; yes, everything. . . ."

It can't be done.

Poe says the paper would scorch and burn if one really told all his life. Maybe it would in my case. But, anyhow, I have discovered rather late in life that there are things that cannot be told; and good things are even more difficult to divulge than bad.

It is for this reason that I must pass by the magic and the beauty of that summer when I found at last a companion . . . that summer when as a "cub" reporter, receiving a salary of fifteen dollars a week, blankly unaware of the responsibilities and duties of real life, I married. . . .

"What a fool you must have been," do I hear you say?

Yes; no doubt I was foolish; and the reasonable side of my own nature looks backward, and is full of wonder; but for good or for bad, prudence and worldly reason do not rule me.

My heart, and my soul, look backward, and regard the present, and then smile into the future,—and they rejoice . . . that piece of "foolishness" was to be worth more to me in the end than most of the calm and reasoned actions of my life.

. . . .

We went, soon afterwards, to New York, where I continued newspaper work. I kept at it for the next five or six years; with intervals during which we made expeditions into country places where rent and living were cheap in order that I might again, and yet again, and again, try to make my way by writing for the magazines.

Also I embarked with Bernard G. Richards upon a singular adventure which was not very lucrative but was surcharged with manifold interest. I had met Richards in Boston, at a time when he was voicing the spiritual life and aspirations of the Ghetto in those wonderful essays, "The Discourses of Kiedansky"; so beautifully written, so vibrant with intellectual power, and at the same time romantic as only literature drawn from authentic life experience may be. We formed a "Jewish-American Literary Bureau." Richards translated articles from Russian and Yiddish newspapers which I transposed into newspaper English and sold to the *Sunday Sun* and other papers. But most of our "work" consisted in sitting in the curious cafés of the East Side; and talking, talking, talking by the hour with the Russian Jewish radicals whose intense intellectual and artistic life supplies such a sharp contrast to the mediocre and vulgar tastes of so large a part of our native Americans. It was the time when Jacob Gordin was the leading figure in East Side drama; and when the far-reaching work of the Russian Revolution was at its most active stage of propaganda. For most of one winter I practically lived on the East Side, and thus learned its life at first hand—even as I had become acquainted with other aspects of New York's singular pageant through passing a year as a reporter at the Mulberry Street police headquarters, and another year at the Criminal Courts, and other years in general work, here, there, and everywhere.

And from these experiences I tried to extract matter for my art. As yet, no other or higher reason for my existence had begun to dawn upon my soul than my desire to transmute my life into terms of literature.

But the same conditions already described still prevailed: I sold quite a number of machine-made stories, but not enough for our support, and I could not sell the things I considered to be the products of my art; and more and more I had to labour at the machine style in fiction. In such labour, however, there is no joy; in this drudgery there arises in the heart and soul no song; and I cannot achieve success in work I do not love, in work that does not march forward to the inward music of the soul. And even in my sketches, be they as "grim" as the editors assure me they are, there was music at their making,—the tones of truth.

But after each effort to force my work to recognition, I was beaten back; my hour had not struck. I was obliged to return to the city and go into the harness of newspaper work.

I left the city, once more, shortly after the birth of the latter of my two children, and during that time of trouble and anxiety I worked for heaven only knows how many hours daily and nightly, writing a book;— one of the several forerunners of this one.

Then, still labouring frantically, like a man in a fever-dream, and punctuating my work with coughs, I wrote a short story and sent it to a magazine editor under an assumed name. I was well nigh desperate of ever making good under my own name. A literary agent told me my case was the most extraordinary he had ever encountered, in that so many editors knew my work, believed I had talent, but felt that I was hopeless for their purposes; some of them, indeed, refused any longer even to read my stuff. I was considered incorrigibly headstrong, densely impervious to reason. I would not—because I could not —take the advice they showered upon me in scores of letters to write more in accordance with conventional models, conventional ideals. I persisted, they complained, in bothering them with stories that were "unpleasant," or "unhappy," or "morbid." They all recognized power in the handling of the work, and originality of ideas and themes, and literary merit (I quote the editors;) but this, it seems, was not enough. So, really afraid that I was taboo, I sent in, as I say, the new story under a false name.

3. Red Hieroglyphic Again

—And one morning as I was tramping through the wet snow to the post office to see what manuscripts had returned, something clicked in my throat; I tasted a peculiar taste, well known to me,—and I remember stopping and staring at that scarlet hieroglyphic of mine enemy, there on the snow, as Crusoe stared at the footprint. I visited the doctors. They all told the same story. The old infected place in my lungs had healed, but there was a new break; tuberculosis was upon me.

And just then there came a gleam of great hope; or what would have been a great hope, if it had come before my breakdown. The magazine accepted my story. S. S. McClure, its editor—one of the few really discerning editors our magazine field can show

—himself wrote glowing words of praise.   He sent a check, and asked for more work.

But for the present I wrote no more stories.   I had more important work.   I had my life to fight for— my life and my family and my art.

The check helped materially to swell the meagre contents of my war-chest; for again I was taking the field, going to the open, to do battle with my sinister and insidious foe, the shadow; and it is only in the field, in the open, that one may hope to overcome that haunter and infector of crowds, of houses, of cities—for when he fights from ambuscade he always wins!

This time I went to Texas.   Since I was obliged to go somewhere, why not choose a new place, why not the sun-drenched romantic plains of the great South-West?   So I argued, with pleasure,—yes, there was pleasure for me even in that going forth, as there is always when I may raise the song of the Open Road. Zest of life has never left me, even at the worst of times.   I say "yes" to life no matter what thorns may be in the bed of our espousals; no matter even if death (her lean bully, according to Henley) is lurking behind the door.

In San Antonio, Texas, I bought a tent and pitched it on a hilltop outside that "city of the sun"—where for twenty-nine days after I arrived the sun was not seen; where "northers" howled across the plains, down from out of Kansas, and rain streamed, and sleet lashed, and ice formed morning after morning in the water pail.

In the lee of my tent, beneath the projecting fly, which I had made six feet longer than the tent cloth itself, I set up my bed; and nightly turned in with all my clothes on even to my boots and hat, and with my overcoat on top of all, wearing, at times, two suits of underwear, and yet sometimes I was forced to get up and stamp about to warm myself. But despite all this I began to improve in health; and when my Lord the Sun (O thou cherisher of life!) at last came back, what an orgy of sun-bathing did I indulge in!

As spring advanced I sent for my family, (there were two children, now), and we camped out together. My health grew steadily better, and I was able to do a good deal of writing, very little of which, however, I was able to sell; and even when you pay no rent your family, to say nothing about yourself, must eat, and be clothed; and money lent by a friend to my wife was all that kept us going, then and many times before then, and later; so as it chanced that a railroad advertised a low rate to San Francisco, my wife and I decided to try our fortunes in that city, where I once more entered newspaper life.

4. San Francisco

I had been only a few months in romantic and lovable San Francisco—a city most congenial to me —when our prospects suddenly improved; from a financial point of view, anyhow.

Late one night, or, rather, early one morning, I was playing poker in the back room of a saloon, with several other men of my paper, when there entered a cub reporter who said the managing editor was looking everywhere for me, and wanted me at once, in his office.

Suspending our game, we looked at each other. Our glances intermingled, electrically communicating our common emotions of surprise, wonder, vague anxiety. Above the green-covered table, above the scattered chips, and cards, the whiskey glasses, the pipes, cigars and cigarettes, through the vitiated, grey atmosphere surcharged with tobacco smoke, our uneasy glances wove jointly a message, clairvoyantly understood by all, and most adequately voiced by one, who said:

"What in hell's broke loose in the office now?"

"You can search me," said the cub reporter, and departed.

Our paper was one where "shake-ups" were frequent. Office politics were fierce and venomous. We were at that time approaching a crisis. I had been engaged in reporting a "story" which was a matter at issue between the contending parties; so no doubt I was to be drawn into the controversy.

"Wait for me, boys," I said, "I'll be back."

Taking a handful of cloves and cinnamon from the bowl on the bar as I passed I emerged into a silent, echoing street deep down among towering office buildings. At the corner, I remember nodding to Con Maguire, the cop; and I exchanged salutations with the drivers of three night-hawk cabs, with Black Tom, the seller of hot sandwiches, and with Darby the Hog, the obese keeper of Little Bohemia, the dance-hall, from which the muffled sounds of shuffling feet, and of piano, cornet and banjo, brassy and acidulous, throbbed out. Turning the corner, I was midmost of one of the white light streets of the town. From a hurrying automobile there came defiant declarations of alcoholic enjoyment. Two young men ostentatiously in evening dress were quarrelling drunkenly with a cab driver, while from the depths of the vehicle two women laughed shrilly. Electric signs advertised cafés, billiard halls, restaurants, and theatres, these latter closed now, but several music halls were still thronged and lighted; and from their widely opened doors the stages were visible, also the audiences. Lamentable comedians evoked raucous laughter by strokes of wit, strokes accomplished with a stuffed club smiting the enormous paunch of a German, or with an ax that clove the property skull of a Tramp; women in tights flourished weary legs above the heads of the beer-drinkers at the slopped tables on the floor, singing in shrill voices and coquetting in ghastly fashion with the spenders and the openers. The tired, irritable waiters hurried through the crowds with their trays, and shook sleeping drunkards, and short-changed the sodden and the careless. There were four of these halls within a space of one hundred yards, and the women of the night and the men of the night went from one unto the other. There were the smells of alcohol, stale beer, the steamy smells from underground kitchens puffing from vent-holes, the smells of tobacco, of musk, of patchouli.

The strange old woman from the East passed me close—she who was said to be the rich wife of a State Supreme Court justice. Her face was ghastly with paint and powder, her costly clothes were in disarray; upheld by drugs she passed, diamonds at her throat, her purse full of money, known in all the big towns of the land as the woman of all the vices. Kid Montanya, the Mexican lightweight pugilist, surrounded by a retinue of parasites, passed me as he hurried from saloon to saloon, hall to hall, on the wave of intoxication that had carried him off his feet after his last fight; his pockets full of gold and silver, —with both hands he would at times scatter it in the music halls; gold and silver would sparkle and glitter through the smoky air and men and women would scramble in the muck of spilled beer, dust, and cigarette ends, on the floor.   Supervisor Jaxon and a group of lawyers, politicians and chorus girls came more or less staggeringly from out the restaurant of the highest prices and entered automobiles for a wild spin through the park to the supper waiting at the ocean road-house famed of sports.   And here and there, up and down, to and fro passed all the noctambulists, of big and little degree, avid or weary, restless, or stolid, doing daily business, or questing frenetically the joys of the night.   And through them all I passed, who knew them all; as I knew the business men by day in the tall office buildings, as I knew the clergymen and the folk of the churches, and the workers in the factories back in Petrero.   And overhead in a sky without a stain of cloud, blue as the deepest of sea water, remote and passionless shone the watching stars.

"Hello, Mike!"

A man shuffling unsteadily across the street spoke in husky accents; and my eyes came down from the stars and met the bleared eyes of my accoster, Ike Davis, a copy reader.   "Come and have a drink."

"No, thanks, not just now, Ike," I said; "the boss wants me."

"Yes, by golly, yes! that's so!" said Davis, his

blood-shot alcoholic eyes glittering in the rays of the arc-light overhead. "There's hell popping tonight."

"What's the particular rumpus, Ike?"

"Hell, *I* don't know! Another run of brain-storms, I suppose. That shop's a madhouse, anyhow; regular dippy-ward, between the Big Boss East, and all the combinations here stabbing each other in the back. I can see poor Bell's finish; and Blinn's, too; Scarratt has had his knife out for a long time; and he'll get them. He'd get me, too, if he could, but he can't. I worked for the Big Boss, and made good, long before he sneaked into the game. Why, once the Big Boss said to me—"

But I had often heard the story of what the Big Boss said to his favourite old toss-pot of a copy reader. "I must break away, Ike," I said. "I'll see you later." Old Ike nodded and shuffled away toward the all-night saloon opposite, and I entered the building and was carried up to the editorial floor by the sleepy elevator man.

In the big city room were the night city editor, the copy readers, sitting in a circle at a big round table; two cub reporters on the late watch; Romaine, the dramatic critic in evening clothes, finishing his special for Sunday which should have been ready two days before, and a squad of copy boys. The last edition was going to press in ten minutes.

"Well, it's about time you showed up," the youthful night editor called out irritably.

"What's the matter?"

"Mr. Murcher wants to see you. He's in his office now—"

The night editor ceased abruptly. The door of a

private office half way down the long room had quickly
opened, and from the doorway there protruded a
bulky head and face; a head round and covered with
a shock of short, coarse, black hair; a face red as raw
beef, mottled with redder pimples, a face lickerish,
humorous and cruel, powerful, violent and ruttish,
the face of John Scarratt, the news editor of the *Daily
News*, who was once its office boy, who had been
managing editor after managing editor come, reign,
abdicate or be overthrown, and had seen city editors
come and go by the score.

"This way," he called out to me in his harsh voice.
Then Scarratt continued speaking to some one within
the room: "Here he is now," and stepped out of the
doorway and closed the door as I approached the
private office. He looked down the long room over
the heads of the bent copy-readers, looking at the man
huddled over his proofs at the city desk. And Scarratt grinned; he grinned, spat noisily on the floor, and
went out to take a drink.

I walked over the soft, rich carpet of Managing
Editor Murcher's private office toward the flat-top desk
by the great window overlooking the street.

"Sit down; I want to talk with you," said Mr.
Murcher.

He was one of the most successful of the various
editors in the service of the Big Boss, the owner and
manager of the paper, and also one of the least pub-
licly known. And he was the one managing editor
who managed John Scarratt instead of being managed by Scarratt.

I sat down, and looked enquiringly at Mr. Murcher.
I already saw that I was not to be "called down," that

I was not here to "stand on the carpet" and be rebuked. Well, then, there must be some special assignment for me. . . .

"How old are you?" asked Mr. Murcher.

All hazy thoughts vanished in my shock of surprise. "I am nearly thirty," I answered.

"Older than I had thought; older than you look, —and old enough to bear responsibility," remarked the editor.

"I hope so," I said.

"Old enough to bear responsibility—" he repeated, scrutinizing me closely. "Mr. Williams," he continued, with a sudden change of key; "I want to tell you something, and to make a proposition—"

I listened for ten minutes in silence. At the end of that time I walked out of the private office into the city room.

Then I stopped, stock still. Suddenly, from deep down beneath the earth, in the bowels of the building, there mounted the first note of a sound; the first, deep, troubling, throbbing note of a sound profound, far-reaching and significant. The final form locked, the last stereotype rushed into place, the foreman had started the presses; and the last edition of the paper was in the printing. Coal burned, water boiled, steam mounted, rods raced, wheels turned, rolls of white paper (for which forests had been felled) spun out their endless ribands; ink smeared the bright plates, which touched with the precision of fate the appointed spaces; and from the ends of the machines dropped in their thousands the newspapers,—filled with the records of the doings of men and women, with the events of American life: murder, marriage, birth,

betrayal, dance, invention, business, politics, games
. . . life, life, life.

Intently I gave ear, thrilling bodily as the whole
building thrilled to the grinding of the machine; my
muscles and nerves tensely strung. The birth-song
of the news of the day!—dear Lord, what a dithyram-
bic chant of pulsating life! and by what a mystic
concatenation was I now hearing it in the minute when,
from out the inchoate mass of the tenders of the great
machine of the news, I had been selected to act as one
of its directors!

Yes.

I was now the city editor of my journal.

The editorial room seemed incredibly strange as I
looked about it, glancing at the weary copy-readers,
at the back-bent night editor, at the office boys. All
its familiarity had fled; for here where I served in
careless, accustomed skill, I was to command. . . .

City editor . . . what a queer chance! I had
always wished that some day I might be city editor;
not for long; not so to remain; but just to reach the
goal aimed for by so many reporters, to taste that
triumph, to drink of authority, responsibility, power
—those strong drinks of men! and to read one more
significant page in the book of life before turning to
my real work—the building of the crystal house.

The night editor called to me as I dreamily passed
the city desk; but although I heard him I did not
stop.

Poor fellow! Scarratt's knife had reached him—
and he didn't know it as yet. And Blinn, the day city
editor, who had once been Murcher's particular pet,
he, too, was to go. Neither was "fired," and that was

good; for I would have disliked to be forced into the places of men put out of a job. Blinn was going to take the head of the copy desk; Bell was going to the capital as the correspondent; politics were his real field, said Murcher. The double city editor system was to be abandoned for the time. I was to manage both jobs. This would not last long, Murcher had promised. Just as soon as a competent man could be found he would be put on at night—that is, if I "made good."

I raised a face of mute wonder to the stars (at which, however, I now was not looking), as I thought over the scene in the office. I had no idea that those "higher up" had been watching me so closely, and that my work had been liked so well.

Unheedingly, unseeingly, I passed through the street. Yet the sub-conscious memory recalls the scene most vividly. Long lines of covered wagons were standing at the curbs and streams of men and youths were already bundling the papers into them, to be carried to ferries, to trains, to distributing stations here, there, and everywhere, so that the news of the day should usher in the day for hundreds of miles around. I bought a copy of the paper—*my* paper; and what a new sense the word had! Through the scattering and disappearing noctambulists I passed on to the saloon in the room back of which my former comrades were still playing poker.

How strange they, too, seemed, as I stood in the door for a moment, looking at them, before they noticed my return. How tired they looked, in spite of their interested faces; how haggard and how lined their faces—and all were young men, the most even younger than I. And just for a breath, there in the smoke-thickened, liquor-tainted air, in the midst of the hour near dawn when the tide of life runs slack and the dying die, to me there came a fear, and it whispered through the flush of my triumphant mood: the fear of exhaustion: the fear of becoming played out. The game was so unresting, so violently head-long, the pace so unrelaxing. Never any rest, never any solitude, never any time for absorption, for con-templation, for the digestion of the news gathered so omnivorously, and so voraciously; gathered crude, dispensed crude—and would I, even I, who dreamed of extracting from this mass of crude facts and expe-riences the essential element of Art be able to do so? . . . but the words of the fear were merely whispered, chillingly, indistinctly, and then the fear passed by. I reached out and poured a drink, and the players stared.

But they did not know what moved me, because I was to keep the secret of my promotion until New Years, two weeks later.

.   .   .   .

Fortunately, the "shake-up" was not a catastrophe. Nobody, this time, lost his job. There was merely a changing about of positions. For me, it meant that for increased pay I shouldered unending work and responsibility.

For in the service of the yellow god of sensational, commercialized journalism there is no cessation; the machine stops never; its directors and tenders never rest. And I never rested. My life sped like a series of biograph pictures.

Between ten and eleven in the forenoon I was at my desk reading the morning papers marked by an assistant, comparing what my paper contained with what the rival newspapers contained; deriving immense satisfaction from the "scoops" scored by us; wincing bitterly over the "scoops" scored by the others. Then as the reporters appeared, there was the anxious and important task of assigning to each man that story for which in my judgment he was best fitted. There were the department reporters to talk to on the 'phone—the ship news man, the police court men, the criminal court men, the city hall man, the Federal bureaus man, the society men and women, the suburban correspondents. Then as the evening papers appeared, edition after edition, there were all the new developments of the day's grist of news to handle. Always the telephone bell was ringing, and reporters called in from a score of places to announce events big or little which I must weigh, sift, and judge. And ever there was a stream of callers filtering through the reception room without; professional tipsters trying to sell stories; men and women with various axes to grind; aggrieved persons threatening libel suits; cranks and stark lunatics. The "higher ups" would appear during the afternoon with suggestions, with criticisms, with orders, with brilliant yellow ideas for stories which already I had "covered" in some other fashion and now had to attack from some new point of view. Then as the afternoon waned, there was the gathering of heads of departments which the irreverent and the scornful dubbed the "Paresis Club"; consisting of managing editor, news editor, telegraph editor, "make-up" man, he who put the paper together amid the clamour of the composing room in the last hurried, feverish hour of the day, and the head of the art department. Then all the stories of the day were discussed, criticized, and weighed, and the space to be given each, and the treatment to be accorded the important stories, or those reflecting the paper's policy, were decided upon; news editor, and telegraph editor, clamouring for space which I considered due to my city news, and the make-up editor fighting us all, with his: "We have eighty columns of ads—cut your stories down, cut 'em down; and make all those two-column cuts one column. Cut to the bone!"

And generally, after all this anxious deliberation, our plans went to pieces long before midnight—shattered by the advent of the always recurring Unexpected. Somebody would surely be murdered, or some train would wreck, some cashier flee, or wife elope, or millionaire be raked with a muck-rake, or some King sneeze thrice at church; and the careful schedule would be smashed into flinders. Over buzzing wires from all the ends of the earth would come the news—the news—the news; throughout the length and breadth of the city men and women were forever weaving the news,—the news—the news.

And often when the columns were filled, and arranged and the presses, oiled and ready, stood waiting for the forms, then . . . "Ting-a-ling-ling" the telephone bell would spring its alarum,—a great fire was raging in the tenement district, and "heroes" were being made amid the smoke and flame; or there was a collision on the bay, or a gun-fight to the death in a music hall. Then would the make-up editor curse the universe, and fast-fire typewriter operators banged their machines to dictation made by a reporter at a telephone, or by myself, and the front page was given another dress.   And sometimes news of such moment "broke" so late, that the order for an "extra" was given, and then the grey daylight would be abroad before I would leave the desk.

So it went on, day after day, night after night, and for me it probably would eventually have brought another breakdown if I had remained long at the city desk.

But that was not to be.

The end—or the beginning of the end of that adventure—came on April 18, 1906.

CHAPTER V

THE CITY THAT NEVER WAS

1. April 18, 1906

I WAS in Coppa's restaurant the night before, dining with James Hopper and Xavier Martinez. They were patrons of the place; members of the Coppa group; I was a newcomer, and Hopper had taken me to dine in the queer little café where for a few happy years there had dwelt a spirit akin to the true-blue-Bohemianism of English taverns in the long ago, and that of the Paris cafés in the days before Montmartre became a side-show of the commercialized vice of Paris. The little "Lark" that sang so blithely, and whose lyric voice carried so far (I remember it reached me away off in Canada, where I was living when Bruce Porter and Gelett Burgess and Porter Garnett and the others sent it winging from the Golden Gate), was itself a "lark" of that gay little company of writers and painters and newspapermen who foregathered in Coppa's, under the weird frescoes, at the tables set apart for their use by a host who knew that artists must eat even if they didn't have the price, and who saw to it that they did. Wherefore, the names of bonanza millionaires, and frock-coated politicians, and many others who in their generation seemed fixed in the seats of the mighty in San Francisco, hath perished from the records, or decorate sumptuous tombs,

maybe; but the name of Joe Coppa is a living name
and will be passed on from writer to writer, and
painter to painter, down the corridors of time, and
pagans will pledge his memory (at least until the bug-
aboo, Prohibition, comes) and Christians will pray
for his friendly soul.   For we who write and you who
read do both in vain if ever we forget that cities and
men do not live in wealth and material power and
pride, but in things that are lovely and of good report.

From Coppa's, that night, I went back to my office;
for my day's work was only beginning.   Not until
long after midnight would my day be over.   Hopper
—that most authentic artist, wielder of a beautiful style
—and I had been talking, I remember, of what chiefly
interested us; which thing was distinctly not the newspaper work which we both were doing; it was art—
in particular, the art of writing.   We had met some
little time before, up on the top of Telegraph Hill,
reporting some murder or other.   Both agreed, however, on the spot, and often afterwards, that if a
writer must do reporting in order that the body shall
have its bread and its raiment while the soul goes
adventuring in other realms, why certainly, no other
city can offer such solace as San Francisco.   And by
and by, we knew, the time would come when the newspaper office would only be remembered as one remem-
bers a dream strangely mingled of pain and pleasure,
romance and deadly drudgery, swampy evil—and a
few, far flights toward the stars.

There once was a time, and old San Francisco
richly knew it—and Boston, and New York, and the
other cities—when the newspaper was what it should
be; when, save for the few out-and-out blackmailers

and political henchmen of the pen, who are always
to be found near the press, the newspaper rested upon
a basis of ethics; when editorial writers were truly
concerned in expressing moral ideas; when there
were journalists in the proper sense, and literary men
of first class quality, thinkers, artists in style—men
like the *Golden Era* group: Bret Harte, Mark Twain,
Prentice Mulford; Noah Brooks; James King of
William; that stalwart and romantic personage,
Ambrose Bierce; Henry George; James V. Coffey;
Arthur McEwen; Edward F. Cahill; Edward H.
Hamilton; and James Tufts.

A few are still with us. Hamilton and Tufts are
yet in the game. Hamilton, one of the truest stylists
who have ever graced the pages of the American daily
press; Tufts, a great editor whose genius was throttled
by the vulgarity of the yellow press. The decline of
the newspaper in San Francisco—or anywhere else—
is not due to the reporters, the writers, the editors. It
is due to the curse of commercialism; the turning of
a great force for enlightenment and enjoyment into
a mechanism for making dollars, or playing politics,
or obtaining personal power.

There were authentic poets, too, in those by-gone
days; such singers as Joaquin Miller, Charles Warren
Stoddard, Ina Coolbrith, and the other men and women
who under Bret Harte and later editors gave the *Over-
land Monthly* a place with the *Atlantic Monthly* in the
hierarchy of American occasional literature. But the
fatal curse of profit-chasing had fallen upon the press,
not only in San Francisco, but almost universally in
the United States, long before 1906. Most newspapers existed for cash first, or the promotion of per-

sonal interests; all other interests trailed a long way
after these; and with this fall from an ethical plane
came a coincidental invasion of screaming sensation-
alism and crude vulgarity.

A few lonely figures—and, here and there in our
country, but not now, alas, in San Francisco, a few
newspapers, still possessing their souls, survive from
that earlier epoch. Perhaps if we are able to overthrow the rotten fabric of commercialism which mas-
querades as civilization, the true newspaper will come
again into its own, in San Francisco as elsewhere; but
as we walked through Montgomery Street that bland
still April evening in 1906, Hopper and I had good
reasons for agreeing that when it was not corrupt the
newspaper was stupid and vulgar, a mechanism for
making money, and no longer an instrument of culture
or of education.

Caruso was singing Don José in Carmen, that
night, with the Metropolitan Opera House company.
My paper was "playing it up," as we say, and when I
reached my desk there was a long list of reporters to
assign to various portions of the grand opera story;
a corps of women to do "society" features; hustling
interviewers who were to gather from "well-known
men-about-town," "first-nighters," and other kinds of
"prominent citizens," their opinions and criticisms of
the occasion. Frank Mulgrew was one of those reporters, and we have often chuckled together since
over his interviews that night with Jerry Dinan, the
Chief of Police, and similar connoisseurs. "What do
I think of Caruso? Will I talk for publication?
Sure! You know what to say, Frank—fix it up for
me." We published columns of the stuff next morn-

ing—next morning when . . . but I'm coming to that a bit later on.

It was two or three o'clock in the morning when I shut up my desk, and left the office. I dropped in at the Old Crow saloon, that "barrel house" so favoured by newspaper workers. Ike Allen, the telegraph editor, was already there, and he introduced me to Joe Mansfield, a brother city editor. Jimmy Britt, the lightweight champion pugilist of the day, and his brother, Willus, were of the group. A little later, leaving Jimmy Britt doing a cakewalk around and about the barrels which served as tables in the Old Crow, to the huge delight of everybody, I walked up Geary Street to my apartment, just the other side of Larkin, not far from Van Ness Avenue. Few and far between were motor cars, in 1906. In the night hours, fantastic horses drew shambling, ambiguous looking cabs, handled by drivers who knew every house in all the Queer Streets of the Latin Quarter, of the Barbary Coast, of Chinatown; and knew equally well all the residences of those who maintained Queer Street as a going business through their habitual patronage.

I am not one of those to whom the name San Francisco is an evocation of all that is disreputable, all that is bold and shameless in sinning, as it seems to be for those who draw their limited ideas of the city from the pages of critics who only saw the meretricious, or the corrupt, aspects of old San Francisco. Every city has these aspects; but most cities are sedulous in whitewashing their charnel-houses, in hiding their shame. San Francisco is very frank, even in her sinning; especially was she so in days gone by.

In the foolish fashion of most young men who would writers be, I spent and wasted many, many nights "studying life" in that blaring block in Pacific Street where roared the high tide of Barbary Coast, or through the sinister alleys and musky streets and lanes of Chinatown and the Latin Quarter, and I watched from the close point of view of a city editor's desk the inner workings of corrupt politics, always such a curse in San Francisco. Wherefore I might write, out of a fund of experience, singular chronicles of the shady side of Queer Street, in this city. But San Francisco's real life was not fully revealed in these accidentals. A very wise old book which sometimes I read when all other books fail me, says, in Latin which I can't read, but which fortunately has a translation paralleling its columns, that "God . . . in creating human nature, hast wonderfully dignified it, and still more wonderfully reformed it"; and whether I mingle with the life of Boston, or of Tucson, New York, Chicago, Vineyard Haven, Reno, or San Francisco—whether in city or country, among rich or poor, I find that evil always is easy to discover, but good is less obtrusive. Perhaps the worst blunder an observer of life can make would be to think that evil is the predominating quality in any particular city, or any particular person. The most subtle artistic intelligence I have ever met—that of Harvey Wickham, my closest comrade in my San Francisco adventures—did more to show me this consoling truth than any other influence. We roamed together through the underworld, and together we watched the stars of many a dawn fade like silver music from the disappearing darkness.

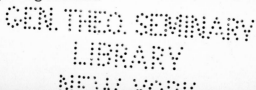

That morning, in San Francisco, as I walked home, Barbary Coast was still wide awake and seething; all the dark places in Queer Street were doing a thriving business; a revised version of the old Vigilante Committee had its secret agents at work trailing the steps of grafting politicians, and in Grant Avenue, the night before, where the anarchists and the Socialists and the religious freaks were wont to do their spouting, Seventh Day Adventists were predicting the destruction of this modern Sodom and Gomorrah; this "Paris of the Pacific," as one loud-mouthed person called her—his feeble mind not holding the thought of the Paris of Notre Dame, or of the Louvre, or Pasteur or of Puvis de Chavannes, but the Paris which used to be maintained by the dirty dollars of such Americans as he.   But this meretricious San Francisco, this San Francisco of Barbary Coast and the cosmopolitan stews—what was it compared to the mighty city of decent people who were sleeping in that still, silent, balmy hour before the dawn; the city of such great works, of such beauty, of such romance and spirituality, of such future greatness?   No, no, no!   Let somebody else write about Barbary Coast, and ambiguous restaurants, if they will; I celebrate, out of my heart and stirred to my soul by faith and hope and love, the true San Francisco, the city where the trails of the high romance of my soul led to so many brave adventures!

2. The Springs Of Goodness

I particularly remember the singular sensation I experienced of realizing how still, now, and how

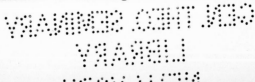

silent, the city was.   It seemed as though I were in the very centre of a circle of stillness and silence.

Now and then, this profound silence would be broken by a sound beginning very far away, like the rumour of a sound.   It would then come near and nearer, rise to its highest, and then pass, and grow lower, softer, and fade away—like the ghost of a sound. . . . Automobiles coming home with merry-makers from the beach resorts.   At that time, the fashion in motor horns ran to something that reminded me, especially at night, of some strange animal—a sort of melodious, gobbling sound, rising and falling, and with something ominous under the rather musical effect.

And as I heard the motor cars, one by one, with a sort of clock-work regularity, passing by, I could imagine, with a vividness like a moving picture play, the scenes in the roadhouses by the beach beyond the great park where the smooth broad roads glimmered pale beneath the high, black trees.   At sloppy tables I saw the drinkers, while on the polished floors men and women danced—or, rather, they "ragged," as they call the up-to-date perversion of the dance; while the piano player, a young, pallid fellow with a fuming cigarette stuck to his lower lip, banged out the rag-time music.

But the last of the motor cars passed by.   The intensified silence drew its circle closer about me.

Night was passing.   Dawn was at hand.   The southern and eastern parts of the sky were paling, and there the stars were dim.   Elsewhere, however, the stars were still big and clear, and the sky darkly and profoundly blue.   A couplet from Wordsworth

came into my mind: "Dear God! the very houses seem
asleep; and all that mighty heart is lying still!"

No doubt, within many indeed of these quiet, darkened houses—in Chinatown, or the Tenderloin quarter, for example—evil was awake and busy—as horrible dreams may go on behind a sleeper's placid fore-
head—but outwardly all was calm, and broodingly
silent.   There came upon me a keen realization of
the wonder of the city's suspended consciousness.
There was a singular magic in the suggestion of rest
that emanated from those shadowy congeries of vacant, criss-crossing streets, and houses darkly slumbering.   In this curious space between night and day
it seemed to me that sleep had finally conquered all
resistance, had worn down the stubbornness of the
most determined noctambulists, just as a quiet,
strong-willed nurse or mother might subdue her ob-
streperous children.

A sense of awe came next.   I felt as if I must be
the only person left awake in all San Francisco, and
as if I had no right to be awake.   I felt like an
intruder.   It was as if I had blundered into some
lodge-room or chapel where a secret rite was about
to be celebrated.   There was something in all this
quietude which troubled me deeply.   The city no
longer seemed merely resting, placidly slumbering,
relaxed and at peace.   It became to me like a city
held in a trance.   It brought back to me the uneasy,
curious, feelings I had once experienced when I saw
a hypnotist put a number of men and women into
deep entrancement and without using any audible
words plant his suggestions in their minds.   Only
now I felt my awe more profoundly.   I seemed

aware of strange things happening behind the veil of
the dusky dawn and the unbroken quiet of the city's
sleep.   I seemed to be on the point of actually knowing just *how* all the hundreds of thousands of men
and women and children slumbering all about me
were being surcharged, like so many living batteries,
with new energy generated by the tremendous, invisible dynamos of sleep and silence.   Streams of fresh
life were pulsing into them all for the use of the
coming day.   Power for thought and for action.
Power more potent, and infinitely more subtle, than
all the electrical currents that could be generated by
a hundred Niagaras!   And soon these living batteries,
each with a place in the vast, complex, living machine
of the city, would awaken and take its part in the
diurnal working of the great organisms and so expend
the energy now pouring into them.

This energy, I wondered—as who of us hasn't wondered!—from where did it come?   And what, really,
was it?   And where was it driving the human machines?

This everlasting, triadic question to which there is
no answer—the whence, and why and where!

How futile to ask it.

It was just as futile as it would be to go upon one
of the city's many hills, and ask the why and wherefore of the tides of the sea, or the system of the
stars, or the secret of the rising sun.

And yet, as I dreamed my way homeward through
the silent city under the mystical stars, I was seized
with a deep, thrilling impression that I was about to
understand the cosmic mystery—that the secrets of
the sky and of the earth and water, and the secret of

man, were about to be revealed. There was the
thought that between the sleepers in the city, and the
stars and the sea and the earth, there was in this moment the closest kind of communion—as though the
tide of life flowing into the sleepers was gathering its
force from sea and air and earth and stars—and
that now: this instant, all were in rapport—and had
come to a crisis; like a clock that had reached its
time to strike the hour.

And this mystical moment left the glow of a thought
in my mind, as a meteor leaves a trail of light, though
its central brightness disappears. It seemed to me
that I understood at least one chief factor that
entered into the wonder of the city's sleep. This
factor was my realization of how united at this
moment all the hundreds of thousands of individual-
ities were in the condition of sleep. So far as
ordinary consciousness was concerned, and the
ordinary affairs of life, egoism—that potent source
of human discordance—was in abeyance. All the
warring and irreconcilable elements that spring from
egoism were withdrawn from manifestation.

What would be the result should the sleepers
awaken *bereft of egoism*—united in waking life as
now they were united in slumber—and if they should
employ *in unity and for unity* the energy they were
now deriving together from the secret springs of
sleep and silence?

Once more my mind gave up a memory—that paragraph of Goethe's which one reads with yearning
wistfulness, and the wish: *"Oh, if it could only
happen!"* I suppose you know the paragraph; it
runs something like this: "There is in man a force

—a spring of goodness—which counterbalances egoism; and if by a miracle it could for a moment suddenly be active in all men, the earth would be at once free from evil."

I was dreaming, as who does not. Dreaming vainly, perhaps, yet I don't disown or repudiate my dream—I only acknowledge that I have not realized my share of it. Yes, that's a good way to express the matter—for my dream was but a share of a bigger dream—which is the dream of this age. It is with us all, in greater or lesser degree. It is the dream of human Betterment—the dream of Brotherhood! I don't use the word "dream" as a symbol of something unreal. No—dreams such as this are what Shelley said poetry was—the mirrors of the great shadows which the future casts upon the troubled surface of the present. All the many dreams by which we think to effect the common end are parts and fragments of the one, great dream. Like the co-operating thoughts of one, gigantic mind, they work together to realize the world's desire, even when they appear to contradict and neutralize each other.

For I believed—and here let me say that I still believe—no matter what anybody may say—no matter how many facts may seem to argue against the truth of my belief—I believed then, and I believe now, that the inscrutable forces of Good are powerful today with the power of the rising tide. They are changing doubt to hope, and fear to faith, and anger and hatred into love, more mightily, perhaps, than at any other time since when the Prince of Peace and Lord of Love Himself expressed the world's desire, when he said: "Thy kingdom come: Thy

will be done in earth as in heaven." The Kingdom
of peace and of brotherly love. Good Will, to the
sway of which the whole creation moves!

My credo . . . and we'll get back to the
story. . . .

. . . .

3. The Shock

But I was too tired, bodily, and in mind, and soul
as well, to maintain my meditation. I had reached
my home; I let myself in and got noiselessly to bed.

I suppose it was nearly four o'clock when at last
my excited brain ceased its working, and sleep came.

And almost at once I came awake again—vaguely
wondering what was the matter?

The big bed in which I lay was trying its best to
imitate a bucking broncho and to throw me out of
the window, toward which it was lurching. The air
itself seemed to be pulling at me, with invisible
fingers clutching from all directions at once, but un-
evenly; the plaster was falling in big chunks; and
there was a vast, crescendic roaring noise, incompre-
hensible: a vast sea of sound.

There was the commingling of the crash of falling
walls, the tumbling of millions of bricks, the rending
and cracking and splintering of wood, the shattering
of window glass by the hundreds of thousands of
sheets and panes, and myriads of other sounds. All
these were based, as it were, on another, unwordable
sound, which was the roaring of the earthquake—
the groaning of the very earth itself.

What a racket!

It was like—well, it was like—let me see, now it was like—Oh, heavens above, *I don't know what it was like!* Nobody knows. Fancy a billion big drays, loaded with iron rails passing along over rough cobble stones, with the rails clangorously falling, and the windows of all the houses being shattered by the concussions, and then fancy—but, no, you can't! Neither can I. That noise is not to be conjured up by fancy—it can only be remembered.

Yet that terrible noise was nothing at all—a mere trifle, a trivial incident, a bagatelle, compared to the impression of the earthquake *as earthquake,* if I may so express myself.

But how can I tell you? I really cannot tell you!

For there was something about that shock that struck, deeper than any sound could penetrate, into the substance of your soul.

—You know how it is when we try to suggest some tremendous emotion or altogether unusual sense of calamity—we say, "It was as if the earth moved under our feet," or, "It was as if the earth trembled."

So what can we say—what is there left to say—when the earth in fact *does* move under our feet, when actually the earth *does* tremble?

For we are so accustomed to the earth being—well, reliable, trustworthy: safe, sane, and conservative, so to speak. We are so used to being its boss, to using it as we please, ploughing and digging it, sowing and reaping it, building our cities with its own stuff, brick and stone and wood—without a mur-

mur from it, without any tricks being played with us, such as the untamable sea and the mysterious air and that dangerous character, fire, take pleasure in perpetrating. We're up against trouble all the time in our dealings with water, and fire, and air—but we consider the earth a straight, clear-cut proposition.

So when *it* cuts loose. . . . Oh, I give it up! There aren't any words for what you feel in an earthquake shock.

Here's a bit of a hint. Suppose you were on a ship at sea, on a long, long, voyage, so that the motion, the fluidity, the freedom of movement, were part of your very being—you are saturated with motion—and suddenly the water becomes a solid substance, and the air becomes rigid, and the ship stops and is held without a quiver, like a toy ship frozen inside a block of ice. Well, the solid earth, that morning in San Francisco, was behaving like the unstable sea—

Oh, but what's the use! The feeling simply can't be described. It dates back to chaos—to a time before there was any law and order or solid substance. This upheaval of the primal powers that bind atom to atom, cell to cell, organism to organism, star to star, and universe to universe, throughout all creation in cohesion, and balance, and system, leaves in the mind that has experienced it a memory which is unique, and a sensation which lies altogether outside the limits of category. Only those who have gone through a 'quake can understand me. I'll just add this, however,—that we who have gone through a big 'quake understand what other people can only think they understand, namely, that the foundation, the underlying principle, of all material things from the ultimate atom to the biggest star in the heavens is nothing that can be seen or touched or handled or known by any sense, but is forever imponderable, and unnamable, and eternally inscrutable. We hint at it in such terms as the cosmic ether, polarity, gravitation, and so forth, and so on. Some of us, however, are still old-fashioned enough to say, the Hand of God.

At any rate it was shaking the city of San Francisco that bright, still dawn, and beneath the falling timbers and stones men and women and children were being crushed to death by hundreds. At a score of points fire was springing up. And there was no water with which the fires could be quenched in this first stages. The water-supplying system had been put out of business by the shock. I have been told that the water mains were not properly constructed, any more than the ruined City Hall was properly constructed—that in both jobs there had been rich, fat graft. You see? It was as if the corruption of the city's life had corroded its very bones, eaten into its very physical structure, so that in the hour of its calamity it lacked the power to save itself. As we now know, if the fires could have been controlled in those first few hours, huge as was the damage of the earthquake, it would have been a trifle in comparison with that which was inflicted by the fire—that fire which was the worst this fire-ravaged world has witnessed, so far as history can show.

·   ·   ·   ·   ·   ·   ·

4. But the Baby is Calm

My little daughter was in the crib by the bed. Her mother gathered her up quickly in her arms, and I arched myself above them both, to ward off the plaster, or the universe, I didn't know which. Our baby boy was in the adjoining room, in a crib by the bedside of a friend who lived with us; a lady who appeared a second or two after the start of the trouble, in her nightdress, in the doorway. She was a maiden lady from New England; so you see how unconventional this occasion must have been. She it was who gave a name to it.

"Earthquake!" she said.

I had vaguely thought of an explosion; of a sudden and awful storm approaching, or a flood, a tidal wave; but, sure enough, now I understood that it was an earthquake. When you come back from sleep after only an hour, you are not as bright-minded as you'd like to be able to say you were.

"The baby!" cried the lady in the doorway.

Then, as neither the plaster nor the universe had crushed us so far, I ceased my imitation of a cat with its back arched, and ran into the outer room.

The force of the shock had been much greater there. All the furniture was crowding into the middle of the room and trying to play a clumsy game of leap-frog. It was bright daylight of a perfect April day outside, but the blinds were drawn in the room and the light was dim, mild, and milky. And through this placid, opalescent light I saw the wide, untroubled eyes of the baby boy, who was perfectly calm, looking at me. He was like a philosopher from some other planet nonchalantly observing a queer human being in pajamas scrambling over a mountain of furniture, in a room which was apparently trying to turn itself inside out. I have often wondered what can go on in the mind of a child in such a moment.

5. Out in the Street

The earthquake came a little after five. It lasted eighteen seconds. According to the scientific gentlemen, it appears that the coast range mountains along a line of some three hundred miles shrugged their shoulders, or made a slight gesture, as it were, and cities and towns and villages along that line behaved very much as a child's building blocks behave when he pulls the table cloth on which they are stacked. Mount Tamalpais, a mass of how many billions of tons only science can tell you, shifted its position. Redwood trees three or four thousand years old were split wide open. Torrents and springs of water or sand leaped from the broken and tortured earth. Landslides streamed down the hills. Trees were overthrown. All this, outside the city. As for the city— Well, let me return to my own adventures; it is hopeless to attempt the description of the city's fate, just yet.

The house I lived in was an old wooden structure, solidly and honestly made. Like all such, it swayed and shook; plaster fell, shelves were emptied; but there was no serious damage. Honestly made steel buildings also stood the racket.

Before the shock had finished its course by more

than a few seconds, we were in the street; part of the
fantastic multitude disgorging out of doorways up
and down all the streets of the city. Some, but these
were the few, were dressed; house-wives or servants
or workers early astir; but the most of us were in all
the stages of extraordinary dishabille. There was
a vacant lot not far from the house, and to this we
ran, and soon the place was crowded with fat men in
nighties, women with children in their arms, blankets
about some of them, others merely in their night-
gowns; and all sorts and conditions of men, women,
and children.

There was a brief pause, as it were; a scant breath-
ing spell, and then, very suddenly, my heart tried
to jump out of my mouth, and then seemed to fall
back, fluttering like a wounded creature.

Another earthquake had begun . . . again the
earth, and the air, and all that was upon the earth,
and in the air, was throbbing, was swaying, was
quivering, was palpitating enormously. It was
frightful! But thank God, it didn't last so long,
nor was it nearly so severe as the first one. Nevertheless, it shook down walls that had been weakened
by the other shock, and bricks from chimneys came
raining down, and people who had ventured back
into their houses came rushing out in fresh dismay.
Some of them didn't come out again; falling walls
or beams pinning them down, killed or badly injured, caught, in some places, like animals in pits
or dead-fall traps.

There came a fresh wave of people rushing through
the streets, but we remained in the open space.

And up the middle of the street, a little bit later,

there walked two well-dressed men; Orientals, or
mulattoes; looking as if they had been up all night
waiting for this moment. They were proclaiming
the end of the world. It was Judgment Day, they
cried; the Book was open, the Book of Life and
Death; and they bade us fall upon our knees and
pray. And, really, you know—we weren't sure they
were not right. Truly, it was like the end of things
mortal. Somebody, looking at the wall of fire marching toward us, later on; that strangely silent, quietly
busy advance of a wall of flame, said: "Yes, it
surely must be Judgment Day." Somebody else replied: "And this must be the gates of hell."

It ought to have been a perfectly tremendous
moment, I suppose . . . but it wasn't.

The trouble was, that we couldn't believe our
prophet. Daylight, I expect, is not congenial to belief in prophets, even when the daylight is one of a
day of disaster. There seems to be something in us,
something that belongs to our very life—perhaps it
is the force of life itself—that utterly refuses to believe in death until death itself says: "Here I am."
Even if April 18, 1906, really had been Doomsday,
you couldn't have got us to believe it, out there in
San Francisco, not if a regiment of black prophets
had been on the job.

I saw a few troubled faces here and there amid
the crowd, but the trouble was more what you might
feel when somebody acts indecorously than anything
deeper.

"That mutt must be crazy," I heard a fat man
wheezing near me.

"Somebody ought to make him shut up—or knock

his block off," answered the man the fat chap spoke
to.   "Say, even if he is right what business has he
to try to scare folks?"

Personally, I felt quite indifferent.   Maybe the
prophet was right.   Quite likely he was.   But if this
was the end of the world—   Oh, very well, it was
the end of the world—but we might just as well carry
on, without any fuss.

And that, you might say, was the common, the
general feeling, not only there in Geary Street, but
throughout the city, and not only then, as we recov-
ered from the first stunning confusion of the shock,
but later on, throughout all the terrible days that
followed.   It was not that we were indifferent to
fears and horrors and disasters; not at all; nor was
it that we were endowed with heroic courage to overcome all things.   No, that was not the case.   We
were full of fears, all the time.   I think there was
hardly one of us who didn't keep in mind the dark
horror of a tidal wave.   Others, I know from what
they told me, felt that at any moment the earth might
open and swallow them.   The menace of shaky walls
loomed always over us.   In the first few days, there
came more than forty minor shocks, and each shock
sent many nervously disordered persons temporarily
insane.   The sand-hills toward the sea were full of
wandering, harmless, mad folk; talking and muttering to themselves, or sitting on the ground staring
at the smoke and crimson reflections of the fire in
the sky.   And we knew the fear of plague, and of
pestilence, and starvation, and sudden death.   And
always there were circulating the most dreadful
rumours.   We believed them, too, more or less.

Why not? Anything might happen, after what had already happened. Anything at all. Nothing was impossible. We heard that Los Angeles had been wiped out completely. Mount Rainier was in eruption; torrents of lava were covering the north country with burning lakes. Chicago had been swallowed by Lake Michigan. The catastrophe was country-wide; maybe it was universal; for London had been smitten, so we heard. There were no telegraph wires working for days, of course, but only a few of us were aware of this. Anyhow, rumours, as we all know, whether false or true, do not need telegraph wires in order to travel about; they seem to use the all-pervading ether, like the waves of the wireless. Or else they spread through telepathy.

But, all the same, we did not get badly excited. We were bewildered; some of us were bedazed; we were all nerve shaken, and we all had our own particular fears to face—but, taking us altogether, by and large, taking us as a crowd of human beings —as a mob, if you like—as a multitude—we stood everything mighty well. There was a calmness; there was a grave, yet kindly, almost smiling kind of acceptance of the situation on the part of the people as a whole, the memory of which remains with me like the memory of noble and harmonic music. For, after all, you see, there was something in San Francisco which the 'quake could not overthrow, nor even agitate very seriously—and this thing was the intangible something which is the spirit of human nature —the spirit of human life—which shows itself in human nature's unbreakable habit of keeping busy at the business of living on in this world just as long as there is any shred of world left on which to live. What is that inner something? That inmost assurance? Mere instinct? Self-preservation? The will-to-live? Or is it Faith?

Anyhow—we do, we will carry on. Some day we'll know why.

6. The Flight

By and by, I ventured back into the house, wondering what moment it would fall in upon me, and secured my clothes. My wife—being one of those extraordinary women whom nothing frightens—except mice—also went back and cooked breakfast.

Then I started to walk toward the office, but on my way I learned that the fire chief had been killed, that the water mains of the city were out of business, and that great fires had started in many directions, and were joining, spreading, and marching along. So I knew, right then and there, that the real name of this calamity was not earthquake, but fire; and I knew that it would march along without any other force being able to stop it. Not remembering the width of Van Ness Avenue (one can't think of everything in such moments, not even a newspaperman!), I thought that the whole city was doomed. So my first duty was toward those waiting for me in Geary Street. On my journey to them I spent what little money I had in buying condensed cream, chocolate, bread, canned stuff, health food (of a particular brand, indispensable to a one year old baby with a weak digestive machine) and trifles of that sort, which I stuffed into the recesses of a canvas shooting coat which I had thrown on that morning, with some vague notion, no doubt, of dressing appropriately. And as I watched the great crowds pouring onward before the drive of flame for the most part so silently, so calmly; dragging trunks, bed-steads, carts, baby-carriages, easy chairs, bundles, baskets, bags, caged parrots, stuffed owls, books, tools, bed-clothes, loaves of bread, live chickens, statues of the saints, jugs, guns, and all manner of things—as I watched this strange multitude, moving through a stranger silence, the silence of a city in which no trolley cars were thundering, I remembered, with gratitude to the giver of all good thoughts, that there were soldiers, Uncle Sam's regular soldiers, out at the Presidio, and that a very good place for a married man and his family to seek for lodging would be a tent near those soldiers. For, like many others, I dreaded looting on the grand scale, and starving mobs, and scarlet anarchy.

Again we ventured into the house, up to the top floor. From the windows at the back we saw the dome of the City Hall against a sky beginning to blacken with smoke, and lurid with flame; a dome like a sinister skeleton, stripped to its ribs of steel; looking like a gigantic bird-cage; and I saw the flames south of Market Street, and out in the Mission, and toward the foot of Geary Street.

Then began that awful tramp to the Presidio, pushing one child in the baby carriage, with the other carried in our arms, or in the foot of the carriage, and dragging all that we could manage to drag, wrapped up in a quilt; up hill, and down hill; that terrible tramp to the Presidio. For a man who had come West in order to patch up a hole in his lungs,

it was tough work; but I didn't think so then. For
when you imagine that at any moment the earth may
open and swallow you up, at one bite (as we heard
it had been doing in many places), or when the sea
is expected to send in a tidal wave, as it was
libellously accused of having done elsewhere, why,
you cease to take much interest in your minor or
major ailments. Many a bedridden invalid leaped
clear out of bed that morning and didn't go back
again; cured by the shock.

What I chiefly worried about was my lack of money.
Strange, I know, that a wandering writer, should feel
such a worry; all the traditions of Bohemia go against
the fact; but yet, so it was, and the first man I knew
by sight was called upon at once to make me a loan.
It was Tom Dillon, the Hatter (I present him with this
advertisement with immense satisfaction). He didn't
know me; but, just like a true San Franciscan, he did
not enquire too closely into this panhandling demand,
he simply, out of the goodness of a San Franciscan's
heart, put a twenty-dollar gold piece in my hand.
(It was a long, long time before he got it back; but
if I ever make any money I think I will walk up and
down Third Street some night, and give away twenty
dollars to the toughest looking hoboes I can discover,
and then ask them all to spend at least part of it in
drinking the health of Tom Dillon.)

Then I bought more food. I point with pride to
this fact. I proclaim it; I write it down in a book
that once in his life, at least, a writing man who from
the dim beginnings down all the coloured years had
sought the far trails of high Romance through all the
western world, was practical! As a result, we did

not have to join the bread-line! But there were millionaires, and capitalists, and even canny politicians, who did.

We obtained a tent, though thousands of late comers were disappointed. All through that night I kept a revolver near my hand, as the thousands of feet went pounding, pounding, pounding—pounding without cessation, pounding all night long, pounding like dull yet mighty drumming, pounding like the sustained and awful sussurance of a mighty ocean—as the crowds poured in from the flaming city. Fifty miles inland and far out at sea that tremendous blaze illuminated the night, reflected back from the huge canopy of smoke that overspread the sky, although elsewhere it was a starry night, bland and still. Detonations of dynamite now and then thudded through the pounding.

With the morning I left my family, and struck out for my office. The three morning newspapers joined forces that day, and produced a joint issue. I got across the bay to Oakland and reported to the superior editors, who were foregathered there, and was immediately ordered back to San Francisco in command of a company of reporters and camera men, to set up local headquarters, and begin the task of newsgathering. The paper was to be printed in Oakland.

We obtained a small tow-boat, which the twenty-odd men on board crowded badly. Among our number was Mr. Samuel Shortridge, the lawyer, who had begged his way across in our company as nobody save soldiers, physicians, priests, nurses, newspapermen, and other regular assistants at disasters, was permitted to get back into the city once he had left it.

It was a gay trip. Our skipper turned out to be blind drunk, and our boat went staggering, and turning eccentric half-circles, and now and then trying to turn a somersault, through a heavy sea. At last two of us had to stand on either side of the wheel, holding up our skipper and making him steer some sort of reasonable course for the other side.

We ricocheted our way close to Alcatraz Island. Telegraph Hill, Nob Hill, Russian Hill, were blazing like cosmic torches, gigantic tongues of red fire going up straight into the still air beneath the black canopy of smoke.

Mr. Shortridge has a very deep voice and a singularly impressive deliberation and distinctness of utterance. He is a celebrated orator. He felt moved to make a speech on this occasion. He said, staring at the three burning hills: "Lord God Almighty!"

I heave heard many speeches; thousands of them I suppose. Perhaps ten of them were good speeches. But this one remains unique at once in its appropriateness and its effect upon those who heard it. All vain words were banished; all useless thoughts were swept away. Today I may string words together, so long after that mighty moment; but then only the high names of God could fit the occasion.

We landed near Fort Mason. I at once set about the business of hiring headquarters. After several vain efforts I finally succeeded in striking a great bargain; I hired Harbor View Park, the whole establishment. This comprised a bathing beach, a bowling alley, a bar-room, a well-stocked larder, enclosed by a high fence. It is vanished now.

I also hired a motor car and sent a reporter—

better known today as Frederick Ferdinand Moore, war correspondent and novelist—to the Presidio for my family. I had heard that the absence of sanitary arrangements among the herded thousands in Golden Gate Park and the Presidio threatened to cause an outbreak of disease. In Harbor View Park we would be safe.

In less than an hour Moore was back again, with my wife and children.

Less than half an hour later, a mounted army officer rode to the gate and demanded speech with whoever was in authority.

"You must immediately vacate these premises," said he, when I appeared. "The United States Army wants them, as a detention camp for contagious diseases. The smallpox patients will be here within the hour."

We heard and perforce obeyed. Very luckily, right at the moment, a tugboat from Santa Cruz put in at the little wharf, and I at once hired it for a despatch boat, to carry copy and orders back and forward between Oakland and San Francisco. So I sent my family across the bay, together with a large number of other refugees. I did not see wife or children again during the next three weeks.

Then came the new search for headquarters. It was ended quickly. Mr. Shortridge, hearing of our predicament, solved it out of hand. He placed his own large and beautiful home completely at my disposal. He threw in his Chinee cook, to make the job complete. So in this luxurious office, sleeping three in a bed with Ah Fung to cook for us, we lived as newspapermen have rarely lived before. Each day a

special detail went out, not for news, but for grub.
The day's work was over at six or seven o'clock,
because the copy had to go over to Oakland very early.
Then we foregathered from our various jobs, and ate
a wonderful dinner, and fleeted the evening hours
away with card games, and stories, a punch bowl,
and Mr. Shortridge's gorgeous grand piano, the one
he had bought especially for Paderewski, his client.
Every now and then a shock of earthquake would
make the house rock and quiver. Sometimes these
blows were so heavy that we went running into the
street. Then we would go back again and Freddy
Moore, or somebody, would play ragtime, in between
the shocks, and we would sing.

> "Through a small Irish town,
> Marched a troop of renown,
> In the year seventeen hundred and forty;
> With a hip, hip, hurray, and a hip, hip, hurray,
> Tirri-row, did-a-dow, did-a-row-dow!"

Ours was the only house in all the district permitted to burn lights after eight or nine o'clock; and
under our glowing windows, on the steps, and along
the curb, the neighbours would gather, listening to our
songs, and taking comfort, I think, in our jollity.
One night we gave a dinner to our host; ah, such
a dinner! We brewed an earthquake punch. The
whole city was scoured for materials. Somebody
went up the hill to Mayor Schmitz's house and returned with beer, and a bottle of Scotch. Into the
big bowl went beer, and Scotch, and benedictine, and
rye, and a bottle of champagne, and brandy, and
creme de menthe—anything, and everything.

7. The City That Never Was

But if we newspapermen had special opportunities to be gay, San Francisco in general was also high-hearted despite the darkness, and the dread of doom.

The fire had on the third day been stopped at Van Ness Avenue.

How many had been lost in the tumbling of walls, and the destruction of cheap tenement houses, and, still more, in the abominable lodging houses south of Market Street and on Barbary Coast, will never be known till the real Doomsday happens along; but many hundreds are known to have perished. As Mary Austin says: "Large figures of adventure moved through the murk of these days—Denman going out with his gun and holding up express wagons with expensively saved goods, which were dumped out on sidewalks that food might be carried to unfed hundreds; Father Ramm cutting away the timbers on St. Mary's tower, while the red glow crept across the cross out of reach of the hose; and the humble sacrifices—the woman who shared her full breasts with the child of another whose fountain had failed from weariness and fright—would that I had her name to hold in remembrance!"

Those were indeed brave, coloured, splendid days! San Francisco's soul will be richer and stronger and warmer and more human till the end of time because of them. They were days when the dream of Utopia, the fabled epoch of the Golden Age, of human brotherhood, were perhaps as nearly realized as ever upon this troubled world.

Save for those whom death had struck with loss

and pain, through taking away loved ones, the vast majority of San Franciscans were not merely stoical—they were gallantly brave, romantically chivalrous, superbly generous. In my goings about through the worst of the stricken districts, I saw many instances of loss and disaster, but my memory of those days is not stained with a single incident of cowardice or of meanness.

The obvious thing to say, is that social conventions and distinctions were laid aside; well, so they were, but that only expresses a small part of the truth. After all, the only place where men are truly, quite literally equal, is in their souls. God made us all, and when the red ruin was raging from the water front on towards Van Ness Avenue, a line of fire ten miles wide, at times, and later, when amid the shards and dust and smoke of the vanished city, men and women no longer felt that doomsday was upon them, they acted toward each other as fellow creatures, as human beings, not merely as employer and employé, rich man, poor man, beggar man, thief.

. . . .

Will Irwin wrote an excellent description of Old San Francisco, which he called "The City-That-Was." Well, the glimpses of Paradise, or of Utopia, which came to me while San Francisco, riven and shattered, was being bound, as it were, upon the monstrous pyre of its burning, was a vision of the City-That-Never-Was—the city of the world-wide dream—the city which John of Patmos saw descending out of heaven to earth—out of aspiration into accomplishment—out

of the ideal into reality—the city of peace and of
brotherly love—of the kingdom of God come upon
earth. The City that never was—that never, never
was—yet which surely is to be—which surely is to be!

. . . .

Perhaps I saw everything magnified by my own
mood—coloured by my own desire—nevertheless, it
is true that for several marvellous days in San Francisco we lived as people might live if they but willed
it so—we lived a life of good-will. Nearly all the
artificial barriers and distinctions with which we iso-
late class from class and person from person were
thrown down more effectually than the 'quake threw
down the walls of houses—the walls of evil houses and
the walls of churches together. For days, there was
no use for money—there was nothing to buy or sell.
Rich and poor were no longer either rich or poor.
The bread line was no respecter of persons. The
women of the Tenderloin were cared for by virtuous
women. Food was in common. He who had not
asked and he who had gave. Your neighbour was as
yourself. You did not see the mote in his eye for
there was no distorting beam in yours. Generosity
—kindness—pity—mercy—tenderness—all the brave
and beautiful angels of the heart of man walked in
the streets of the shattered city. Oh, yes, there were
exceptions, no doubt. I've heard of them—but I
did not myself see them—but it is God's own truth I'm
telling you when I say that the great disaster which
for several days shut off San Francisco from the
world that still went on in the ordinary way, brought

out what is best, and what is strongest, and what will finally prevail in mankind—that which is good. Those three or four days, despite all the dreadful things that happened were days of the Golden Age returned again—and to me their memories remain as prophecies of the time to come, when we shall all together so live without change or shadow of turning.

Indeed, it almost seemed as if Goethe's dream was realized, and that San Francisco had been shocked out of its egoism and had found in the midst of this apocryphal overthrowal the poet's spring of goodness, and had become quite literally the City of Brotherly Love, the City of Peace—the City-that-Never-Has-Been. . . .

Ah me!

It was wonderful to hear city officials who were more than merely suspected of the most brazen graft declare that for them, "The history of San Francisco begins on April 18, 1906!" It was thrilling to see sworn foes and bitterly opposed factions uniting in the new bonds of mutual service.

It was sublime!

.   .   .   .

And it was also evanescent as a dream.

Violent reformations of cities or of individuals are dramatic, but impermanent. . . .

I well remember how frantically we had to work, one night not long after the worst of the disaster was over, to hurry the news to Oakland, where our paper was being printed, that the Board of City Supervisors had just jammed through a very nefarious piece of special privilege legislation. . . .

—And we know how soon afterwards the malodorous graft cases made the name of San Francisco scandalous throughout civilization.

No. Apparently it requires something more profound, more energetic, than an earthquake, to reform a city, or a soul. An earthquake may destroy; yes; and so will many other things. . . .

But what will save us?

CHAPTER VI

HELICON HALL

1. Back In New York

SIX weeks after the shock, my turn came to fall into disfavour with my superiors, and in the row that followed, I quit my post, and returned to the East. For a while I left my family in a country town, while I adventured to New York again; penniless, yet determined not to retreat to newspaper work save as a last resource.

A friend (what would have become of me all my life had it not been for my friends?) took me in and gave me shelter until I could earn enough money to hire a room and a typewriter.

A sympathetic magazine editor realized my position and promised to read and pass upon a story at once. "So go home and get busy," said he.

I went home; sat up all night (drinking coffee to imitate Balzac in at least one particular!), and wrote two stories. By nine o'clock I was at the editor's office.

"Come back at ten," said he.

For an hour I sat on a bench in Madison Square Park juggling with my nerves in an effort to achieve equilibrium of spirit—and of body, too, for I shivered despite the warm September sun.

I had only one dime left, and my friend's house

was far away in the remoter parts of Brooklyn. If the stories did not suit, I would be in a desperate fix.

Yet, I wanted a drink.

Should I or should I not spend my dime, and take a chance?

I tossed for it. Heads came—or tails—I forget which. Anyhow, it meant, "Take a drink." And I did so. I drank to the success of the stories.

At ten I entered the office. "A cent a word for one yarn. So here's a check for thirty dollars; the other story is a lemon. For God's sake never offer such a story anywhere," said the concise editor.

I thanked him for the check; then my blood stirred; and I offered to bet him a dinner that the story he had turned down was the better of the two; and I would prove it by selling it somewhere else.

And a few weeks later I had the ineffable satisfaction of asking him please would he cash a check for one hundred and twenty-five dollars, as another magazine had given me three cents a word for the tale despised and rejected of him on the one cent basis.

I hope the editor did not consider me too cocky, but I fear perhaps he did, to judge by the note he sent me.

. . . "Was glad to hear you have got the half-Nelson-strangle hold on the publishers. Get them down on the floor three points and keep them there. It might occasionally help things along if you break a back or two, or slip an ear out of place. In any event, dislocate an arm once in a while, and do a little gouging."

This letter tells its authorship plainly; only Robert

H. Davis—that stalwart friend of the writers—can
do this sort of thing so well.

2. An Expensive Coincidence

It was about this time that Madame Fate displayed
herself in her most mordantly ironical mood.   Yet,
for such an accomplished artist in arranging human
trouble, it must be said that she did it rather crudely
in that she resorted to that expedient which experts in
dramatic technic agree to deplore—the long, strong
arm of coincidence.   Nevertheless, it was a very remarkable coincidence.   Even the theatrical manager
who—as it were—staged the affair, admitted that
fact; and surely his great experience, in drama and
in other ways, fitted him to judge the matter.

I had sold a story to *Everybody's Magazine* which
when published achieved quite a success; mostly because of circumstances having nothing to do with its
literary merits.   The story dealt with an anarchist
inventor who devises a machine that will disintegrate
the physical atom, or neutralize the power of gravity
—I really forget which; but something, anyhow,
very dreadful and ultra-scientific.   After giving due
warning of his purpose by means of signals written
on the clouds above New York, he proceeds to
destroy the city, this modern Babylon, as he terms
it; beginning with the Flatiron Building, and finally
wrecking most of the town before he is captured
and disposed of.   The magazine gave the story
several full-page pictures, and it caught the fancy of
many readers.   The *Evening World* seized upon the
occasion to print a lurid half-page special, based on

the idea: "What if somebody DOES discover such a thing, and then—goes to it?" The cigar store in the Flatiron Building borrowed the artist's paintings from which the illustrations were reproduced, and exhibited them in its windows.

In the midst of all this, my wife said to me: "Why don't you make a play from it?"

"A play? Why—"

"Oh, I don't mean a real play; I mean a Coney Island spectacle, or vaudeville stunt. The idea has great possibilities."

She was right—as she so often is. I agreed with her; which doesn't happen quite so often. Not knowing the theatrical ropes, I went to a friend who did. He, too, thought that the idea had possibilities. He agreed to collaborate; he to attend to the business side, I to write the play, with his assistance in construction.

"The Mortimers are looking for an idea right now," said my friend. "Something to use as the central feature of the new show which will be opening soon. I'll get busy."

A day or two later he called me on the 'phone to tell me that he had seen the press agent for the Mortimers, and the various managers of the theatre, including the man who handled the electrical and mechanical effects. "And they're all strong for our stuff," said my collaborator. "They haven't an idea outside of ours; they all say so. It certainly looks good. Mortimer himself is out of town, but will be back in a day or two. They think he will jump for this. It will mean a run all winter, and all next summer at Coney Island."

I was living directly opposite the theatre in question, and my wife and I would sit near the window and figure out what we would do with all the royalty money which would soon be streaming into the huge building over the way. Of course, this wasn't Art; but, anyhow, it looked like real money; and even Art looks at her lover with a singular feebleness of appeal when her rival, Golden Dollars, begins to make eyes.

"Hello, hello!" my friend telephoned one day. "Come right down to my office. Mortimer is back, and wants to see you right away."

I was in his office promptly, you may believe me.

"You're to see Mortimer at twelve o'clock. Now, remember—don't sign any contract; don't agree to any terms. Leave all that to me. You're simply to talk to him about the play, and how to handle it. Get back here as soon as you can, and I'll get busy."

I was at the office of the great manager at the appointed time. I sent in my card. I was kept waiting some little while; not long enough to make me feel slighted, but long enough, oh, quite, to make me understand that it was Mortimer at whose door I sat; the great Mortimer; who was, if not the foster-father of American drama, at least its uncle.

By and by, I was sent for. I was led through office after office, until at last the sanctum sanctorum was achieved; where the great man sat enthroned at his desk, with his heads of department, ten or twelve of them at least, seated by and about him.

Most courteously he received me. There was no hint of that haughtiness which great men in the world of drama and literature are fabled to display toward

the timid aspirants.   On the contrary, no uncle could
have been kinder, or more considerate in his manner.

"So, this is the author of that wonderful story!"
he exclaimed, heartily wringing my hand.   "I read
it with such pleasure, Mr. Williams.   And it has been
so successful, too.   Well, well!   And now, let us
get down to business.   We are soon going to open,
and we are about to rush work on our central feature.
That's where you come in, Mr. Williams.   You see,
it's most amazing, really—you see, your little idea—
why, upon my word, it's a wonderful coincidence, but
your idea is absolutely the duplicate of a play which
we've had in our safe for the past three months
or more.   The author, however, is quite unknown,
and as your story has created such wide attention, I
would like to use your name on our bill-boards and
program and newspaper notices, as the real author.
It will give you great publicity, Mr. Williams.   But,
of course, as you are not the author—well, you will
see for yourself that I couldn't offer you any
money. . . ."

I am afraid my crude, Occidental mind had difficulty in taking this in, and assimilating it, in a proper
manner.   I am even afraid I jumped up and said rude
and nasty things about robbery, and coincidence be
damned.   Why I did not rush at great little Mortimer, in my hasty wrath, due to my inability to recognize the wonderful nature of the literary coincidence
which he was relating, I to this day cannot understand. . . .

I went back to my collaborator.   He threw up his
hands, slumped into his chair, looked at me help-

lessly, and murmured: "Anarchists destroying New
York won't be just a magazine yarn, if this sort of
thing keeps on!"   And so hard was it for him to understand the coincidence, that he sent me to one of
the leading lawyers of the town, to see if "something
couldn't be done."

The lawyer listened carefully, then he sighed,
offered me a choice cigar, and said: "I wonder if
you will take my advice?   You are a young man—
and one of your names is Irish, so I daresay you
won't; but if you could take my advice, you'd go back
to Mr. Mortimer, and get the advertising.   You
haven't a chance on earth to get any money."

But I could not take his advice.   From our windows, a little later, my wife and I watched the crowds
pouring into the theatre, where the coincidental play
ran all winter long; and all the ways we might have
used the money we did not get, mocked us like a flight
of chimeræ. . . .

But it *was* a remarkable coincidence.

3. The Red Flag Of Revolt

I went on with hack work.   I did Sunday newspaper "specials," and more short stories for cheap
magazines; I wrote a serial of 30,000 words in five
days; and another in twelve days, and sold them both
at a cent a word.   I wrote a handbook for the use of
commercial travellers; I wrote a hundred leaflets for
an advertising manager.   Soon my family was with
me; we rented a flat, and furnished it, partly with
new things, partly with furniture left in storage when
we went West.   All this was more or less magnificent

(for us!), but it was not war as we wished to make
war. I was not writing what I wanted to write; still
I was a slave to the machine-made in writing.

So I seized every possible chance to work upon a
new novel which I had begun immediately after my
return from San Francisco, and at last I finished it,
and began to offer it to the publishers.

Upon the success of this novel we built our hopes.
It was making a decidedly good impression. Several
publishers seriously considered its purchase; and one
house at last said that if I would make the book longer,
and strengthen it in certain places, they would issue
it among the spring books of 1907. I went to work
upon it zealously. At last the dawn of my real life
seemed breaking.

That novel was to speak the magic word, the "Open
Sesame," which would throw down the rocky walls
hemming me in, and give me the long-sought treasure
of success. I called it "The Red Flag of Revolt,"
and it was drawn very largely from my own experiences, expressing my own philosophy. It was in
essence a glorification of the power of the human
will. Its hero was (of course!) a consumptive writer,
burdened with poverty, crippled by ignorance, surrounded with unsympathetic conditions, yet dimly
conscious of a higher destiny. He breaks down with
a hemorrhage. Instead of regarding it as the signal
of failure, the symbol of death, he wills to make it
the red flag of his revolt—the revolt of his will, of his
soul, against all that would hamper or drag him down
to defeat with his message still unspoken. So he sets
his will: and goes forth into the wilderness: he fights,
and he conquers; he gains love, health, and success;

the red flag of revolt becomes the brilliant banner of his triumph, the symbol of his personal power, the heraldic device betokening the self-sufficient and dominating "I." . . .

And now, with my hero (a self-portrait, Oh, of course!) I, too, was at last conquering my own way, by the strength of my own will. Or so, anyhow, it then seemed to me. The dawn of a new day appeared to be at hand.

And so indeed it was—only, again, as so often before, it came in a form of which I had not dreamed; it brought the opening of a new adventure instead of the ending of the old.

4. The Co-operative Home Colony

While with high hopes I was working upon my novel, I joined the "co-operative home colony" established by Upton Sinclair and a group of other radicals and "advanced thinkers," at Englewood, in New Jersey; a pleasant suburb of well-to-do business and "leisure class" people (as we of Helicon Hall would say), and their parasites and purveyors. It was snugly situated behind the Palisades, overlooking the Ramapo Valley, and only an hour's travel from the heart of New York.

I was not formally a Socialist, then—or even later on—however much I sympathized with the point of view of Socialism, and thoroughly as I shared its hostility toward commercialism. So it was not as a Socialist that I joined the colony. I went in the expectation of finding congenial society, pleasant surroundings, and relief from the worries and cares of housekeeping in a New York flat, in which I had to do my own work, and where there were two children to be considered when I desired privacy and quiet. Also, of course, there was the interest of the adventure itself. Helicon Hall was a social experiment; and it attracted great attention in the press.

Upton Sinclair I had known through correspondence for some time. An essay of his attacking the superficial and mediocre aspects of American magazine literature had drawn from me a warm message of approval and congratulation. He responded, and we kept up an interchange of letters for some time. Then I drifted westward, and lost touch with the literary world of New York; while Sinclair emerged from his garrets and tents—wherein for years he had been making his fight—and achieved the tremendous success of "The Jungle."

It was shortly after this event that I returned from wrecked and ruined San Francisco, and found Sinclair famous, and established in Helicon Hall. So I wrote to him asking if his roster of colonists was complete.

"Come and see for yourself," he replied.

So we went, my wife and I; we saw; and we were conquered by the varied attractions of the colony. It would be a rare and rather wonderful adventure, so we thought, to live in Helicon Hall.

So it proved to be, indeed; and if it turned out to be much more of an adventure than in our most adventurous mood we would have bargained for, well, there is no sense in complaining; such is the inevitable hazard of all forms of adventure; namely, the risk of getting too much of a good thing.

5. The Suburb, And The Colony

Both Helicon Hall and Englewood were in their way typical and significant products of the time-spirit. Englewood was a pleasant suburb, secluded, yet convenient, with its Country Club and golf course and private schools and motor cars, and college-bred business men going to and returning from Wall Street, or the Courts, or the great commercial houses of New York, and their fashionable women-folk and children. It was one of the many similar strongholds of the employing, or official and professional classes, near New York; homes of the average aristocracy of the commercial world, not the great millionaires, but the rank and file of the hierarchy of our dollar system of society. Safe, sane, conservative; average, normal, suave, smooth, conventional; all the words and phrases of this ilk belong to Englewood. On the other hand, Helicon Hall, stranded in the midst of all this, like a gypsy van stopping in a Methodist camp-meeting, and throbbing with a perpetual brain-storm of radicalitis!

6. The House Of Strange Souls

It was a queer place surely; this Helicon Hall! Incongruous, yet ironically appropriate as well, to find it in an ultra-respectable, ultra-conventional, bourgeois suburb like Englewood.

I've been told—heaven only knows with what truth —that it owed its existence to a dream—the dream of a schoolmaster at that! According to the legend, this schoolmaster was plagued by restless ideas and ideals;

poor man, the Time spirit had thrown one of its many tentacles about him. He was not content to teach as he had been taught, and to trot along the main highway of his profession, safely, soundly, and conservatively, and thus make a quiet living, and get through the world with the minimum of botheration and trouble. No; he felt obliged to experiment, and to seek out many inventions; a restless item of a restless age.

The education of boys in aristocracy seems to have been his obsession. His boys were to be made into "gentlemen," after some rather vague, neo-Nietzschean notions of gentility and individualism. Each was to have his valet, if he so desired; and each was to be treated with the most distinguished consideration, on the part of the tutors, and other servants, and encouraged to express his own innate temperament.

The plan and construction of the school building which was to be the outward and visible manifestation of the inward grace of American aristocracy was revealed to this Nietzschean shaper of souls while he was voyaging on the river Nile.

Perhaps the spirit of some sardonic old Egyptian adept of black magic overbrooded the spirit of this Yankee "professor," as he dreamed of his new-fangled school, and of the boys in whose persons he would influence his country and his age. Anyhow, he dreamed his dream, and coming back to America— where ideas need only to be money-producing or else starkly fantastic to find support—he secured a patron (probably a patroness!) to back him, and built Helicon Hall, and started his school for suckling aristocrats.

It failed. I don't know just why. I did not get all the story. Maybe the dreamer's chemical constituents wore out, and he died, or perhaps his immortal soul got tired of the task of inoculating the sons of American business men with the virus of an artistic aristocracy, and shook off the clumsy encumbrance of its chemical apparatus and went forth seeking other adventures through vistas impossible to New Jersey. I don't know; but, at any rate, Helicon Hall shut up shop as a school. I think it was a boarding house for a while; but it was empty when Upton Sinclair came along, just after the success of his book, "The Jungle" had made him rich and famous—in the relative sense—and bought it for his "co-operative colony," and he and a mixed assemblage of socialists, "intellectual anarchists," single taxers, vegetarians, spiritualists, mental scientists, Free Lovers, suffragists, and other varieties of Ism-ites, moved in and took the place of the neo-Nietzschean schoolmaster and his brood of infant aristocrats.

Many of the colonists, of course, were writers of one type or another. They expressed their immortal souls, or their chemical reactions, in novels and plays, and poems, and speech; especially in speech.

Never since the episode of the tower of Babel, I dare say, has there existed a place so saturated in language as Helicon Hall. Everybody there was more or less of the "advanced," or "radical" order of chemical make-up, or of soul development; and it is a scientific fact that this type is continually effervescing in monologue, sizzling in conversation, detonating in debate, fuming in argument, flashing in expressions of opinion, and exploding in many theories.

The Hall was a tremendous, oblong, wooden building with a huge court in its centre roofed with glass, with a fountain and miniature brooks, and rubber trees and palms growing twenty or thirty feet high. Little fish of gold and silver swam in the brooks. At one end was a vast fireplace open on all four sides, about which fifty or sixty people could sit or lounge. Near this was a pipe organ. Sometimes by night, when a glowing fire of crimson coals was suspended in the iron basket in the fireplace, and the lights were turned out, and the moon streamed dimly through the glass roof, splashing like noiseless silver water on the palm trees in the court, and some one played a violin, or something on the organ, and the talk mellowed and modulated from sociological arguments to a more meditative mood, then it seemed as if some influence sweet and pensive, friendly and melting, flowed like incense over and through us all; and for a while we could dream that our dreams could and would be realized—and the Socialist lived for the moment in his co-operative commonwealth, and the anarchist in Egoland, and the spiritualists divined the presence of their departed friends in the swaying shadows by the fountain, and all the ideals and dreams and fantasies, and all the impossible illusions of that assemblage of modern dreamers seemed to materialize, seemed to be real things, and the world of fact evaporated quite out of existence.

—At other times, though—Ah, then matters were different! For one thing the partitions were of the

thinnest between many of the rooms; and nearly
every second room (to draw it mildly) contained a
temperamental person with a pen or a typewriter and
a message for the world—or else a definite job of
literary work to be put out of hand as soon as possible.
That flimsy house fairly throbbed with criss-cross currents of diverse temperaments and purposes; also
with the shouts and yells of children, and, of course,
with Talk, Talk, Talk!   In one corner of the second
floor, where most of the living rooms were, Grace
MacGowan Cooke and her sister Alice MacGowan
were industriously dictating novels.   A door or two
away Edwin Björkman was philosophizing amid walls
packed to the ceiling with books in Swedish, Norwegian, Danish, German, French, and English.

Sinclair Lewis and Allen Updegraff were down in
the cellar, neglecting the furnace as they sought for
rhymes or stories.   Somewhere else, Professor William Pepperell Montagu was working at his problem
of a Thinking Machine which was to prove the chem-
ico-mechanical theory of the origin of human intelligence.

Never shall I forget the wild night when Sadakichi
Hartmann,   the   German-American-Japanese   poet-
painter, visited us.   Seven or eight feet tall, (or so
he seemed) with a face like a grotesque mask.   With
him was his friend, Jo Davidson, the East Side
sculptor, and another friend, the Tramp Madonna,
and also a big, black bottle of whiskey.

He sat by the fire theorizing on Art and Life and
Love—Free art, Free life, and Free love, of course
—until long after midnight, filling the sonorous shell
of the court with talk,—talk—talk; until at last Ed-

ward Björkman, in a fluttering bathrobe, with flashing eyes and a head looking like the head of a refined and elegant Ibsen, rushed forth from his bedroom and drove Sadakichi and the sculptor and the lady and the bottle out into the bitter night, and into the newspapers next day.

.   .   .   .

7. Strange Souls

The room next to mine was occupied by a stout, elderly widow, whose walls were hung with "spirit portraits," and who was ardent in the faith of that most pitiable of all cults, the Spiritualists. Existing in a continuous tremor of morbid sentiment, she saw forms that the air gave up for her vision only, and faces, smiling or sad, appeared and disappeared in dusky corners, and she heard voices that said: "Deary, I am so happy over here—all your friends are with me, deary!"

There were Christian Scientists, also; and "Mental" Scientists—who believed in the transforming power of "affirmations," like the New Thought people, but, they said, in a much more logical, more intellectual mode. An elderly semi-hobo man-of-all-trades who attended to the furnaces after the youthful socialist poets from Yale were relieved from the task, was one of our most advanced radicals. There was a young Southerner who having run through nearly all other formulas was thinking of trying sequestration in a Benedictine monastery. There were, of course, numerous feminists, devotees of Mrs. Charlotte Perkins Gilman, and George Bernard Shaw. "Bernard Shaw says—" was a phrase you heard at Helicon Hall as in less advanced homes you hear, "mother says that . . ."

And always there was a coming and going of visitors, who for the most part were themselves representatives of the "advanced movements"; singular cults and experiments in life and thought. Lecturers and writers on Sex, on Sociology, on Anarchism, on Dress Reform, Child Training, Vegetarianism, Fletcherism, Socialism, and all the other modes and manifestations of the restless mind of the age, all defiled through Helicon Hall, like a Pageant of Eccentrics.

There were also a few first-class intellects there. Edwin Björkman, for instance. I shall always feel a sense of solid satisfaction in my memories of my communions of spirit concerning matters of art and of life with Edwin. He has, indeed, a deep vein of the truest artistry running through his complex temperament of a philosopher-reformer-poet-religious-mystic searcher after the Absolute. And Professor Montagu was not one of the intellectual eccentrics; but his rigid mechanical view of life had no appeal for me.

Sinclair and the others, in varying degrees, represented interests with which it was not in my nature to affiliate, but yet for a time they all were deeply and sympathetically interesting to me, who came among these radicals, these advanced thinkers and heresiarchs after my lonely years in newspaper offices, and wanderings here and there in many parts of the country. And Helicon Hall was a vestibule, as it were, through which I entered a curious tract of modern American life, and from it radiated many of the vistas of ad-

venture which we shall follow as these pages expand
—the tract occupied by believers in strange ideas and
the followers of singular systems of Life, which it
fell to my lot to explore—I will not say thoroughly,
but at any rate most adventurously, as I sought the
trails of the high romance which eluded me in Helicon
Hall, as it had elsewhere.

8. The River

For it was at Helicon Hall that the problem with
which so much of my life has been concerned—the
problem, namely, of whether we are immortal souls
or merely ephemeral products of a casual chemico-
mechanical process, began to press upon me with an
irresistible urgency. My quest was stimulated by
the vertiginous mixture of ideas in Helicon Hall, and
also by many solitary communions with silence and
solitude, on the verge of the Palisades, overlooking
the river, gazing at the great city which has given me
so many adventures.

Helicon Hall stood amid a grove of trees apart
from the village and not very far from the top of the
Palisades. A short walk brought one to their verge,
and I often took that walk, in the afternoon, after
working on my novel during the day.

The snow crunched beneath my tread; the naked
trees threw inky shadows; withered leaves clung to
a few desolate branches. The broad flood of the
Hudson looked drab, or a steely-grey, or a murky
brown; sometimes dabbled with streaks of white foam
or blotched with grey fields of drifting ice; and how
solitary was its atmosphere! How different from
its summer suggestion, when long strings of loaded

or empty barges and canal boats are briskly drawn
up and down, and the passenger steamers pass covered with flags, and swift sailboats and rushing motor
boats dot it all over with accents of energy.   Now
there was only the solitary ferryboat crossing from
One Hundred and Twenty-eighth Street.   In the
evening when it was lighted up it somehow seemed a
mournful thing, like a funeral barge, very lonely on
the immense width of the dusky stream, on which, as
it slowly passed from shore to shore, it threw the
wavering reflections of its lights.

Advancing to the very edge of the cliff, I would
stand there.   Used as I am to New York, there is
an irresistible attraction for me in almost all of its
aspects, and few of its exterior points of view, I
should think, can surpass in interest the one of which
I am speaking.

It is invested with an air of fine style; touched with
the influence of something elegaic, something romantic, almost psychic; as though some magic casement
opened in the atmosphere at this point to permit the
vision to pierce beneath the surface aspects of the
scene.   I suppose the rugged romantic rocks and
splendid forest trees of the Palisades, and the broad
river, are responsible for the subtle quality of the
view of the city from this point; and, also, there is
always a sort of hypnotic effect produced by the
running water of a river.

Across the stream there is the pepper box ugliness
of Grant's Tomb; there are the squat, mushroom
shapes of the huge gas-tanks; a train crawls along the
shore trailing a snaky, black ribbon of smoke; the

cliff-like formation of the apartment houses along
Riverside Drive glitters at a thousand points where the
windows catch the light; beyond these there is the emanating suggestion, rather than the actual appearances
of the crushed-together vastness of New York. And
how many times I have wondered at the effect of
silence, and of immobility as well; as though all that
has been said of the roar of the city, and of its
frenzy of action, were fables. It is as though the
hypnotic river had woven a barrier of silence around
New York, or as though its population had been en-
chanted.

At the hour of sunset the wizardry is intensified.
Then the thousands of windows in the tall houses flame
or smoulder in lines of blood and of gold; they are
blurred and lurid, smoky and fuming; or clear, hard,
glittering, and cold, according to atmospheric conditions. Or the hour after sunset, when the electric
lights along the Drive, and in the windows, begin to
shine; beaming steadily or pulsating, after the fashion
of stars and planets; appearing to be of many colours,
all pale, like lemon, and dim violet, and withered
lilac, and faint mauve; sometimes diffused and misty,
like vague, ghostly radiations; at other times sharply
defined, like a myriad of clear, emphatic dots and
dashes.

These were the best hours for one to stand, prefer-
ably alone, at this point of view. Or in the nights
when the mystery of moonlight transmuted the river
from grey water into a flood of ether, and the trees
dripped with its magic foam, and the lights across the
stream of silver and dusky ether seemed no longer to

be those of New York, but of Sarrass, the Spiritual City, or of Mount Salvatch.

.   .   .   .

9. Visions And Desires

And my thoughts shaped themselves:—"Millions of human beings are massed together over there. Millions, and each one unique; each one an individual, not-to-be-duplicated spark of immortal spirit clothed about with tenements of flesh and bone; a Soul that can never die; a Person, destined for endless experiences, of which living in New York is a mere momentary fragment.

"Or else, they are nothing of the sort; they are but casual ephemera, produced (according to Professor Schaffer of the British Association for the Advancement of Science, that most learned man!) as a mechanical result of certain actions and reactions of chemical substances; they are swirling together intricately, over there, each one seeking its own instinctive desires (these also being the result of chemical agencies), like a swarm of summer gnats!"

And then a wider vision would come. I would grow almost objectively aware of the population of the great city in a way never to be forgotten. I felt the tides of being moving around and about me; the people going to and fro in the streets, and beneath the streets; and across the North and East rivers and the harbour to Staten Island, to Jersey, and Brooklyn, and Long Island; and under the rivers in the tunnels; and on the rivers in the ferry boats; and in the trolley cars, and the "L" trains, and the subways, and the steam and electric railroad trains, and the cabs, automobiles, stages. Men, women, youths, maidens, girls and boys. To and fro they pulsed. They thronged the theatres; or the parks, or the streets; and their houses, everywhere; from the Waldorf-Astoria or the roof garden of the Hotel Astor to the fetid tenements of the Ghetto. Millions of bodies—bedecked in silk; or hung with a dirty rag;—lithe, well-nourished, gleaming in health; or gaunt, breaking down, torn by the assaults of disease. Millions of souls—from the soul joyously ascending in ecstatic aspirations to the heights of life; to the purblind, wounded, scarred and ignorant soul struggling still in the slime. (But struggling, always struggling to rise, to escape!) To and fro they swept on the tide of life that pulsed through the great town; myriads of them eddying, swirling, jostling together upon interweaving currents of destiny; the strong, the weak, the alert, the dull, the noble, the base: each and every one a distinct and different element in the huge alembic—the alembic in which life with innumerable reagents was testing all, and from which would issue the men and women of the future. And of all these myriads the greater number by far were doomed to suffer, were sentenced to ignoble and endless toil, and were banished from beauty. Yet all these poor men and women, and all the others, too, the strong, the haughty, the proud ones of wealth and wider life; all, all were my brothers and sisters; and all were awakening to a dim, troubling, bitterly-sweet and ever-growing knowledge of their relationship as brothers and sisters. All were made of the same flesh and blood, and mind and soul;

and they were ever moving forward to a completer realization of this fact of facts—the truth that shall make men free, the truth of human brotherhood. And those who knew the truth must proclaim it far and wide! . . .

And as I saw, here and there upon the river, lights flashing forth as the darkness grew deeper, I would think of the light-houses on the shore of the sea into which the river runs, and the swords of their lamps that pierce the night; swords of the Will of Man; of man in his long warfare against the dark forces that oppress him.

.   .   .   .

Let me be in my little world a sword, O Will of Man, a weapon of life!

So I prayed; and I prayed also:

When I forget that sad company of the poor and lowly whom I left behind me in the subcellars and stores and shops and tenements from which I have fought upward toward free life, then may life slay me utterly!

As Life would do, I know, if I proved traitor, no matter how high the apparent place my apostacy might temporarily gain me. . . .

.   .   .   .

And so, too, for the most part, though not so fantastically and feverishly, did my comrades of Helicon Hall meditate and dream. Like one of the best of the modern writers whose ideas greatly moved us, H. G. Wells, we desired, one way or another, to add something to the Book of the Samurai.

Nobody can understand this statement who has not

read "Modern Utopia," so for their benefit, unfortunate souls! let me recall that in this book Wells points out the fact that no worlds are ever conquered save by men who carry bibles in their hands. Those who find and conquer Utopia, then, must possess a Bible; a Book of Power. In this book will be put such words, said or written by men and women, as embody the idea of the Order; the order of men and women who are at work today re-shaping the world, and who by and by shall rule it.

And, Wells goes on to say, at first the book must necessarily contain much namby-pamby and mistaken stuff—it cannot be at once made beautiful and noble and perfect. . . . Which is an encouraging remark to some of its would-be contributors!

The only editors the book can have will be those who need its message. These editors—I may put the case—are the discerning men and women who recognize and act upon the Great Idea—which is, that the Will of Man can make a world fit for Man—a happy and contented world of true men and women, a real Utopia. They seek and utilize the inspiration and the plans of those ever-increasing writers who see with Walt Whitman that though each man is unique, yet all men are brothers; and that men can truly make new worlds out of old—all that is necessary is to realize, and act upon the realization of, the truth whispered by the Sea Lady, that "there are better dreams" than this dream of the poor, wretched world we have.

So, therefore, even my dreams may be useful. My tale of myself in pursuit of my dreams is not a singular and bizarre phenomenon. It is part of a great group movement, the most characteristic and important movement of thought and of literature in these troubled times.   Which fact gives what I say an importance it would otherwise lack.   For a multitudinous chorus of many voices, many of them out of tune, and uttering frightful discords, it is true, strives today to find unity and harmony as the Voice of Man. . . .

All who are instruments of the Voice of Life— all those poets, philosophers, musicians, tale tellers, and other creative artists, who are moved by life to be the voices of humanity—consciously, or unconsciously, work toward self revelation.   And even although I realize that my own effort may be in vain, I still think the effort itself may be of some value.

It is one more story of the human soul facing the ineluctable Mystery.

For to me the final fact of all facts, the core of all things, whether of a sun sparkle on a wave, or the light of Sirius, the movements of an insect, or the nature of man or superman, is Mystery.

Nothing can be more self-evident than that all things in life are but parts, phenomena, of the pilgrimage of the soul of man in quest of mystery's Solution. And ever as we pilgrims of the quest, we searchers after the answer to the riddle of existence, solve this or that minor puzzle, our very activities, being actions of life, weave other and more intricate patterns of Mystery—our creative labour generates harder and deeper tasks in the womb of eternity; and ever, always, the great loom of life spins on, weaving the curtains that hang before the shrine of the Eternal. . . .

.   .   .   .

—A little picture flashes before my eyes as I write of ourselves being pilgrims of that quest whose object is to find the answer to the riddle of existence; a little picture evoked by the word "pilgrims."

—I see a vast desert; night at hand, and the sands are grey. A caravan has travelled a great distance. It has stopped at many oases; and now, reaching a camping place, it rests, but soon will go on again—on—on—on. . . . And the caravan will reach other oases, but it will leave them, for the caravan must go on. The pilgrims rest; some cook; others kneel in prayer, the brown, lean faces turned toward Mecca; camp fires twinkle, and the stars come out; and around the fires sighs mingle with laughter. And with intent eyes watching the flames, or lifted up at times to look at the stars, or to peer into the surrounding darkness, the men and women and children gather together; and now appear those who tell fortunes, and who write letters home for the pilgrims, and who sing songs, and tell stories.

. . . .

—I, too, would tell a story, O my fellow pilgrims, a story of myself, a story of many adventures, some very strange, some very common, some evil, some that shame me, and others that gladden me to remember—the adventures of a man who roamed the world in search of his soul. Far away from this beautiful shore where now I write did the tale of my quest begin—as I will soon relate—far east and north, in bleak New England, where the Pilgrims landed—again that word, pilgrims—how strange! Can it be that I who have hated the Puritans of New England with impatient, hot hatred, can gain a truer vision of them by remembering that they, too, were pilgrims of a quest?

10. End Of Helicon Hall

Perhaps those solitary hours of brooding on the Palisades were the best things that I gained by my sojourn at Helicon Hall. Perhaps the sense of great wonder, and the adumbrations of the inner mysteries of Life, which came to me during those hours, with such irresistible persuasions of their power to affect human life, were after all connected closely with the people and the happenings at the Hall. The vistas of many of my spiritual adventures were opened for me in my wanderings by the mighty river, and my sojourn in the fantastic Hall.

.   .   .   .

The colony, with its ideals and dreams, its beauties and mistakes, its errors and its ignobilities, ran its brief, feverish course of a few months,—lamentably to end as a flaring story for the newspapers in the disastrous fire that swept it away between dark and dawn one cold, winter morning.

A red symbol of the dawn! Such was Helicon Hall —symbol of the dawn of a new day and a new way of living; a new life which *must* come, else the yearning soul of man but deludes him with vain dreams. . .

.   .   .   .

And in the fire my wife and I lost our all—our clothes, furniture, our books. . . .

.   .   .   .

And my manuscripts!

Every shred and scrap of my manuscripts; including the accepted novel and the book I had written in the year before I went to Texas; seventy thousand words of another book at which I had been working at intervals for more than ten years; the forerunner, in fact, of this book; three short plays, and a mass of stories, poems, prose sketches, essays, note-books; all the literary baggage of my life's work, save for a few unimportant short stories then going the rounds of the magazines.

The insurance on our property had lapsed; we faced the world that winter morning, the four of us, man, wife, and babies, in our night gear.

Why had I not saved my manuscripts?

There was no chance. That great wooden barn of a place was a hell of roaring flame within ten minutes of my awakening; and my awakening came where I was sleeping on a balcony on the third floor, with my books and papers in a room far away at the other end. And my wife and children were downstairs. The children were on the ground floor; my wife on the floor above. She knew the babies were safe; so she came to me; to warn me, just as I was starting to seek her. We bumped together in the smoke and flame—in which two poor souls went out from their bodies on the final adventure of all—and we just barely managed to escape, after one sickening moment of horror when we blundered down the staircase choked with smoke, at the end of which was a locked door.

. . . .

Grace MacGowan Cooke and Alice MacGowan, her

sister, were badly injured jumping from the windows; and many others were slightly hurt; while all the writers and students suffered more or less seriously through the loss of their work.

So ended Helicon Hall.

Destitute now, and utterly so, with the book that was to open the door of success destroyed, my chance gone, I turned once more to face the bitter struggle.

I resumed my literary free-lancing in New York; but when summer came we went to the Island of Martha's Vineyard.

CHAPTER VII

THE CALL OF THE QUEST

1. A Hut Upon a Hill

I T was at Martha's Vineyard that the turning point arrived and my Quest of the High Romance definitely shaped itself, and became conscious instead of merely instinctive.

On a little hill by the shore of this island—where we went nearly every summer—I had built a hut which I used for a work-room. It was not far from our cottage, yet far enough to permit me to escape from children and neighbours—translate, noises and nuisances when one is working!

It was my wont to sleep in good weather on a mat outside the door of this hut. When the first dawn light came, I would awaken, and as the birds began to sing, I would begin my work.

And so it was at dawn of that day among days which led me to a new, strange trail in my quest of the high romance.

In the doorway of my hut—that smelled sweetly of new-sawn pine—I stood in the cool crystalline stillness, and wondered—as ever I shall wonder—at the miracle of sunrise.

(I am sealed with the sense of wonder . . . for me nothing grows stale.)

Across the dimly blue-grey water, smooth as silver,

in the lighter sky, there extended a broad, undulating band of rich crimson, from which slowly spread upward—like a curtain rising—a ruddy glow, waxing lighter and brighter and more aerial in its ascension to where it was transmuted, in the high alembic of the cloudless heavens, into the pure gold of the sun.

My mood, despite the solemnity of the moment, was whimsical. I felt something that was akin to the shallow flood of complacency that a city man on a vacation in the country might feel as the reward of his unaccustomed virtue of rising early. And as a city business man might indulge in a few leaps, or do physical culture movements, under the stimulation of such a mood, I, being a literary person, must needs exercise myself by juggling with a few phrases to celebrate the occasion.

"My Lord the Sun still sleeps," I said, making as good an imitation of the genuflexion of a Parsee as I could improvise, "in his pavilion magically built by the genii of water, fire, and air. Its floor is of lapis-lazuli, the walls are of purple, the roof cloth is crimson, and the canopy is of gold. But when my Lord deigns to appear, forthwith the pavilion will be dismantled and overthrown, for this arrogant Majesty suffers no lesser glories to flaunt before his face."

Having witnessed my Lord mount the throne of day, I knew it to be time for his subject to go to work —for even devout Parsees, I suppose, have to work for a living; so, considering my devotions accomplished, I turned and went into my hut, and took the cover from my typewriter. I was at work on a Sunday newspaper article. The subject was well formed in my mind; I expected to finish the task that morning. . . .

2. The Inner Voice

But . . . but something happened. I do not know how to speak of it. For nothing outwardly happened, nothing at all; yet inwardly something quite momentous happened. All my life was from that instant changed; that moment was like the hinge on which invisibly, noiselessly and inscrutably, the door of Time swung open to admit me to a new existence.

And yet it was all so impalpable, so casual, too. As I have said, I was about to sit down at my typewriter, my mind filled with a sort of light, careless joyousness inspired by the freshness of the buoyant air of dawn.

Instead of doing so, I turned, all at once, toward the open door—very quietly—as though I had been touched by some invisible hand,—by the hand of somebody who had an urgent message; somebody who wanted me. It was—this is all I can definitely say, an impulse; a new kind of impulse; an impulse to do something as yet unknown; an impulse accompanied by an emotion of clear and thrilling joy—the joy which the beginning of an adventure always brings to the true follower of Romance.

I stared expectantly towards the door. But there was nothing, there was nobody there; only a clear space of sunshine, and the silence. The thrill of the moment passed; yet I remained there, feeling the sun, and, as it were, listening to the silence, in a sort of dream-condition. I am not as yet a master of moods; I am a poor disciplinarian of my energies.

Into the midst of the busiest humdrum my vagrant dreams intrude; they come—dream shapes, and dream voices, whispering poppied words, and they beckon, they entice my soul to follow them to a far region where only those things happen that are as you would have befall; and I follow them, I cannot help but follow.

So it was with me in that dawn. The magical draught of light and life, ever pouring from the golden beaker in the sky, entranced me—the wine of white magic was it! And then—and then I knew that the hour had struck. The conviction was suddenly and irresistibly borne in upon me that the time had come in which I must make my testament—my confession of the faith to which I hold—nay, which holds me and will not let me go until I have worked its will, to the fullest extent of my power. And the power comes. The soul does not send its servants forth to fight unarmed and unprotected—it gives both buckler and the sword. I am certain that in this moment of pulsating life my greatest, my most essential need found imperative voice.

And I obeyed the call.

What I had to do became clear to me. I must take a blanket and food, pen, ink, and paper, and go out of my house, go away from family and friends, neighbours and strangers, go away where there would only be the sea and the sky and the lonely land, and myself, and write to my friends—to all my friends —the story of my adventures on my pilgrimage. When I recognized and assented to the call my agitation waned; peace was with me; I set about the plain business of my mission.

3. On Taking To The Open Road

If I were not a writer, I would like to be a tramp, or a sailor,—but, verily, I'm pretty much of a vagabond as it is. The open sky—the roof of my house of life—has arched above my bed and board in many a land, on many seas. Canada, North Carolina, New England, Texas, West Indies, California, Mexico— these sonorous geographical names evoke remembrances of many adventures—they conjure up recollections of ships, and camps, work and play, in heat and cold, sun and rain, calm, storm, day and night— perils — pleasures — fights — fires — earthquakes! Great Walt, beloved R. L. S., sombre George Borrow, I, too, may raise a chant of the open road.

But I was not simply going on a tramp—I had business in hand; and as my pack was heavy, I was easy with myself, not wishing to get tired, and the first six miles of the journey were made as a passenger on the stage that runs between Oak Bluffs and Edgartown, the old whaling port at the base of Cape Pogue, the northeast point of the island. From Edgartown I meant to strike out on foot for South Beach, on the ocean side of the island, with an old, abandoned hotel at Katama Bay as my objective point. I felt that it would be well to keep within a mile or two of the deserted house so that I might readily reach shelter in case of a storm. And, indeed, caution was suggested by a change in the weather. Already the brilliancy of the day (a day among ten thousand for clarity of atmosphere and unclouded sun) had faded; clouds had gathered, and I read a threat in this frown of the heavens at the outset of my journey. My mood subtly attuned itself to the new key of grey. I became sober, serious, and somewhat sad. I felt a distinct shrinking back within my mind from the prospect of solitude; there was after all something darkly enigmatical in the thought of voluntary loneliness. The stability of purpose that a man's accustomed chair supports, the definiteness that keys up your work at your familiar desk, the comfort of a well-ordered household—could I really work without all that? Perhaps my intention was not wise after all; perhaps it was even foolish—my guiding dream might be a pixie, freakish and malicious, and not a serene messenger from the blue hall of the gods!

How was I to know? The little devils of doubt had seized me already! As matters stood, every hour's work was of urgent practical importance. I had no money; I needed money;—one day's work must pay for the morrow's food and shelter, fire and light, books and music—all the necessaries of life. My desk was piled high with work. Was it not foolish, recklessly foolish, to run away, at the beck of a dream, from real work?

And, musingly, I considered that chilling, dark chasm in the dim world of thought which I knew so well,—the chasm that yawns between desire and fulfilment, the idea and its accomplishment; descending deeper, extending wider still, between the ideal and its attainment. I considered it seriously. I recognized full well the difficulties, labours and dangers of its passage; and knew that I might thrill to my soul with realization of how goodly a thing I had conceived and yet fail most lamentably to demonstrate its goodness. . . .

But even in that time of doubt, of hesitation on the threshold, I knew that doubt and hesitation would be but momentary. Even then, deep within me, beneath my sombreness, a song of affirmation was thrilling as a bird sings above a cloud, in the sun; and when there is a song in my heart all goes well. Nothing daunts the soul that sings; for then it is in tune with life; and life's truest voice is music,—such music as men hear, or dream, and write down on paper to release again in violins, in drums, in brass and wood-wind, and in human voice. And there is music in the wind moving in the grass, in the brush, and the trees; there is music in waters falling in rain, purling in streams, crashing on the strand; there is music in all natural sounds, but all is inarticulate—it is song in limbo; song that must rise upward through the heart, the brain, and the soul of man, as through an alembic, before it is made living. Surely, the spirit of life speaks in and through all things; but from man comes its most noble words, its greatest messages, its highest songs, since man is its most perfected instrument,—though, indeed, merely the chief, the leading instrument in the orchestra. I dream of music as saints dream of heaven. I dream of so placing words together, of so choosing words, that from one unto the other will flow my thought, undulating, chanting its message musically.

4. The House of Quiet

—I was the only passenger on the stage. My driver was a boy of fifteen. As we drew near Edgartown we fell into talk. Previously, I had been silently drinking in the beauty of gracious colours suffusing sand and sea, wind-bent oaks, high, yellow grass and tufted rushes—and of the graceful lines traced by the deeply inset bay and low, curving hills, the moorland, and the linked garland of little ponds along the shore. I asked my driver the shortest route to Katama Bay. He gave me intelligent directions; and then asked me what I was going to do down there, where nobody lived. I told him I meant to tramp and loaf by day; and by night sleep under the sky. You should have seen that lad's eyes brighten, and heard how his voice rang the bell of his heart's interest! That was what he'd like to do, you bet, said he; and told me of his own past excursions.

What a pity all boys cannot do likewise, and from time to time go away to the woods, the hills, the waters, and roam them, sleeping where the day's end befalls. No doubt a few would drown; some necks would be cracked by tumbles from rocks and trees; and they might occasionally pot each other with guns not known to be loaded,—but do they not die, the boys, die like flies; die weak, vicious, diseased, by countless thousands in our cities?—thousands whom open air and play might save?

It was past six o'clock when we reached Edgartown. My boy driver kindly went out of his way to carry me to a place where he could point out the best route cross-lots towards Katama.

"Thanks, and good night—good luck, friend!"

"Good night—good luck!" he sang out in his piping treble.

I hoisted my bag on my shoulders and set my face

to the open places. I walked across a great, bare, swelling, wind-swept moor. Only a scattered house or two, far off, and widely separated; not a soul in sight.

Now was I indeed alone, in the house of the open; night at hand, sky grey, the rain already being cast into my face in brief spats by a fitful wind that whistled dryly in the stiff, short grass and the scattered patches of brush. Against the grey skyline to my right arose a tall water-tower, impressing solitude upon me like a symbol.

I had walked perhaps a mile and a half when suddenly I became aware of a sound that brought me to a dead stop, listening, peering forward—could it be—Yes! It was the low, deep, still, distant booming of the surf, sonorous and profound. Ho! how I thrilled,—how it always thrills me, that sound—I, who was born by the sea, who have sailed it, who have been threatened many times with death by it, and whose father and brother have it now for their graves. Both father and brother were sailors; so was my father's father, and his father—oh, if I might put the suggestion of that melodious thundering into words, back of all other sounds, like a gravely noble bass accompaniment!

Shortly after sunset I reached the deserted hotel at Katama, standing on the sand of the bay about a short mile from the sea beach. The sky was quite black save for one little place low down in the west where a dim, faint gleam of gold was fading; it was like the last hope left in a sorrowful heart. A chilly wind, salt and moist, was blowing in from the sea. The booming of the surf waxed louder.

Loose boards clattered in the ruined house. The wind in a cracked voice hummed banshee strains, or in husky accents whispered secretively through the shattered glass windows, the broken chimneys; and wandered through the empty rooms where once at such an hour as this bright lights shone, and men, women, and children laughed out the holidays of their work-a-day lives. Some great night bird, an owl, perhaps, blundered heavily down upon the roof of the veranda, startling me for a breath; and all about me were the queer, strange, anonymous little voices of nocturnal nature.

I took a bath of solitude. My soul and I sat like two Arabs in silent communion, secrets passing without words between us.

No man knows himself until he goes away from the crowd, and even then he learns but little for a long and weary time.

The dark, the low-breathing night leaned close to me, like a hooded priest toward a penitent. What is your message for me? Rest—rest—rest—so I translated what I heard, and I laid myself, dear night, upon thy bosom. . . .

I love the night; but my love for it is like unto the sentiment one retains for an old, past love affair. Truly, for many years I was a noctambulist, and wooed the adorable, moody, secretive mistress of dark hours who is veiled and has jewels in her hair, she whose cool caresses infect you with a singular and restless fever—but now I have a new love and pay court to her frank, joyous, wholesome, warm-hearted sister, day. . . .

5. How Joy Came With The Morning

I put myself between the folds of my blanket, drew on my sweater, got out my bundle of writing paper, and doubling a towel about it, used that for a pillow; and it pleased me to think I was like unto a soldier lying on his arms in the field. The conceit soothed me; and I slept, fitfully, it is true; but at last for several hours. On my final awakening I found the sky hinting of dawn, although it was still overcast, still threatening rain. But the wind was warmer, and there were dim penumbras of colours low in the east, across the black sea; the faint intimations of sunrise struggling through the clouds. I took the water pail and a towel and walked toward the sea.

On the sandy beach the waves were rolling in miles-long regiments of breakers, crested with curling foam. Flying sand and spin-drift stung my face. In this wan, grey light the effect produced on me by the sudden explosions of white wave crests was enthralling, it was deeply exciting. I lay down in the shelter of a sand bank to watch the wild yet ordered movement of the waves, dancing to their own secret rhythms. I was waiting for the light to increase in order that I might bathe. My wife's last words had been a warning against uncautious bathing on the South Beach, where the undertow is most powerful; and indeed one look at the swirling of these big smashers was enough to convince me it would be folly to risk swimming in them. But I conceived an idea. There was a fragment of an old wreck on the shore, and it occurred to me that I might wade out to the

lee side of this as one wave receded, cling to a plank
and allow the succeeding waves to drench me as they
breached against the seaward side of the stout, deeply·
sunken timbers.

After a little while the sun cleared a path through
the clouds and shone down upon me brightly.   The
moment was auspicious, I undressed and soon was
rushing at the tail of a retreating wave for the wreck.
Thigh-deep in the swirling back-rush, I clung to the
projecting plant I had marked, and in another instant—

Boom and crash!

The timbers shook, and a sheet of cold, sharp
spray fell heavily upon me. . . . Whew-w! what a
shock; and what a morning bracer for a man who
once upon a time depended upon dry Manhattan cock-
tails!   I allowed a few more waves to dash over me,
and then raced for the shore, dancing and leaping;
warm, tingling all over; and then I scampered back
for more.

After a brisk rub-down I pushed back to the hotel.
The sun had again disappeared; again it looked like
rain.   In a snug corner of the veranda I drew forth
my pen and began to work:

.   .   .   .

—And in my heart I offered up a pagan's prayer:
*"Blow, O wind of the morning, shine, O rising sun
upon me!   Freshen and fructify me with your keen
joyousness, your prepotent vitality, your irresistible
life—so that from me may spring my testament to
life as from this earth there comes the grass on which
I tread and the flowers that turn toward the east!*

*"For I have come to the shrine of the morning as
one who enters a confessional in the holiest of holy
Churches, to cleanse my heart by my confession—and,
if I am found penitent—and if I receive absolution—
I will partake of the communion—and then swear the
vow—and upon that shall follow the great Adventure,
of which this book is the shadow cast before. . . ."*

6. Mystery

The next night I slept far away from the dismal
ruin that complained to itself all night long,
querulously bemoaning its by-gone comforts; even
on calm nights it sighed and groaned. I spread my
blanket on the sand at South Beach, and listened to
the sea; and watched the moon, huge and ruddy and
round, coming up out of the water like a slow fire
balloon into a sky of rich, dim violet, losing its ruddi-
ness and becoming luminously silvern—like a blonde
girl losing the glow brought to her slender, white body
by a plunge into the sea.

The moor, with its covering of short, spare yellow
grass and its patches of pallid sand, and of dusky
brush, was drenched in a mysterious flood of mystical
sheen, a glimmering of singularly rich, dim, un-
nameable faint hues and suggestions of colours. On
the still inner water of Katama Bay the moonlight
was entrancing—one's soul plunged deep into that
silver current of dreams. A thick, sombre grove of
dwarf oaks and scrub pine lay to my right, black
and sinister. Now and then, fireflies sparkled in its
brooding gloom, unexpectedly and erratically as witty
thoughts issuing from a misanthrope. As I strolled

along the beach I heard the laughter of picnicers, and I made a long detour to avoid them. Then in the lee of a sandbank I again spread my blanket, and lay there contemplating old ocean—that ancient of days, hoarsely talking to himself along the sand—and drinking my fill of the night's freely proffered beauty. . . .

I think I was nearly asleep, when I heard gay voices, laughter, little ecstatic cries, and I hurriedly sat up. . . . I am very glad I was not sleeping! Three girls had stolen away from the other picnicers, and were racing along the hard sand by the very edge of the breakers; their shoes and stockings off, and their light summer dresses kilted up around their thighs. The distance softened their (perhaps) shrill, Yankee voices; the moonlight made their white legs gleam like silver, their draperies fluttered about them. . . . They are not Yankee maids, I cried, they are Nereids! Hark! in the surf the "blue Tritons sound their twisted shells." Old ocean (and who shall blame him?) clutched at their twinkling ankles as they sped along . . . and passed. . . . I saw them no more, I was sleeping, I suppose, when they returned. . . .

For a long time, I lay thinking of these communications before I fell asleep. I thought of my friends; I sent my love toward them. My thoughts went up into the air, through the moonlight, and sped on, like homing birds, their homes your hearts, dear friends. And, believe me, there is more than an evanescent conceit in these words,—for how many of my thoughts came from your hearts, were born and were given life through acts of kindness, of friendliness, on your part towards me! They are innumerable. We live in our friends. We are all unique beings, each and every one of us, but yet how much we gain, how much we add to what we are and what we do through the inter-play and interweaving of our common dreams, our thoughts, our acts, our sins, our dooms and destinies! One man alone would be no man; he would be an It, a Thing; the bees or the ants would capture and put him in a wax case, stuffed and neatly labelled as the monstrous curiosity of the earth. The word man to me signifies family.

．　　．　　．　　．　　．　　．　　．

When I awoke on the sand bank in the morning, lightning was flashing and thunder rolling in the east. It was two o'clock. I hastened for shelter from the storm. These electrical phenomena exercise a singular influence upon me, strongly exciting my nerves, and stirring up curious thoughts. And although the storm died out in the distance before daybreak, I was in a state of mind not braced for the continuance of writing. So I built a roaring fire— the morning was the coldest I had experienced— and stripped by it, and took a plunge. Then I raced back to the fire, and soon I was warm, glowing all over, feeling light and clean and happy, inside and outside.

And like a Brahmin contemplating the universe with his eyes for ever bent upon his navel, I sat by the blaze, the three elements of fire, water, and air having their will upon my body—and I was struck into awe by the wonder of this structure of bone, blood, and cell, in which I live. To think of the heart pumping blood through all these veins; the lungs and

all the intricate organism at work in strange
chemistry, transforming the air I breathe, the food
and drink I take, the sunshine that touches me, into
that other mystery—the energy which animates my
body's movement, and the thoughts and dreams that
move through the strange chambers of the brain!

Once dressed, I threw myself upon the turf.
There was a clump of daisies near me.   I thought of
their roots, reaching down into the soil, and of the
mystic chemistry there operating, to be expressed
finally in the blossom of white and gold that seems
(or is it fancy?) to be turning toward the East, toward
the sun. A gull screamed, wheeled sharply, and
dived into the water, seeking its food—a winged
mystery in the mystery of the air!   And the stars I
watched last night, the stars! . . . O mystery . . .
mystery! . . .

The profoundest chord in the symphony of life is
mystery.   Where it sounds in art you may know the
artist has drawn near the veiled source of all things.

Voices seemed to whisper secret words; I strained
to listen, to mark, to remember.

No.

I could not understand.

I cannot understand.

I do not think it possible to understand.

But in all I create may there be intimations of that
august, impenetrable Mystery.

7. Words of the Night

That same day, I returned to my home. I was
temporarily written out, and my strange, new mood

had relaxed its tension, although I had in mind
further things I wished to say. But for some time
after my return I was obliged to devote myself to my
bread-and-butter work. It was not until two months
later that I again took up the task begun at Katama
Bay.

Once more I feverishly wrought at my communications, because things that I desired to tell crowded
upon my attention at every turn, at every moment,
for months after the visitation of that curious wander-
lust. I could not meet even the most casual
stranger; I could not look to the right or left, up
or down, at star or gutter, upon open sea or city
street, without finding some new thing; something
that I felt I must write about, as though it had never
been described before; as though it had just been
born, and I had just been born, and must tell other
souls newly born about all these wonders, all these
things, and deeds, and happenings and personages of
this mystery-play of human life!

.   .   .   .

Night after night I brooded over them; in a far
different mood, however, and in very different circumstances, than during my trip into the solitude and
beauty of South Beach.

The storm that threatened but did not descend
all the time I was gipsying had now broken in all its
violence, and blew day after day and night after
night. The house in which I lived, a single-boarded,
unshingled, summer cottage, shook and quivered
continuously. The doors and windows rattled without cessation.

And night after night it was my duty to sit up, sleepless, and see the night through. I felt a deep disturbance of nerve, a feverish agitation of thought, —in reaction, no doubt, from my exalted condition during my South Beach adventure.

How it went to my heart to imagine—as each night I most vividly did—that out there in the bitter weather men were struggling and strangling, with flooded lungs and bursting hearts. All their agonies in vain, I could see them sink; down they went, down into the strange depths beyond which they might not sink; down among the tangled skeletons of the sea; down where the bones of my father and of my brother were swirling to and fro.

—In the depths of the sea—I told myself—there are great sub-oceanic rivers, with powerful currents (like the Gulf Stream) and these move along bearing with them everlastingly the bodies of the drowned; true rivers of Lethe! . . . And these men who were drowning, they were fathers, or sons, or husbands, or lovers, or friends; and their parents or wives or children or sweethearts or comrades were on shore; and they did not hear the passing cries of the drowning upon the wild wind, yet surely some of them felt strange tremblings—and yearning trouble; and tomorrow or the next day the news would reach them.

.   .   .   .

So I, who wrote in the morning, in calm, in peace, of the joys of my new life, my morning life, now in a night of storm wrote of the grim welter of the sea, where in the midst of the surf the withering faces of the drowning disappear, like bursting foam bells, and the wild wind howls over them.

．　　．　　．　　．　　．　　．　　．

Something had happened beyond the reaction from my other mood to make me feel like this.

I was watching beside a bed of sickness. My little son was burning in fever. I nursed him by night. In the intervals, when he was asleep or at ease, I kept on with my writing. Every little while, I would break off and go to his side when he moved, or moaned, or cried out, or needed attention. Just so long as I could hold myself to the task, I had kept at my bread-and-butter work, to the articles I was writing for the magazines. But ever since that call out of the dawn I had been singularly excited, or perhaps merely feverish, in spirit. Thoughts kept rushing through my head, even as in that autumn time the wild ducks were rushing out of the mystic solitude of the North; and when I heard the whirring of their wings—my wild bird thoughts!—perforce I stopped my work-a-day toil, and added something, if even but a few lines or words, to the book of my adventures.

And night after night I wrote, or read, as I watched by the sick boy, and thought or dreamed.

Like a river of unequal depth and varying strength and rapidity of current, is life; and during those strange nights I rushed through whirlpools and rapids; or in beatific calms, or wild vertigoes of spirit, I swept under sheer rocks, looking up into skies where eagles winged, or shuddered at the profound depths over which I floated—an atom, aware of its infinitesimal unimportance.

Yet surely the atom is important to itself, and to other human souls? At least I am something to my friends; as they are to me; as we are to each other in this world of which we know so little—this world which, like us, is rushing down the great river of life through the shadow land of eternity.

Every human soul is an exploration.

.   .   .   .

About three o'clock, one morning, the sick boy, after a dolorous spell of pain, went to sleep. What a blessed relief!

The night had grown colder, or perhaps it was I who was colder. They say, you know, that in that dismal hour before the dawn one's vigour is at its lowest ebb. I felt chilled, although I hugged the stove. I felt somewhat down in the mouth, a little nervous, and inclined to be irritable. I could see that I had not yet shaken off all traces of the shock impressed upon my nervous system by the earthquake, and the fire at Helicon Hall. I still find myself, in moments when vitality ebbs, troubled by fears of cataclysmic disasters impending. And that morning the quivering of the frail house alarmed me. I dreaded an overthrow, and fire starting up in the rooms from lamps—and I have had my fill of burning houses and of rushing out into cold dawns, homeless and stripped bare! And the rain was leaking dismally through walls and ceiling in half a score of places. This thing I consider damnable; there is something sickly, something suggestive of a mean disease, connected with a house that does not fulfil the true functions of a house; which is, to protect us

from the weather. Do you remember how Edward
Carpenter points out somewhere in one of his essays
that our house is one of our skins? . . . and a house
should be whole for life's sake, for decency's sake,
and for honour's sake. . . . After placing basins,
cups and other vessels beneath the more copious leaks,
I huddled up in a rug near the stove and read
Metchnikoff's "Nature of Man"; for I could write no
more, I had written myself out.

Metchnikoff's book is a great one. It is one of the
most inspiring and hopeful messages that science has
delivered to mankind in the course of many years.
It is one of those books from which material could
be drawn for the formation of that Book of The
Samurai of which H. G. Wells speaks; that book
which will be a Bible in the new civilization that is
to dawn, a book in which the finest and most hopeful
and truest words will be marshalled for the use of us
all.

But in my dismal mood that morning I came upon
an appropriately dismal portion of Metchnikoff's
otherwise stimulating message; that in which he deals
with the subject of death, and the instinctive human
fear of death. . . .

When you have a sick child on your hands you
do not like even to see that grizzly word, Death, in
print; you avert your thoughts with a shiver from the
idea—which is another instance that Metchnikoff
might use in support of his contention that there is
an instinctive fear of death implanted in human nature.

Nevertheless, the subject of death has always been
one of deep interest for me, and I returned to its

contemplation that morning. Indeed, it became uppermost in my thoughts. I laid the big book aside and sat musingly by the fireside; musing and re-membering. Scenes and conversations came vividly to mind; scenes in which Death and myself, or Death and others, played leading parts; conversations in which Death was the subject of the talk. I found myself synthesizing these memories, reflections and inquiries on death, in an effort to define what Death meant to me.

And as I sat there silently, all these memories be-came vivid pictures, and they defiled before my eyes like a panorama; or perhaps I might say that I sat there like unto a man in a strange house who studies the designs and figures in the tapestry upon the wall of a room of mystery. . . .

.   .   .   .

But as I brooded thus, my boy awoke and called me, and I hurried to him.

"I want a drink," he whispered.

I put the prepared draught to his scorched lips and he drank avidly. His head sank back on his pillow. He seemed not so feverish as on my last visit. In the dim light in which I kept him, his eyes seemed clear, and as he looked up at me he smiled—a queer odd, piteous grimace; and then, in a voice of unimaginable softness, he murmured:

"Daddy, I love you!"

I should like to reproduce the accents of his voice. But I cannot. I try "baby-talk" spelling; writing down, in an effort to be phonetic, "I yuve you;" but this is not right; no, I do not catch it; he did not, it is true, say "I love you" with just the clearness conveyed by the written words; there was that untranslatable, that adorable lisping accent. . . . But I cannot convey the unconveyable.

This, however, is a fact which can be told, namely, that even in the night, in storm, even when I thought of death, my grey familiar, I was in the midst of life and knew the joy of it.

.   .   .   .

And I thought:—

What a goodly thing it would be for a man to be writing so that he might "pass the time" and keep keenly awake in such a service as this attendance upon a child, and in so doing write something true, write something worthy, write something worth while! . . .

Can it be, after all, that to do some little act of service is better and more worth while than to write something beautiful?

Little boy, do you know the answer to this question? You smile as you dream—tell me what you dream about? Of coming life? I dream of it also, and I dream that perhaps again I may be as you are, and know the life that is to be. . . .

What is that saying I have somewhere heard, that we must be born again to know the truth. That we must become as little children? But if we become as children, there must somewhere, somehow, be a Father!

Ah, but that is only illusion?

.   .   .   .

Yet, illusion has its place.

Personally I delight to play at make-believe. I imagine myself a true Lavengro; a real master of words; a gipsy word-master; and when I play this game I seem to see myself so weaving words together as to suggest voices that sing like the violins in Tristan, or that roar like the surf on South Beach, or shine like certain spaces of star-set sky I can remember, or that are coloured like the slender, black masts of the schooners against the clear golden dawn in Vineyard Haven, when each mast is like unto the spear or banneret of a knight, drawn by an artist to serve as a design for the initial letter of a story of adventure.

Ah, if I could only find words of a beauty like unto the beauty of the lips and the dear eyes of a child!

But I am a dreamer of impossible dreams. . . .

Do you know, sometimes I fancy I am able to think the thoughts of a child. I wish I could be sure, for I would write them down; but, of course, I must be mistaken, and I do not want to make myself ridiculous. For one thing, I am always wanting people to play *my* play; to come into *my* game. But I must not cherish illusions when there are so many real wonders about me. . . .

None the less, I feel that my game is much more interesting than most of the stupid games being played around me. . . . Money-making, for example; and the chase after the folly of fame.

*   *   *   *   *   *   *

And of all the games I desired to play, the game of games was life itself. Oh, to live as something within me passionately desired to live—to live exuberantly, boldly, splendidly! Ah, it was not enough to dream; and still less worth while only to write down the dreams.

No; no; there was something in me that rebelled against the best that was offered to me by life as so far I had known it.

There must be something else; somewhere, or somehow, if I could only find it. What was it? Where was it to be found?

. . . .

But, as the wind howled about the house, I grew weary of my longings after the intangible, the unknown.

I thought of how the surf must be smashing and shouting upon South Beach.

And I longed to escape from myself, and go out to the sea and the wind.

I felt a desire to rush through the sedge grass at the end of Long Pond and gaze out into the hillbroth of white foam, boiling, seething and crashing in the weltering blackness, under the scud of flying rack, with the wind cutting off the white heads of the breakers as if the swords of the Princes of the Air were at war!

The clock neared four o'clock. Soon it would be day. When I was writing at South Beach, I used to arise at this hour to write of my morning joy.

Now I sat up in the night writing of my quest after the Grail of Joy. Well, in night as in morning, in sickness as in health, in cold, killing storms, as in the bland, caressing sunshine I must maintain my quest.

Let night make me think of day; let sickness remind me of health. I will fight on against all sickness. I will fight it in other ways than in words. The storm evokes the remembrance of, and the longing for, the warm, gladdening, life-cherishing sunshine; and storm and darkness and disease bring up the thought that from man's life should never go:—

From storm and darkness and disease, and death, O man deliver thyself!

CHAPTER VIII

A DARK NIGHT OF THE SOUL

1. Boiling The Pot

THE summer was over, winter was near; the flimsy seaside cottage would soon be quite uninhabitable; we had no furniture, no roof of our own; it was time to seek shelter for the boreal months.

For part of the time after my expedition to Katama beach I had been away from the island travelling for a magazine, gathering material for special articles. I had deplorably failed with these, from the magazine's point of view. My articles had been too personal in tone. What the magazine wanted was its own tone, which, it appears, I was unable to catch; as a matter of fact, I was unable to hear it. My articles had interested me so much that I could only write them in my own way. I recognized the right of the magazine to demand its own way; and relations were broken off. One of my commissions had been to visit and investigate a great sanitarium. When the magazine refused to accept my account of this institution, I interested another magazine in the same story, and I decided to go to the sanitarium again with my family, as I could live very cheaply there. As to plans beyond a month or two, I had none. Perhaps we would go to New York for the winter; or maybe we would buy a tent and roam about in Southwestern

Texas, or Arizona, or Southern California; living a gipsy life such as we lived in old days outside San Antonio.

My mind was working furiously, and so was my hand in writing down what the mind was thinking; there was confusion both in mind and in writing, but amid the welter of ideas, of desires, and the clamant voices of urgent immediate needs, there was always the inner voice of my firmest idea, my strongest desire, my most imperious need—the inner voice that commanded the building of my house of crystal; and it seemed to me that only by going away into some country place, or into the wilderness, could I secure the time and leisure necessary. However, first of all, I had to make some money; so, in New York, I boiled the pot for Sunday newspapers, and secured commissions from magazines for articles and short stories.

At this time I once more met Upton Sinclair. He had just finished his novel, "The Metropolis," and was, like myself, desirous of forming some plan for the winter that would be more congenial than living in New York. I told him of my idea of living in a tent in the Southwest, or of travelling with a wagon; we put our heads together and evolved the following plan, which a magazine approved of to the extent of signing an agreement to accept a number of articles describing our project as it proceeded. I will copy our prospectus, for it shows the state of my mind at that time.

2. Utopia on the Trek

"INTRODUCTION: The talking out of the plan; introduce the Revolutionist (Sinclair) and the

Dreamer (myself) with their families. They have spent their lives in a battle with the evil forces of Society; with poverty, sickness and despair. They have come out of the social pit. One had been a hack writer, living in garrets and shanties. The other began life as an errand boy in a department store; has been a journalist and a literary free-lance; has had a death-grapple with consumption, and cured himself by the outdoor life. They had won their right to live, and were seeking for some happier way to bring up their children than civilization afforded; but their efforts ended in a disastrous fire (Helicon Hall) from which they escaped with nothing except their lives and the knowledge they had painfully gained on the road to happiness. They rendezvous at Battle Creek, (a sort of headquarters for the "nature cure" enthusiast) and take stock of their physical condition, and set out once more to seek a way to live out their convictions.

"Our plan is a perambulating colony, a Helicon Hall on the hoof; a migratory home, warranted fireproof, and free from landlords and steam-heat, and taxes. Our wives will escape flat-hunting; the servant problem will be solved, and dress will cease to worry us. We shall set out about the first of the year, with a couple of big surveying wagons and teams in South California. We shall have our wives and three children, between the ages of three and six: also a governess and a stenographer and a cook, and two young poets, who will help with the men's work. They are all friends, and all but one or two were at Helicon Hall. We plan to wander here and there, living out-doors all the time, camping now and then, by the seashore or up in the mountains, while we do our writing. We shall go north as the summer advances, seeing everything on the Pacific Coast that interests us; the Point Loma Colony; the Carmel group of literary people, the Anarchist "Freeland," San Francisco, Berkeley, and the Yosemite Valley. (Williams was a city editor in San Francisco at the time of the earthquake, and will have interesting impressions to review.)

"The story of the trip will not be in any sense a mere record of travel. It will be an intimate and personal account of a new life experience, that will be a life experience open to all in the new civilization whose dawn we hope to greet while on the trek. It will be a health pilgrimage, a pæan to the outdoor life. There will be brown-legged babies, and camp adventures galore; we shall tell how we live and what we eat and how much it costs us, and what are the ideas behind all our ways. We are worshippers of sunshine and fresh air and cold water and the simple life; we use no alcohol nor tobacco, tea nor coffee, nor the corpses of our fellow-creatures. We shall have books and music and a panoramic school for our children; and glimpses of these will appear in our record; but whatever sociological or philosophical opinions may be voiced will begin and end with good humour.

"The story will be, from first to last, full of enthusiasm and the spirit of adventure. We plan this method of life as something which others may follow, and we expect to follow it ourselves in other parts of the world—next year in England, France and Italy."

3. The Book of Good Health

Our plans became known and how the press roasted us; the vials of ridicule being poured out, of course, more especially on Sinclair's head; I being comparatively unknown. However, all this fuss had its commercial value as advertising, so we could afford to shrug our shoulders.

But there were certain reasons of a personal kind, concerning my collaborator more than me, which prevented an immediate start on the trek; so Sinclair proposed that we should all go to Bermuda for the first months of the winter, making our start in California in the spring. It would be an expensive project, to be sure; but perhaps after all no more expensive than living in New York, and we could recuperate, financially, while on the trek. So we adopted this plan, and went to Bermuda; and were barely settled in a beautiful bay in Somerset before events befell of a kind which caused my collaborator to feel that the trek plan must be abandoned. We decided to write another book together, to take the place of the trek adventures; a book relating in a popular way those ideas and methods of modern hygiene in which we both believed and which appeared to us as part and parcel of the effort of the human race, consciously and by power of will, to banish unnecessary suffering and disease, and to create for itself a real Utopia.

Good Health, and How We Found It; was our title.

I was, of course, quite positive that the title exactly expressed the case—so far as I was concerned, at least; therefore, was I not plainly called upon to give the world my message?

Obviously!

4. Humpty Dumpty Has a Great Fall

When the health book was written I returned to New York. The financial panic of 1908 was rumbling like an expiring storm on the national horizon, and I found New York still frightened and very cautious in buying anything. It was impossible to get a magazine to purchase the health book for serial publication; all I could do was to obtain a book publisher. However, there were magazine editors who wanted stories, so once again I sat down to write things to sell.

An editor of a popular magazine told me one day that he had to have a new serial in hand within six weeks or so, and that he was in despair—he could not find the novel he wanted; a novel full of action, with "something doing" in every chapter, and a crisis, at the end of each instalment.

On the spur of the moment I said: "I'll write you such a novel."

He said (looking at me over his spectacles, his kind, grizzled face smiling): "Have you one on the stocks?"

"No, I haven't; but I can write one."

"Dear boy, don't try such a thing; because, first of all, you ought not to work like that; and I can promise you absolutely nothing—"

I said: "I ask for no promise, but I have made up my mind to write that novel."

He said: "Go to it, then, and the best of luck."

So I went home, and sat down to write a novel in six weeks.

I resolved not to leave the house until it was written. My wife was to manage the meals. The roof-top was to supply air and exercise, in the coolth of the summer nights. We were living in two rooms on the top floor of a lodging house. I was so certain that I was going to write and sell my novel, that I engaged a stenographer, and day after day, night after night, I dictated or wrote, to the amount of from three to six thousand words daily.

I had conceived the plot of a mystery tale; jewels; Oriental secret circles of fanatic assassins (an unconscious plagiarism of Wilkie Collins, no doubt); exciting, rapid, tense.

I had hardly got into the third chapter, however, before the confounded thing that ought to have been a rattling, pot-boiling serial yarn turned around on me with a new face—the face of my dreams,—and the passion that is in my soul, the passionate quest for truth, boiled up and overmastered me.

I said to myself with arrogant wilfulness: "Never mind! I'll go on and do both things; I will write a book that will be a popular slam-bang novel; and it will also express my real interests! It will be a tale of material adventures which shall symbolize the higher adventures of the soul. It will be a book of the new and better age, the dawn of which is opening dimly yet certainly in America."

And with this mood upon me, and daily growing more tense and urgent, I forged ahead with the work.

Our rooms were next to the roof of the house, with

nothing between us and the sun but the flimsy plastering; and—but you know your New York in the hot days; and the nights were worse; even when we went upon the roof and talked, and watched the dim stars in the smoky sky, or the yellowish moon, and dreamed our dreams.

And thus I spilled myself out on paper, wasting my soul in feverish words, and as I walked upon the roof, under the towering cliffs of surrounding sky scrapers, in this canyon among mountainous houses, with the hot clamour of the town beating upon and around me, and the lights from Broadway streaming high into the sky, and the lives of four millions boiling and seething for many miles in all directions— as thus I walked, I say, there were moments when I felt that I held the city in the hollow of my hand, studying it as a sculptor might study a lump of clay, and that with my fingers I could mould it into what shape I choose. . . . I was, you see—the Artist; the new master of the new life of men!

.   .   .   .

Having reached which exalted condition, it was, of course, time for a fall.

It came, in a familiar fashion; a hard, far, shattering fall.

I remember the moment with stark vividness.

I was alone in the house one very hot afternoon.   I was working on a page in one of the chapters which dealt with the efforts of one of my characters to cure himself of tuberculosis, when all of a sudden there was a click, or gurgle, deep down in my throat; my mouth filled with something hot, something with a taste that I recognized; I coughed and then something spattered the page and the paragraph dealing with my consumptive character—and the something was red.

.   .   .   .

Do you remember Crusoe staring at the footprint in the sand of his lonely island?   Figure me, staring at this red warning—staring; but I'll spare you any description of my thoughts; indeed, to describe them would necessitate the invention of sentiments appropriate to the occasion, since, in reality, my cerebration was suspended, and, like Crusoe, I stood like one confounded, or as if I had seen an apparition.

Some of my readers may be soldiers, hunters, adventurers.   Blood does not affright you, even your own.   That's all right.   That is as it should be.   But I wish that I could lose my blood on a battle field; in   some   stand-up-and-have-it-out-and-may-the-best-man-win kind of fight; losing it through some clean fierce sword thrust or bullet hole, rather than in this miserable fashion.   It makes me angry to have some confounded blood-vessel spring a leak, and put me on my back; I feel as some commander must feel when one of his trusted men fails him at some critical juncture.   I need all my blood in my work.   I am ashamed, too, when it fails; because it is a part of me; and I want to be sound—I *will* be sound—I *shall* be sound!—I want to be sound through and through, up and down, inside and outside, body, and mind, and soul.

.   .   .   .

5. The Dark Night

But I had to go on with my work, anyhow.

So I pulled myself together; the chief factor in my rally being my sheer incredulity—I simply could not believe that my lungs were affected again. I had been examined several times during the past year; everything was sound and I was in fine shape, the doctors had assured me; my lung capacity having been increased so that it was distinctly above the average. And I had written the health book on the assumption that I was a cured man, a well man; I had written scores of articles on the same assumption; I had planned and already written a large part of the book of the Crystal House on that foundation.

It was utterly absurd to believe that I was wrong. I was a fool to be afraid.

I had been overworking in the heat and airlessness of the city room; this would explain matters; some little blood-vessel had burst; it was a warning; it could be nothing more.

And so firmly did I hold to this view of the matter, that I did not have a physician examine me; and after a week or so I had well nigh forgotten the episode.

There were times, though, when the red hieroglyphic came before my mental vision; then I deliberately turned away from it.

My wife, however, wanted me to get away from the city; and so we made up our minds to return to Martha's Vineyard, where I could sleep out of doors.

So we got out of town right away, and at Martha's Vineyard, I finished my book.

What a book!

Neither fish nor flesh nor good red herring. The most impossible book, I think, that ever was written. In all my long career of writing unsalable manuscripts I had never created anything quite so impossible as this new novel, which finally, I threw in the fire.

But at the time, of course, I would not recognize facts, and I tried hard to sell the thing. When its failure was palpable, I cursed the editors, and packed my bag for the journey back to New York, back to the market place.

I well remember that morning!

I had left my bed feeling irritable and disgusted with myself; precisely why, I did not know. There were a score of reasons for feeling blue, and how was I to decide between their conflicting and sneering claims? They ran through my head, these reasons, intolerably chattering, and quarrelling; exhibiting their vulgarities, their frailties, and disagreeable stupidities with all the naïve rudeness, the smutchy brazenness of a mob of ill-bred urchins shrilling their contentions concerning some trivial yet offensive subject. And each one of them, down to the most obscure and feeblest voice, assumed to speak, for the time, with the voice of my very self. Going to my writing room, I drank strong coffee, and smoked a cigarette or two and languidly toyed with my work; and then gave myself up to this mood of disenchantment—as completely as I abandoned, without the pre-

tence of a struggle, my hygienic program of absti-
nence from drugs like nicotine and caffein and alcohol, and I said something like this, to myself:

"What the devil was the use?

"Here's a pretty kettle of fish. I can't go on working at a magazine article, because the very thought
of clattering the keys of a typewriter makes me ill.
Yet I know very well that I ought to be doing so—
I need the money; and never, never shall I be able
to give myself up to the writing of anything better
than a magazine article unless I first get some money.
And I can't attempt anything better, in such a state
of mind as this, for I would be like unto a lover expressing his passion to his mistress through the
cachinnations of a bad cold in his head; or like a
singer trying to achieve pure tone with a quinsy sore
throat; in fine, I am utterly disgusted with myself!"

And I would not listen to the inner voice which
tried to tell me that even out of my grey moods I
might weave purple banners; that out of my doubts
and despondencies and despairs I might extract the
quintessential oil of art.—

I threw some manuscripts together, and fled back to
town.

   .   .   .   .

In going to New York from Martha's Vineyard, it
is necessary to change boats at New Bedford. It was
on a Sunday when I made the journey, and travel
was so heavy that I found it impossible to procure a
stateroom, or even a berth in a stateroom. The notion
of passing the night in the fetid atmosphere below
decks in the common cabin repelled me utterly, so I

resolved to stay on deck the most of the time, taking cat-naps in the main cabin.

It was a windless night; the atmosphere clogged with the fumes of the great forest fires burning everywhere along the coast from Cape Cod to Maine. The West when the invisible sun went down was thickly horrible with a red like old blood; the air was heavy; sounds like the swash of waves, the throbbing of the machinery, the tolling of a reef bell, the far-off whistle of a passing steamship, came to my ears as through a muffling of crepe. It was a night made for a lamentable and gigantic disaster; but this portentous impression faded as the west died out into grey, and then into black; and, as I sat on deck muffled in a coat, my mind turned to other thoughts.

I said to myself that I was a pretty poor specimen of a man—of a man such as I wished to be; and was it worth while trying to be other than the scallawag and weakling that at bottom I knew myself to be?

But was I wholly a scallawag and a weakling at bottom?

At bottom, did I not also have a goodly share of the qualities which make up a decent man?

I didn't know; I was sure of nothing; only this was I sure of—the big ship was carrying me along with it, on, on, on—towards the unknown, towards life still to be lived; that was all of which I could be sure.

And I turned toward this thought. I tried to extract new courage and hope from it.

Life—life in the future, towards which the throbbing ship was bearing me,—surely it would claim more from me than weak thoughts; more than the dreams of a feverish artist, more than the troubled meditations and the feeble works of a self-made, perchance self-ruined, egotistical writer.

Action of a forthright nature would be asked of me as well as the written word.

What would this action be?

I did not know; ah, would I ever know?

When would this restless wandering of body and mind and soul be over?

Health was fled again. In my heart, despite my obstinate refusal to recognize the fact, I knew that I was breaking down.

And my work was getting farther and farther away, it seemed, from all chance of success.

After all my vain dreamings, was I now to face and acknowledge failure most positive and permanent?

.   .   .   .

For more than three hours I walked up and down, that night, on the deck of the boat, trying to get at grips with myself, and to see things as they really were; my troubled soliloquy running something like this:—

"I am now more than thirty years old, poor and heavily in debt. I am sick, and getting worse, for my youthful energy is failing. I have written much, but nearly everything that amounted to anything was destroyed in the Helicon Hall disaster. The publishers and editors apparently believe in my talent, and are helping me to achieve mastery of my instrument of expression; but they do not understand what I want to write; they seemingly want me to write what they want.   They are kind, and try to be helpful, and they are doubtless right in many of their criticisms of my work—yet I know they are not wholly right. Literature is not produced by writing for the market. Art is not commercialism.   I must make a definite choice; either I must write for myself, despite everything; or write for the market.

"As for all the mistakes, and blunders, and sins of the past—all that matters little, save as I make use of what has happened.   I still hope to turn all that to good account.

"I am saturated with life.   My feet know city pavements equally with country earth and the unstable decks of ships at sea; I have sat with the poor at bread and water and with the rich at meat and wine; I have been lover and husband and father; I have toiled in the world's work in many fashions; I suffer from the most characteristic disease of the time; I am steeped in the peculiar sins of the age; also, however, I dream the dream of the age, and share at least partially the possession of the virtues of to-day—the dream of true Brotherhood, the virtues of faith, hope, and love.

"And I know I have ability to write; I have ability to do even more positive acts.   Therefore, I may hope to be a truthful voice of my age, in that I am equipped with knowledge, experience, sympathy, ability; but the crucial question is:—Have I the requisite strength and endurance, bodily, mental, spiritual, left over from the endless and often foolish expenditures of energy in many forms which my life has known; the energy I need in order to shape adequately the utterance which a voice of the age must give?

"There is only one way in which I can answer this question—by putting myself to the test."

And, after all,—I thought—this period of failure is but one more lesson in that course in life's university, the object of which is to fit me (if the task be possible!) to perform the work of an artist—a lesson the text of which is: "Nothing that happens to you has any value or significance unless it is something you can make use of as an artist."

.   .   .   .

Quite true, O my soul, I said to myself, thou calm one, serene philosopher!—but, first of all, please stanch the bleeding of the wound in my heart; still that sound as of sobbing which goes on in the shadowy places of my being.

It is like the sobbing of a child.

For there is a child in my heart, eager to play, fain to trust and to love; a child always looking out wonderingly and joyfully upon a world ever new and ever-changing, a world where everything is possible.

.   .   .   .

Let me hasten to an ending.

I grow weary.

When I grow weary, I begin to cough.   And then I think of things not pleasant to face.

.   .   .   .

Yes, I grow weary.   The past few months have severely taxed me; I have drawn heavily on my reserve store of energy; yet I must go on spending for some time at least,

—The little, blue devils of melancholia make many attempts to seize my soul.   O, shapes of gloom, why do you haunt me?

So, during those three, long hours, on that bitter night, each second of which was a great misery, I descended into the hell of my own soul and was tormented.

Three hours!   Three times the slow pointers circled the innumerable clocks of the world; and the seconds ticked and tocked.   I walked without resting, up and down; I watched the foam-flecked sea; I sought to hide my dark spirit in the darkness of the night; and I drank deeply of my bitter pain.

I felt myself a tiny speck amid a billion, billion, trillion, tiny specks; restless on the surface of a restless earth; pursuing a blind voyage nowhither. Who was I?   What did I matter?   Nothing at all.

Tick-tock: the seconds swung; the three, dark hours accomplished their part in the progress of time's unfathomable destiny.

And as each second swung its slow pendulum, there was the gasp of a dying man, or woman, or child; there was the agony of a birth; there was the cry of a new-born child; assassins thrust or shot; gold was mined; toilers toiled; ships sank at sea; the keels of new ships were laid; poets dreamed; prophets were enrapt—

So Life surged, throughout the earth: and throughout a billion billion universes, life surged.

And during those three hours, the earth moved onward a certain space, and swung through a certain segment of its circle on its poles; and so moved and so swung a billion billion worlds.

—And I—the speck of flesh and the spark of spirit
—there on the sea, dark in the dark night, drinking
my pain—I said to myself that there could be no
profit in wasting this strange time which is all the
Eternity man can yet dimly know, unless I could bring
back with me from my descent into hell a measure
of words, to be arranged on paper.   I am a reporter;
a war correspondent of the war of Man with Darkness,
and I will and must report what I find, to the limits
of my vision, as best I may; even in the infernal regions, blaze they never so damnably!

.   .   .   .

Now I must go to work again.   How do matters
stand?

Let me try to understand the adventure which was
begun at dawn in that mystic moment when I felt as
if a hand had been laid upon my shoulder by Somebody who desired me to follow, a Somebody who had
a message for me.   I followed, thank God! I followed, although I faltered, I stumbled, I fell, I
groaned, I complained, I failed in task after task,
still I followed in order to communicate what I might
be able to learn: and further communications will
follow these stammering and faulty utterances if I
may live to shape them; and I believe, despite everything, I believe I am to live for many years yet.

Let me try to sum up!

.   .   .   .

I am a dreamer of dreams; and I have been too
long merely the slave of my fancies; I who would be
the master of my moods remain a led captive, and in

a sense my book is my battle for freedom. Yes, I have dreamed too much, and my waking hours have been barren of fruitful work as I tried to remember and to piece together into words the fragments of my dreams—into words that should evoke something of the lustral beauty of the visions. And time who helps you to realize your dreams if your will be strong enough, but who ages the unworking dreamer in the midst of his dreams, which fade and pass like the vain dreams of slumber, inexorable time goes on and I have little or nothing to show for all my dreams. Therefore, who shall believe in them? Dreams are no literary assets. You cannot play showman to the phantasmagoria of thought. You must dress your puppets; you must write the play for them. . . . And yet I still believe that my dreams are not pinchbeck, but true gold only requiring pressure in the mint of mental assimilation, and the stamp of the right words, the coinage of art, to win appraisal at high worth . . .

.   .   .   .

But when am I ever to essay the great work of realization?

Upon me, now, as many times before, there falls captivity unto the unloved task. But I shall not moil blindly and bitterly, as in the past. Poverty, and Death's henchman and grey familiars, Sickness and Death itself, my seeming enemies, may even yet prove to be my friends—they may be my rescuers; they may inspire me afresh with knowledge of the necessity for this unending struggle for existence. In this period of failure and of imprisonment to illness and poverty, I must not chafe or repine; and whatever happens in the future, I must not yield. I must remain assured that in the midst of all the doubts, the darkness, the barriers, the uncertainties which surround me, there is something to which I can rally for support—there is my true self: the upright and unyielding I—the only reality of which I can be certain in a universe of illusion and ceaseless change.

Myself, and own will: that is my creed—with this necessary corollary: that I am one of many others, all of them sparks of Spirit; incarnate items of the Will of Life; and we are brothers and sisters who must strive to console ourselves for our ineluctable, essential loneliness, by mutual service and love; each doing his or her own work; each fulfilling his or her own function; artist, prophet, workman, healer; whatever the vocation may be.

Can there be—may there be—Something beyond, and higher, than self-consciousness? Is there perhaps a power greater than that of human will?

Dimly, feebly, these questions raised themselves; but I only passed them by. I returned to the more fascinating theme—the subject of myself.

.   .   .   .

So passed the black night. In this fashion, I consoled myself.

But Fact is stubborn material, and resists the moulding of our desirous hopes. I could not escape the consequences of my wilful folly, even if I disguised them in the coloured garments of my self-willed interpretations.

Cold, calm medical science pronounced its verdict: physically, anyhow, I was badly damaged. And so once more, I left the city, and went into the open places; Arizona, Mexico, California,—defeated and broken down.

.   .   .   .

—But, at least, there was art, and there was alcohol; and when their mingled magic was at work, the golden dreams again were mine, and the shining vistas of adventure opened before me.

PART II
THE HOMEWARD WAY

CHAPTER IX

A TESTAMENT OF EGOTISM

1. California

ALTHOUGH my return to the West was in one sense a retreat after a lost battle, it was not reluctantly that I went, nor with sorrow; because it was California that offered sanctuary to my wounded and fleeing soul, and there was healing in her protective hands, and consolation in her beauty. Even for obtuse travellers, even for the material-minded, there is a magical charm in California which uniquely sets her apart from all other American scenes. For artists and souls awakened to the spiritual and romantic influences of fair, stately, or historic places, the mystical emanation of California's personality is ineluctable. From the beginning, for me, it was a case of love at first sight, and my passion was perdurable. How well I recall my first pangs of pleasure in the journey out of the Texas plains, through the Arizona desert, northward along the vast Pacific's verge, through the coast range hills into the Santa Clara valley, riant with peach and plum trees blossoming in millions, and on to San Francisco. The potent gramarye of this most beautiful among the States cast a glamour upon me which has never waned.

Who that has crossed the Sierra Nevadas has not experienced this penetrating impression, this wizardry of a land whose soul is sealed with romantic beauty? But who shall define it? Who may weave the verbal nets which shall capture the delicate birds of beauty which sing in the secret places of the soul? I for one shall not attempt the impossible. The essence of beauty, like the secret of personality, is a true mystery.

The peculiar quality of California's charm is, no doubt, traceable to many material sources and factors—the space relations and splendid shapes of many mountains, the curving lines of the gracious valleys, the immense amplitude of wonderful plains, the opulence and mystery of the forests, the clarity and purity of the light, the mightiness of the sea which protects its coast, the mysterious veils of the great grey fogs which hang about its beauty the curtains of illusion, and the ever present power of the ardent sun—Ah, yes, to be sure: but what of the spirit underlying all these things, the strange spirit which, blowing where it lists, has elected to place a special seal of romantic beauty upon this lonely, lovely land, this California? Its haunting, occult bewitchment yearns and throbs in the songs of many poets, and from these wells of wonder and vistas of high romance which California opens for the thirsty souls of the children of America our literature is being enriched—think of Miller, of certain stanzas of Markham, of songs by Ina Coolbrith, of the verbal splendour and great imagination of George Sterling, of the murmurous monotone, so full of elegaic tristness, of Charles Warren Stoddard, and of the lyrical though sad ecstasy of Nora May French.

As for the painters, legion is their name, who seek

to express California. Knight errants of the ever-baffled quest for what can never be attained, they seem as wistful as lovers admitted to the presence of the beloved only to be denied the consummation of their dreams. So the pictures hint; the poems whisper their musical suggestions; there are great revelations in certain pages of Bret Harte; Stevenson at Silerrado and at Monterey wrought pages pulsatory with the psychic presence of California's soul; Frank Norris has mirrored much of its mystery and its striving drama in his novels; Charles F. Lummis, Mary Austin, James Hopper, are prose artists who spread the creative inspiration of California; yet none make known the inner secret; nor may they do so. True beauty, I say again, is a mystery, and mystery is communicable but not explicable. I am certain that in that good time which is coming when the United States shall have become a great, true nation bound together by something deeper even than the bond of blood, united by will, California's function among her sister states will be comparable to the function of Italy or of Greece or France in Europe. We of America must make truly our own that which is ours yet now neglected. We must weave into the national consciousness the rich strains of Californian legend, the high romance of Spanish exploration, of Spanish faith, and of the Boston sailors who sought out this far land, and of the Missouri hunters who followed the trails of sunset over the hills and far away, and through the burning deserts to the limits of the west, blazing the path for the Argonauts of '49.

California was invented by an artist. Montalvo was his name. He conjured up in the magic mirror of his art an image which later on more "practical" men made a reality.   You will find Montalvo's pen portrait of the soul of this state in his novel, "The Deeds of Esplandian, the Son of Amadis of Gaul," published in 1510, eight years after Columbus sailed forth from Spain, his mission being to fulfil ancient prophecies, or so he believed, by discovering new lands for Christ to conquer.   Yet there are solemn pundits who talk about the Genoese as the opener of new trade routes to the Indies, as a mere pawn of "Economic Necessity," that most bizarre and bloodless of all the gods—despite the facts that stare you in the face in the records of Columbus—the great fact being that spiritual and ideal interests led him out on the trails of his high romance.   To be sure, he threw sops to the lords of finance and of commerce, by showing that, incidentally, his voyage would be good for their business.   Poor Columbus!   Unescapable compromise, everlasting entanglement of the ideal and the material!

In one of the earliest of his reports to Isabella —the great soul who understood his soul when the only ones who else would listen to him were cloistered monks—Columbus gave the name of the Earthly Paradise to the mesa region lying near the headquarters of the Orinoco River.   (Let us also remember that when the early explorers were not apostles, they were very apt to be dreamers and romanticists who went forth to look for the Fountain of Youth, for the Islands of the Blessed, for the land that always seems to lie just over the edge of the receding horizon.) Montalve read Columbus' report.   His imagination flamed.   He drew forth his pen, instead of a sword;

he embarked upon the galleon of reverie instead of a ship, and fully a quarter of a century before Cortes saw Lower California, and longer yet before Cabrillo landed at San Diego, Montalvo, the poet, discovered California, and named it, too, leaving it to others to actualize his spiritual conquest. Listen to what he says:—

"Know then, that on the right hand of the Indies, there is an island called California, very close to the Terrestrial Paradise. . . ."

(No Californian will gainsay this description of place, unless, of course, it is contended by the more ardent lovers that this is the earthly paradise in very fact. Well, it is certainly as close to it as we may arrive.)

Montalvo goes on to say that of this wonderful land, where precious gems were found in great abundance, and where the only metal was gold, Califia was Queen, and after her was the country named. And this is how he describes her: "Very large in person, the most beautiful of all, of blooming years, and in her thoughts desirous of achieving great things; strong of limb, and of great courage."

Tons of ink have been used in writing about California; but has any writer ever bettered Montalvo's clairvoyant and verdical description of the soul of this lovely land?

"Most beautiful, of blooming years, and in her thoughts desirous of achieving great things, strong of limb and of great courage!"

2. Carmel

At first I did not go back to San Francisco. We settled in the country, in a village called Carmel-by-the-Sea, a few miles away from the railroad, near Monterey, and there I resumed the struggle; the triple struggle; first, to make a living; second, to succeed as an artist; third—to find that which I was seeking, to achieve my Quest.

I was in a shattered condition, truly; so also was my Book, the chronicle of the Quest, the legend of my efforts to build, or to find, I hardly knew which, the Crystal House. Its whole point, its meaning, its message, had been that I had conquered; that I was a victor—blow the trumpets, beat the drums!—I, the upright and unconquerable, I.

And now, here was this upright and unconquerable person bowled over, and the book was deplorably out of harmony with facts. However, I was not ready to admit that I was beaten. I was down, but I was not yet counted out; and so the struggle went on, year after year, with flights to the dry, warm deserts of Arizona from time to time, when once again the physical machine would fail me.

There was an old, broken-down summer house upon the ocean beach which I begged from its owner, and this I carted back into the pine woods on the slope of Mount Carmel, and converted into a hut. It reminded me of the hut on the other side of the world, on the Atlantic coast, where the voice of the Quest had lured me forth that mystical summer dawn; and in this hut the Quest continued.

Here I found how true was that saying of a modern

mystic, with whom about this time I began to correspond, after being keenly interested in his work, together with that of another mystical author who was even more sympathetic to me, because more of an artist. The first was Arthur Edward Waite; the second, Francis Grierson. In one of Waite's books I discovered and made this my own: "The world of mind is wider than the world of matter, as it is indeed older. In the unsounded depths of its oceans lies the past of all the universes; on its heights are stars that we never see in the common daylight of consciousness. What fields for exploration—what vistas of great adventure!"

Yes. It was so.

In a very literal sense, it was truly in the world of mind, of intellectual effort, that I began to adventure; that is to say, I began at last, at long last indeed, to consider myself, and the world, and the invisible universe in which I moved, from a less emotional, less impulsive, calmer, and more reasonable point of view. I did more thinking; in fact, it may be said that I began to think. Everything I had written up to this time, and the motives upon which I acted or spoke or wrote, were spontaneous, instinctive, intuitive; whether for right or for wrong. It was as if my reckless soul had run away from its calmer companion, the mind; so eager to enjoy the high romance that it simply threw itself into any path, turned aside for any new experience, no meadow escaping its riot. But it had bruised itself; it had weakened, if not broken, its wings; and though still it cried, Onward! in its own interior it knew that it was weary, and somewhat dreary, too.

Yet, even then, it could sing:—as it did from a hospital bed to which one day I was carried when a hemorrhage came upon me in the street.

When I bethink me of my weakened state,
    I seem a soldier in whose fighting hand,
    At mid-most stress of battle, snaps the brand
While fierce his foe is pressing, all elate
Because of his misfortune—while the fate
Maybe of all that issues high and grand
By this one conflict needs must fall or stand—
Lo, if he doth not yield now he is great!

Lord God of unseen battles, I'll not yield!
    I'll make this bed a forge for a new sword;
    My faith its steel, and pain its point shall **grind**
For knightly service on the world's grim field,
    Fighting for God and smiting Evil's horde,
    As Heine did, a cripple, and Milton, blind.

Thus the wounded spirit strove; but now my mind was allowed to examine the situation; to look back upon the campaigns, and endeavour to judge the results, and, more particularly, the morale of the fighter. Above all, it did its best to arrive at some clear understanding of what the long struggle was all about!

For it felt that at the bottom of the business, back of the weltering confusion of efforts and failures, there was something resembling a definite philosophy.

While examining the huge mass of manuscripts resulting from these attempts to get at myself, and explain myself to myself, and to express the result in terms of art, I have found one paper which today I look upon as a man might look upon something excessively fantastic which he has done during a fit of fever, or a nightmare, or when drugged or drunk. It is really almost incredible in its effrontery of self-conceit; yet it so aptly illustrates that fashion in which I tried to apply my philosophy of self-will: my belief in the power of affirmative egotism, to my own life and work, that I shall copy it, although it would please me much better to put it into the fire, here in my hut among the pines of Carmel—the fire that has now consumed so great a part of this amazing mass of morbidity and poisonous products of selfishness: these excretions of the auto-intoxication of my soul.

R. L. S. (who used to roam these very pine woods, upon a time, coughing and dreaming, and seeking the paths of his high romance), has said somewhere that the young man who hasn't had courage to make a fool of himself, now and then, hasn't lived at all. Well, I've lived, anyhow! And these are the rules by which I tried to guide my life:—

My Book Of Canons

Believing that I am one of those men to whom are given power to affect human life profoundly through their written and spoken words, I deem it necessary to set down for my own guidance towards the performance of my best possible acts of service to mankind, the chief of those principles which I consider to be the basis of my work, together with the most essential rules of conduct derived from these principles.

Creed

I believe in Love. I seek it. I will the Brother-hood of Man. I am a romantic, and an idealist. I believe the beauty and the joy to be found here and there in this present phase of human life may be vastly increased, and made general and common for all; and that most of the ugly and wretched and pain-ful aspects of life may be removed. All Property that depends upon Poverty must be abolished. Life must be re-established on a foundation of Love, not of Profits. Truth must be recognized as man's only safe guide. Mutual aid among men I hold (with Kropotkin) to be the chief factor in evolution, and I deny that the dominating factor is the false idea of the "survival of the fittest," or the "struggle for ex-istence," which are merely excuses for crime, cruelty and stupidity. Mankind is progressing constantly towards a condition of life-in-love, and Art must be made the ruling influence in all things. Then man in general shall know a life wider and deeper and more glorious than any men save a few prophetic artists now dream of. My ideal, then, is to help to advance the race on its journey to its destined end.

Practical Work

My practical work is to write as best I may my own thoughts, ideas, experiences, and aspirations. It must never be actuated principally by desires for money or for fame. Yet I must also consider my own claims upon my own efforts. He who succeeds in truly bettering his own condition does the highest thing that lies in his power to do for the betterment of humanity.

Conditions Of Good Work

Thoughts, ideas, fancies, creations—these come to me, I know not how; I know not from whither; out of the blue; out of the country of the soul. My mind seizes these in its nets of memory; it shapes them, in words. My hand writes them down. Thus I discern three elements, or factors, working together: the body, the mind, the soul. It is obvious that good work will only be done when these three are one, that is, practically, when body, mind and soul co-operate with the least possible amount of friction, and the greatest possible amount of harmony; in other words, when I achieve the greatest possible condition of health. It follows that therefore it is my duty to be as Healthy as I can. (Oh, for health; for the power of good health!)

Concerning My Body

It is now thirty-three years old. It has been shaken and racked and badly damaged by tuberculosis; unquestionably, the germs of the disease are still within its veins and cells, only awaiting the next time I overwork, or dissipate to excess, in order to smash it some more. I have also, since boyhood, soaked myself with nicotine and alcohol. My nerves have been jangled and tampered with. Hence, if any good work is to be got out of this damaged instrument, it is necessary to discipline it and master its unruly tendencies.

As To My Mind

Well, first of all, it altogether lacks training, education, and discipline; but apparently it has an innate ability to transform the ideas generated by the soul —or communicated through the soul, I know not which—into art forms, some quite good, others very poor. Hence, it is plain that I should use my mind to the limit of its power, without, however, injuring it by over-work. I should practice it in Concentration; which is not the forcing of the mind to work at some particular task or other, but is the directing of its attention to the task in hand, whatever that may be, to the exclusion of all competing interests.

It should be borne in mind, however, that a powerful impulse to turn from one task to another task may be a signal from the high places of the soul.

The conscious will should only with great caution interfere in this action and interaction of the mind and the soul in creation and in work.

My Soul

All I can say about my soul is, that I know very well there is something within me which is more than the life of the body and the mind, and which will not die with the dissolution of the body. It is not to be expressed in words, but no words are to be expressed without it. It is that which recognizes Beauty and which knows Love. It is that which my work must ever seek and strive to communicate. The law of the soul is love. If I may write true and beautiful words men will gain glimpses of the crystal house of the spirit—vistas will open into man's real life, which transcends this material life.

Conclusion

I hereby promise myself that I shall try to read this book of Canons daily and follow its rule as best I may. I must add, that many failures do not debar efforts to try again. To write one, little, true and beautiful thing would be worth the longest life-time of poverty, and sickness and sorrow. One thing I must avoid; self-pity: for it is the morphine of the soul, which I must put to one side for ever.

That bad habit, anyhow, I shall cut out.

I am, just now, at the bottom of a high and very steep hill—but I shall climb to its top.

Looking upward, from this valley of failure, I see gleams of a sunshine warmer and purer and brighter than any that appear in my valley. They glint above the edge of the summit, up yonder; and now and then there drift downward breaths of an air that is sweeter and cleaner and clearer than any I have ever tasted, faintly perfumed with scents of unknown flowers. Surely, over the top of this hill, there is an upland country where those things happen that you would have befall; where live those whom you would love to know—yes, and know to love—a region where great adventures are to be had, where romance walks hand in hand with truth, and beauty rules all from a throne made visible at last! A country where the folk do not toil and moil and sweat and cheat and lie and steal and harm each other; a land that is over this hill and far away, the country of tomorrow, the realm of the future, the kingdom of heaven when it comes upon earth, and of good will done by men!

To that hill, I address myself. I must win to its height, even if there are many lions in the way, and though there are no paths up the dangerous steeps save those each lonely climber makes, each for himself.

CHAPTER X

THE QUEST OF TRUTH

1. Gleams

A ND my hut at the foot of Mount Carmel, surrounded by the peace of the pines, with the muted thundering of the incessant surf along the marge of the Pacific ever in the air, was not only a place where my mind busied itself to find the truth concerning this mysterious questing of my soul, it also proved to be a sort of postern door, opening upon secret places of the inner life. Gleams of truth came, very faintly at first, and confused, yet with increasing breadth and force of illumination. I did at last begin to see some part of the truth concerning myself, and my quest, and my Book.

Indeed, I made great discoveries concerning Truth itself, and the power possessed by those who speak or write Truth.

I mean, that these were discoveries, for me. For others, they were obvious facts. Which situation gives a writer as he grows older some highly ironic moments, when he looks backward along the vistas of time and beholds himself frantically singing or fighting because of some wonderful thing which is wonderful to none save himself, and the others who happen to be living outside the circle wherein this thing has always been visible and known!

Nevertheless, these discoveries of truth were still most valuable, even when I could see that it was only because I had been blind that I had not made them before.

For I saw that words of truth spoken by anybody, no matter who, gentle or simple, cultured or ignorant, artist or dullard, were mighty and went on living with mighty force, even when disregarded at the time they were uttered.

A commonplace? Yes; but some of the most wonderful discoveries in the universe, some of the most marvellous adventures to be chanced upon in the high romance of the soul, come through revelations of the beauty and the force and the tremendous meanings of disregarded commonplaces.

For instance—

I was walking with Walter Prichard Eaton through Newspaper Row in Boston, in the days when we were twenty-one—Ah, over the hills of time, and far away! Eaton was displeased with me. We had both been reporting some disgusting murder trial or other, and in order to make my court room story interesting, I had paraphrased one of Walter Pater's most delicately eloquent passages, and applied it to one of the women witnesses; and Eaton, concerned in those days, as in later and more authoritative years, with the dignity of letters, and the responsibility of the writer to maintain the integrity of literature, was annoyed. But, even more, he was justly sorry for something else I was doing that was wrong. Without any heat, or personal scorn, simply telling the truth, this good champion of good causes, said to me: "Your brain is too fine to be injured, as you are injuring it, with alcohol." That was all. I made no answer. It went in one ear, and out the other; but, in passing through, with that mystical virtue possessed by the word of truth, it traced an indelible and potent mark upon my soul. Though for nearly twenty years they remained quiescent, those words, they were simply patient, not passive; and in the hour of my need, in the time when I was making my fight, they came to me with helpfulness and with inspiration. They bore a message of faith. They worked the good will of their speaker, in the measure of his intention. And thus it was made plain to me that deeds of intellectual charity, the acts of kindness and of consolation which we may accomplish in spoken or written speech, are to the full as real and tangible as the giving of bread and wine, or money. Wherefore, the good Samaritans of art and literature walk down the roads of time as long as time shall last, helping the wounded and the fallen.

Again:—

I chanced to go to a little California village, on some journalistic adventure, and stayed there several days, and made a most congenial acquaintance with a Catholic priest. Unable in any degree to share his faith, quite outside the circle of his sacramental life, I was still able to appreciate his personal charm. Also there was a bond uniting us. It was obvious that he too had fought with tuberculosis. And though he was a very modest man, I obtained his story.

For many, many weary years he had dragged his wasted form and failing body from sanitarium to sanitarium, in Colorado, Arizona, California. And the fight went against him. Finally he could no longer leave his bed; in fact, he could hardly lift a finger. Then to him, stretched upon the bed of death, there came a Thought, on the trail of which he kept his mind during a long, long time. This Thought, was an idea of how he might invent a new form of sputum cup, one which might enable conscientious invalids to be careful in regard to spreading the contagion, yet which would be less of a drain upon their purses than existing contrivances. For years he had thought about such a thing, hoping that out of his own trouble he might make something that would help other people. And now the Idea arrived. He sent out for card-board. With his feeble fingers he bent and moulded the paper into this shape, and that shape; scores, even hundreds of shapes; until at last he evolved the shape that embodied his Thought. (Ah, that's a great moment, in art, in science, in labour—the union of the thought and the mechanism for the thought!) But by this time he was up out of bed, and on his feet. He had switched his mind from his disease to his invention. And he sent out for copper; by and by he set up a little forge in his room; and with his own hands made his own model. Then there came a Congress of the American Medical Association, to Los Angeles. He went there; he showed his model to many of the most famous specialists; they commended it highly.

He had it with him, this model when I visited him; some day he meant to go to New York, or place it with somebody in New York, to present to the one firm of manufacturers who handled such devices. I was on my way to New York—bound on one of my literary adventures; so I offered to act as his agent.

Which I did, with this sad result—that the manufacturers declared his invention was indeed a great improvement, but that they did not care to put it on the market.

I do not know when I have written a letter that gave me such difficulty to write, and such pain, as the letter in which I had to tell my friend of this failure of the object which I supposed had been the central part of his life for so long.

But there was a centre in that man's life deeper and higher than any I knew about.   Never shall I forget the wonderful letter which he sent to me, condoling me for *my* disappointment; saying, most simply, that as God had given him back his health through his work, he had from the very start resolved that success or failure, in a material way, with his device, should not be allowed to perturb his spirit.

Here was another great discovery, over which I brooded in my hut among the pines, namely, that he who forgot himself found himself; he who put others before himself, found what was greater than what is usually termed success: he found peace, happiness, life.

.   .   .   .

—But this vision was blurred, even as the sun-lighted vistas of my Carmel woods and hills would often be blurred by the invading fogs.   I admired, I wondered; but . . . but what about my upright and invincible ego?   What about the creative power of my own will?

I evaded the issue; I shunned these obtrusive and disconcerting thoughts.

2. The Book Of The Quest

Also, there was my Book; this Book which was the chronicle of my life.   The time had come when I must revalue my own values concerning this central point of my artistic and spiritual life.   The time had come to search out the truth about my work as well as about myself.

There was, for example, the verdict passed upon the manuscript by one of the chief readers for an important firm of publishers whom Witter Bynner had fairly pestered to publish the thing.   He did not succeed, and he sent me the report which caused the publishers to reject the manuscript.   It came to me while I was working in my Carmel hut, and I read it with blank amazement that anybody could so regard my work.

Its essential portion ran as follows:—

"In character, though not in quality, the MS belongs with Rousseau's Confessions, Marie Bashkirtseff's Journal, any one of those self revelations that the Celtic and Latin races excel in, but the package of sheets contains much else.   Part of it is in the form of letters, the interludes interrupt the main narrative to present nature pictures, sketches of chance companions, a medley of aspirations, reflections, experiences, friendships, reveries, rhapsodies, prose poems, and physical detail, fact and fancy—resembling a flood of rather muddy water, sometimes bearing precious things upon its bosom, sometimes, flotsam and jetsam, sometimes, the objects of daily life.

"Technically speaking, the MS has nearly every

possible fault,—extreme verbosity, no order, wild confusion, no sense of proportion, errors in taste, trash and gems of thought and expression mixed together with no appreciation of values, different sorts of literary forms, no unity, no harmony, wild outpourings, imaginative flights, autobiographical detail,—a heterogeneous compound of dissimilar elements—as the old phrase goes.

"Yet the merits embedded in this mass are undeniable, evident, and could some one, other than the author, attempt the task of selection, of revision, of pruning, the MS might be made over into a contribution of some value to the literature of psychology, of self revelation, of human documents. The author, himself, is entitled to be heard and he describes his purpose as that of trying to write 'as truthful a statement of myself in relation to life, and of life in relation to myself as I can compass,' 'a book of the open air,' 'a chant of the morning sun,' 'to give enough facts of his life to serve as foundation stones,' 'My wish is to trace in firm lines the course of my physical career, sounding therein the motive phrases of my spiritual career, Art, Death, Intoxications, Women, the Infinite, taking them up one by one, like parts of a symphony, developing them fully, pursuing them to the limits of their flight in any direction, solos for the various voices of my many selves, with variations on certain themes for some of the instruments in my orchestra; blending, fusing, harmonizing, all voices, all instruments, all parts; the word-music of my Ego in its relations to life.' This last quotation may serve a two-fold purpose, show the aim of the MS, and the author's fanciful, redundant style. Again he says that this MS is simply a big magazine, himself the sole editor, and well nigh its sole contributor.

"The author complains not once but many times, and bitterly, of rejected contributions, of editors who acknowledge that his work has power, originality, literary merit, but allege that it is morbid, unhappy, unpleasant. Judging from this present MS, the fault may be also placed upon lack of mental training, of mental control, of order, of unity. There is beauty, as for example, in that cry of the artist in the throes of creation, or in many of the thumb-nail nature pictures, or in scattered phrases and expressions, in poetical feeling, and yet—the moods often are akin to the sensations experienced through opium or alcohol.

"On the side of actual facts, the MS is a narrative of a fatherless boyhood, of uncongenial work from the age of twelve, of literary tastes and longings, of the horrors of existence in the basement of a Boston five cent store, of the inspiration of Philip Hale's articles, of cutting loose from business, and relying on his pen, of repeated hemorrhages, journeys for health, in Texas, California, Bermuda, etc.; of the destruction of all his MSS in the fires of the San Francisco earthquake and at Helicon Hall, of the unrelenting pressure of impecuniosity, of the makeshifts of the machine fiction produced as pot boilers, of the indestructible yearning to write after his own way, of the final settlement in California, and of the farewell that sounds as if the shadow of the Faceless Stranger, Death, that has haunted the writer all his life, were near at hand. It is a pitiful, squalid record on the material side, a losing fight with disease, poverty, untoward circumstances, dissipation,— and yet there blooms the flower of the ideal, of hope, of work, to redeem, to uplift, to ennoble, to make worth while, this story of a life.

"Valuable portions, fine descriptions, poetical sketches, beautiful phrases, much prose poetry, could be disentangled from the mass in which they are embedded, and a story of great human interest, of literary quality, of psychological importance produced, but the work would amount to a thorough rewriting of the MS. It would be a task to which few editors would wish to apply themselves. The appeal to the sympathy is so great, the beauty of much of the MS is so plain, that it is with real regret that the reader condemns the MS, and with a real hope that some way may be found to utilize the MS. In its present shape, it seems impossible."

This criticism—which today I can see to have been most fair, most thorough, erring where it did err only on the side of kindness and of eagerness to recognize what was worth while in the amazing manuscript through which that poor lady (whose name I do not know) was obliged to wade—this criticism, I say, appeared to me simply as one more of the obtuse refusals of the conventional publisher, and I threw it aside disdainfully.

The fact is, I was not arrived at the point where I could see the truth regarding my work, and I rejected even such helpful criticisms as the one quoted above with the same impatience with which I bolted from publishers and editors who did, in fact, attempt to influence me toward commercial compromises.

Many indeed were these efforts of men who quite frankly regarded writing as a part of the almost universal profit-making system of the age, to have me take what they regarded as a sensible attitude.

I was at this time writing occasional contributions for a London weekly journal, *The New Age*, which that brilliant champion of the rights of the poor, that leader of the Guild revival in England, A. R. Orage, was editor—an editor who possessed much of the intuitive genius of W. E. Henley in divining and encouraging literary talent. Hilaire Belloc, H. G. Wells, Bernard Shaw, Gilbert and Cecil Chesterton; that great exponent of beautiful style, Francis Grierson (one of the true masters of modern literature), and other makers and shakers of world-thought were among Orage's band of writers. So too was Arnold Bennett, writing under the name of Jacob Tonson. His weekly column was stimulating to a degree, and I wrote to him, and we exchanged several communications. I had recently tried a novel, which was largely autobiographical in its matter; another version, in fact, of the theme I was struggling with in my book of books; and I had received a letter from a New York publisher which was so frank an example of the commercial attitude toward literature that I sent it to Bennett, knowing he would make some characteristic use of it in his inimitable column. He did so, and I take the following passage from his department in the *New Age:*

"Authentic documents are always precious to the student, and here is one which strikes me as precious beyond ordinary. It is a letter received from a well known publisher by a correspondent of mine who is a journalist:

" 'I am awfully sorry that we cannot take your novel, which is immensely clever and which interested my partner more than anything he has read in a good while. He agrees with me, however, that it has not got the qualities that make for a sale, and you know that this is the great desideratum with the publisher. Now, don't get peevish and send us nothing else. I know you have a lot of talent, and your difficulty is in applying this talent to really practical problems rather than to the more attractive products of the imagination. Get down to facts, my son, and study your market. Find out what the people like to read and then write a story along those lines. This will bring you success, for you have a talent for success. Above all things, don't follow the lead of our headstrong friend who insists upon doing exactly what you have done in this novel— namely, neglecting the practical market and working out the fanciful dictates of imagination. Remember that novel writing is as much of a business as making calico. If you write the novels that people want you are going to sell them in bales. When you have made your name and your market, then you can afford to let your imagination run riot, and then people will look at you admiringly and say: 'I don't understand this genius at all, but isn't he great?' Do you see the point? You must do this AFTER you have won your market, in the first place, by writing what folks want to buy. Sincerely yours——.'

"The writer is American. But the attitude of the average English publisher could not have been more accurately expressed than in this letter sent by one New Yorker to another. The only thing that puzzles me is why the man originally chose books instead of calico. He would have understood calico better. In my opinion, many publishers would have understood calico better than books. There are two things which a publisher ought to know about novel producers—things which do not, curiously enough, apply to calico producers and which few publishers have ever grasped. I have known publishers to go into the bankruptcy court and come out again safely and yet never grasp the significance of those two things. The first is that it is intensely stupid to ask a novelist to study the market with a view to obtaining large circulations. If he does not write to please himself—if his own taste does not naturally coincide with the taste of the million—he will never reach the million by taking thought. The Hall Caines, the Miss Corellis and the Mrs. Humphrey Wards are born, not made. It may seem odd, even to a publisher, that they write as they do write—by sheer glad instinct. But it is so. The second thing is that when a novelist has made 'his name and his market' by doing one kind of thing he can't successfully go off at a tangent and do another kind of thing. To make the largest possible amount of money out of an artist the only way is to leave him alone. When will publishers grasp this? To make the largest possible amount of money out of an imitative hack, the only way is to leave him alone. When will publishers grasp that an imitative hack knows by the grace of God forty times more about the public taste than a publishers knows?"

Yet, I could at last begin to see that although I was right in not complaisantly adopting the commercial point of view, I was not right in my reckless insistence upon an absolutely egotistical attitude. More disconcerting still, was the gathering suspicion, and more than suspicion, the growing certainty, that my work itself was not all that I cracked it up to myself as being.

William Aspenwall Bradley, who, like Bynner, in the friendly spirit of one writer trying to help another, had read my book in the interest of a publisher, gave me a leg up over this wall of blind egotism.

"The conviction has grown upon me," he wrote, "that your book contains some of the best writing you have yet done. But for that very reason it seems to me that to centre so much that is beautiful around an appeal for the particular form of social philosophy which you have adopted, while it may have personal justification, is bad art. Now, I am not descrying this or other forms of social experimentation, as you know; nor am I quarrelling with the way in which you have written the book, for I am aware that it has a very deep personal meaning for you. I am simply forced to consider the matter as an outsider, and try to ascertain through my own feeling, just how the matter would present itself to the public. I can see how, if you gave a more profound philosophical basis for the change that occurred in you, making your adhesion to your special theory merely incidental, the book would be greatly improved, without losing any of the force you wish to give it. Indeed, I remember you making a particular point of the fact that there was something deeper than this theory of yours about the power of optimistic new thought in your experiences—that you have already tried to apply its influence to your life without success—and that it was only because you had approached it in a new light that you finally found it helpful."

3. Seven Years Later

Never was there more discerning criticism and advice given to a young and unformed writer; yet he was totally unable to avail himself of the words of truth, for he could not see the truth, therefore, it could not set him free from the talons of his chimera —of indeed, a flock of chimeras, which bore him away upon wild and whirling and vertiginous courses, dashing to and fro among all the isms and illusions, all the fads and follies of the fantastic age, now drawing nigher and nigher to the abyss of the Catastrophe the ominous shadow of which was even then, though we knew it not, darkling upon the world.

But though I disregarded good advice, and ignored the truthful criticism of my book, as well as the merely commercial advice, I knew that for the time, at least, the game was up; the book was no go; and I put it away, and did not look at it again for seven years.

Seven years, you know, is a mystic period!

For now, my dear Bradley, seven years after I threw down my book, and nearly ten after you sent me your kindly letter, I not only confess that you were quite right, and that you told me the truth— which I could not recognize (the seed falling upon

stony ground indeed)—but, what is more to the purpose, so does my book confess it. That really fundamental basis for my book, the lack of which you
discerned, and which I could not supply, for I did not
know what it could be, is now at last mine to build
upon. At the time you read my screamingly egotistical *olla podrida* of autobiography, auto-psychology,
literary essay, book of adventure, book of kicking
against the pricks, I was, as you were just enough to
recognize, trying in my nakedly personal fashion to
contribute something to the great task of social re-
construction which is so absolutely necessary. But
what I could contribute of any real value, was not
so apparent. I waved so many banners, I shouted
so confused a medley of war cries—Socialism,
Vegetarianism, Anarchism, Fletcherism, New
Thought, Psychic Research, Mysticism!—that no
wonder you couldn't make head or tail of it all;
any more than the poor world could make head or
tail of the babble of contentious systems and formulas
of the rest of the literary world-makers and world-
shakers so busy among us—the Tolstois, the Nietz-
sches, the Shaws, the Ibsens, the Metchnikoffs, the
Kropotkins, the Strindbergs, the Gorkis, the Maeter-
lincks, the Gorkis, down to the Bertie Russells, and
the Norman Angells, and the Walter Lippmanns, etc.,
etc.—the would-be social saviours, the Prophets, the
Voices, the Visionaries.

And my book was the mirror of this confusion and
fantasy of mind and of life.

There was only one thing which justified its baffled
efforts—namely, the fact that it was after all bound
upon an adventure in search of truth.

So, too, the same thing is true of those greater and more adequately equipped minds and souls, whose personal testaments so bizarrely bear witness to the frightful confusion of our world as the Catastrophe approached; they too were seeking the Light.

But I was blind, utterly blind, during all those years of reckless roving as I adventured in my search after the high romance among books and among men, among ideas, and personalities, here, there and everywhere in our country, from Canada to Mexico, from Boston to San Francisco, from Whitman to Neitzsche, from Yeats and Wells to William James, from Frederick Myers and his ghosts to Wincenty Lutoslawski, and his Christian Yoga!

Yes, I was blind, utterly blind, to the fact that all Seekers, the great as well as the little, the proud and the humble, seek but one thing, and sooner or later must make a choice. . . .

The thing that we seek is God.

The choice we must make is, Shall I follow Him?

—In my little hut at the foot of Mount Carmel, as in my hut on the Massachusetts island, and as everywhere else, I was struggling with a myriad of questions, which at root resolved themselves into one or two, namely:

Is there a God?

If there is, what are my relations to Him?

Around these fundamental questions, all others gather. I can see now that from the beginning, I was committed to this deepest of all concerns, but

I did not realize that fact—my eyes were holden so I could not see; my soul was urging me onward, but my mind was not in communion with my soul, save brokenly and confusedly; wherefore, like millions of others, before my time, and in my time, and never more than in these days of War, I followed wandering, betraying lights, and fascinating shadows, through highways and byways, and over the hills of life and time, far, far away. I roamed toward vague vistas of adventure, ever opening in new directions. There was no fixed star known to me by which I might safely guide my quest.

Nevertheless, it was after all, a Quest; it was the Great Quest. It was the supreme adventure. It was the real, the only worth-while romance and high adventure of the soul. And the time for its crisis was now at hand.

CHAPTER XI

1. The Artist as Hierophant

M ANY things, however, were to happen upon my adventurous road, before the great thing of all came to pass. . . .

And as I look back upon that time of confusion, and clearly see that what I had to give the world was of no particular value, nevertheless it would be an affectation if I did not also recognize that in my persistent attempts to achieve literary self-expression I was, in my humble fashion, in *rapport* with the spirit of my age. I unconsciously sought to become one of its mediums of expression, one of the channels for its communications; a Voice of its desire; and a part, therefore, of the most powerful and predominating movement in modern art.

For, without raising the question of the relative merits or demerits of modern art (especially literary art) as compared with that of past days, surely nobody will dispute the statement that never in the history of the world have writers, purely as writers —quite apart from their positions as proponents or expounders of religious creeds, or scientific knowledge, or systems of government—ever claimed or attained such influence and power as they exercise today.

Artists have assumed, and been freely accorded by

public opinion, positions of almost dogmatical, pontifical authority in human society. They claim and are granted a right hardly short of divine to criticize all values, all institutions and all laws, and to overthrow those they condemn, and set up new ones of their own creation.

At the centre, as the animating principle, of all social and religious movements and revolutions—both those which renovate and reform and those which wreck and destroy—you will find the writer. That large and constantly growing portion of humanity which, as W. B. Yeats puts the case, "makes its soul" out of books, and music, and painting, and dancing, and drama, instead of the religions which it has cast into the dust-bin of Time, fully accepts free and individualistic Art as the revelation of the innermost truth and power of Life.

A new dynamic religion is thus being created: a religion of the mystical recognition of the power, beauty, and right-to-be-free, of human life. It claims for the artist full liberty to utter, in any form, whatever he and none other deems best to say. The creeds and regulations and organizations of society must follow and be moulded after his visions and revisions. He is at once the prophet and the only permissible priest of the high service of human progress. Therefore it greatly behooves all who are concerned in any way with bettering the race-soul (upon the betterment of which depends the improvement of all the institutions of government, law, and social service) to be keenly attentive to the voices of all authentic artists.

This, I am confident is not an over-statement of the belief in advanced and radical intellectual circles today.

2. The Chief Issue

It is, of course, obvious that humanity is standing at the gateway of some tremendous new epoch, one in which all the past struggles of all those ideas which debase or uplift mankind will be eclipsed by the gigantic scope and relentless nature of the coming conflict of opposing wills and antagonistic spiritual forces.

America will unquestionably be the greatest of all the psychic battlefields of the future, and the voices of our artists today are uttering the omens and the prophecies of the impending crisis. They formulate the watchwords and phrase the battle cries. . . . If you would know what is to be tomorrow, study the artists of today. . . .

Already, I think, it is quite clear that minor issues are being brushed aside, and that the basic principle of the warfare being waged by most modern writers who count for anything, intellectually and artistically, can be plainly discerned as a demand for absolute liberty of expression, and the overthrow of all attempts to maintain traditional and institutional forms of moral and spiritual Authority.

Ultimately, all forms of moral and spiritual authority are based upon the dogma of a personal God; who has revealed His dictates to His creatures, who are bound to follow these or meet with inevitable disaster.

Christianity is the expression, and the Catholic

Church is the organism, for the working-out of this idea, and all forms of society which claim "legitimate authority," save one (a new-comer to the hierarchy of modern ideas), derive directly or indirectly their spiritual or moral sanction from this source.

The one exception among modern forms of social organism claiming "legitimate authority" which does not derive sanction from Christianity, is Socialism, which would set up the authority not of "God," but of the "State."

This idea of the innate and sovereign power of "the State" ceases more and more to remain the mere abstraction it was for long, and tends more and more to become positively deific in the minds of ever increasing multitudes.

This deifying process is largely the work of modern artists, poets and prose prophets especially, who have breathed an energetic life into what would be only a cold mental abstraction without the fire and passion and power they have given to it.

Now, with this particular source of authority, modern non-Christian thought (with the exception of pure anarchy: but that grows constantly less active) has no quarrel, but rather a deep affinity; because both at bottom are in opposition to dogmatic religion, to Christianity.

Hence, it is day by day becoming clearer that the great task which modern art has set all its forces to accomplish, is to get rid of the power of Christianity, and to permit all that which Christian morality would prohibit or shackle—all the forces of free sensual life —to seek and find expression untrammeled save by considerations of expediency, or of a purely social,

and non-Christian, decorum. For, since Christianity
claims the power and the sanction of an Almighty
God to guide and mould human life, and asserts that
disaster follows any least slackening of its control,
modern art must of necessity wage war against
Christianity—save, of course, when modern art is
itself Christian, explicitly, or in nature, and purpose.

But modern American art has shown little Christian
character or direction. France has its Huysman, its
Brunetiere, its Paul Claudel, its Francis Jammes, its
Maurice Barres, its Paul Bourget, and many other
Christian forces; England its Newman, its Francis
Thompson, its Hilaire Belloc, its Benson, its Chester-
tons, its Martindale, its Alice Meynell, its Shane
Leslie, its Francis Grierson; but only a few and,
as yet, quite local and minor Christian artists are today ranged against the powerful brigade of English,
French, German, Jewish, Russian, and native artists
who in America wage war against the Christian ethic
—avowedly, or implicitly.

It is impossible, however, to doubt that a reaction
is near at hand, and that soon the champions of
Christ in art will step forth to face Apollo. . . . For
the inevitability of reaction, in all movements, is a
phenomenon that must be granted by all students and
champions of humanitarianism, and as the New
Paganism, which is creating the mystical religion of
the state, continues its career it is bound to face at
last the one power which dares to say to Man: "You
have a Master—a Supernatural Creator Who demands
Obedience, and Who has given to me His Authority
over you!" For such is the voice of the Catholic
Church; and, strange to say, it has ever been able

to gain poets, and other artists, to express its ancient and unchanging mind. A few of the keener-minded and far-sighted leaders of modern humanitarianism are aware of this singular recrudescence of Christian supernaturalism in American art and thought; and are calling attention to the fact that the one thing, and the only thing, which can prevent the overthrow of all forms of dogmatical, authoritative, moral conventions, habits, customs, and beliefs,—namely, the influence of the Catholic Church, is now exerting itself in a great new movement of artistic and cultural forces. In this age, the fourth centenary of Luther, it is plain to demonstration that Protestantism has failed. Only the religion of Rome has retained power. Rome alone opposes the free development and ultimate triumph of the New Paganism. Rome is the true enemy of that ascendant force in modern art which would lead humanity away from Christian ideas of good and evil in search not of a Heaven in the sky, but of the Earthly Paradise: Utopia: in other words, the fully accomplished Brotherhood of Man in the Socialist State of the World. For nothing short of that consummation of the dreams of the literary rebels of all the ages can be accepted as the ideal of the New Paganism.

—No more definite and noteworthy utterance of this ideal has been made than the confession of faith which one of the most influential and typical artist-prophets of the new dispensation, H. G. Wells, makes in the most recent of his books, as follows:—

"I conceive myself to be thinking as the world thinks, and if I find no great facts, I find a hundred little indications to reassure me that God comes.

*Even those who have neither the imagination nor the
faith to apprehend God as a reality will, I think, realize presently that the Kingdom of God over a world-
wide system of republican States is the only possible
formula under which we may hope to unify and save
mankind."*

He comes to this conclusion after studying "the
sub-surface religious movement" which he believes is
going on, a "movement entirely outside any existing
church or religious form," a movement he deems to
be a turning of the minds and hearts of ordinary men
toward God, a yearning after righteousness that prom-
ises much for the good of the world.   Mr. Wells,
after many books, and years of search and experiment
in life and art and thought, has come at last to
Religion: to the Religion of the State.

In this, he is a true prophet, a true pioneer.   His
new religion is definitely here, and the great task
which it attempts is the final overthrow of Christianity,
which it declares to have failed in the work which
it, the New Religion, will surely accomplish, namely,
the "unifying" and the "saving" of mankind.   This
is the result, says Wells, and the only possible
result, of the modern movement of revolt; of mankind's great and never-ceasing quest for life—for
more life; the life more abundant—for liberty: true
liberty, unshackled, unquestioned, and permanent—
and for happiness, real and lasting happiness—after
which all human hearts are ever searching.

And this is the great quest in which nearly all
modern writers unite, however else they may disagree.
Of course, I refer now to "serious" writers, writers
conscious of responsibility and of definite social pur-

pose. Thousands of writers work merely to supply the huge modern demand for entertainment, and for something to "pass away the time." Apart from these, there is that constantly increasing number of writers who definitely and consciously are "artists," and who consider their work to be socially important. And these writers, I repeat, nearly all concur in that dogma which Wells has so forcibly phrased, and I have quoted above.

Again, I say, it is obvious that Mr. Wells, in common with most of the more forcible and influential writers of today, has come at last, after many years of restless wandering among the systems and the formulæ invented by men, to Religion; he has returned to God, as the only possible solution of the mystery of human suffering and subjection and degradation in the world as it is today.

—And I, too, at last made that discovery, I, too, found my Religion, and it is how I did so, and with what result, that now remains to be told.

3. A Man in Search of his Soul

I have often been struck by the fact that you may (or you might until quite recently) read most modern American and English literature—novels, poetry, essays, biographies, etc., without ever being made aware that men are concerned in other matters than material, or sensual, things and interests. There is much vague talk of "spirituality," it is true, especially of late, but very little serious examination of fundamental questions dealing in a concrete way with the mystery of man. Few modern writers, until quite lately, squarely and honestly faced the queries which nearly every individual some time or other must examine, namely,—

Did I or did I not come into existence accidentally?

Am I a product of mechanical forces?

Am I mortal or immortal?

Is there conscious life for me after the happening we call death?

What is the meaning of my life?

What is the answer to the riddle of existence?

But this silence on fundamental subjects is broken. The books begin to multiply in which these questions are treated. Indeed we are now in the dawn of an epoch when these questions will give us no rest. Willy-nilly, we must face them. The soul-hunger and the soul-thirst of humanity will no longer be denied. Strange foods are offered it, and are eagerly devoured; for if the soul is cut away from its true nourishment it will turn to anything to satisfy its ineluctable cravings.

And, as I go through the records of my own blundering and febrile existence, I see that from first to last what I have been trying to tell is the story of a man wandering in search of his soul: looking everywhere for God.

But when I was writing of my earlier adventures, I did not know this palmary face, and therefore I omitted mention of many vital things which now I can see were essential to the understanding of my story, and necessary for me to consider, if I were to bring my quest to a happy ending. . . .

These facts I now propose briefly to muster together, passing rapidly through them to the conclusion of all. . . .

Among these facts, for example, were these, namely, that as a child I was baptized, and partook of the sacraments of penance, communion, and confirmation, in the Catholic Church.

Yet these facts are barely mentioned in my record; because for most of my life they seemed to me to be only most negligible, accidental facts; of which I had ceased even to think. Before I was thirteen years old, all religious interest had completely left me. My mother had been a Church of England woman, joining the Roman communion when she married my father, but never really consenting to its claims, and giving them up after her husband's death. Therefore, I was brought up at a public school instead of the parochial school, in spite of the objections of my father and the Catholic friends of the family. For a little while after my father died I went to mass and the Catechism class on Sundays, but they made only an evanescent impression upon me.

For a brief period, a month or two at most, while I was at the Catholic school, in the infirmary, nursing my broken leg, the personal influence of a kindly old priest who used to visit me every day brought about a brief phase of piety. It was, however, merely of an emotional and "literary" type. All my dreams were of living a hermit's life in the woods and putting up crosses over springs of water so that those who drank should think of the God who died for man. On my return to Halifax this streak of religious emotionalism faded away.

I liked the rites and ceremonies of the church, but

merely for artistic reasons; yet even this slight hold upon me was soon broken after I went a few times to hear an American Universalist minister who was then the sensation in "liberal" circles in Halifax.

From him, and from a very self-conscious Catholic apostate who took me to these meetings, I received the infection of the spirit of "science."

4. A Pageant of Mystagogues

It was in the air, this spirit, twenty-five years ago, almost as powerfully as it had been some years before, in the period following the work of Darwin, and Huxley, when God was dethroned.

This spirit did not really lead its victims to a serious personal study of real science, or of religion; save in a few exceptional cases. It simply communicated itself from soul to soul; all souls that were not awake and obedient to God being at once occupied by the spirit of materialistic natural "science." So far as I was concerned, I simply accepted all the easy denials of religion which were the effects of the new dispensation upon ignorant and un-educated egotists; and soon the subject of religion completely dropped out of my mind.

From my fourteenth to my thirtieth year I cannot recall feeling any, even the slightest interest or concern in the Christian religion, or in any other. Art was the only thing that mattered: art and my self.

The only bond by which I was spiritually attached to others was formed when in my first years in Boston I fell into a loose and sentimental, not a reasoned-out or firm, connection with Socialism.

But it was not until the days of Helicon Hall, when I came to share the same conviction that was animating so many modern writers, namely, that the Spirit of Life was striving to express itself through us, through the medium of art, that I consciously experienced any psychic life.

Art and self were really my gods; but still I was not satisfied; I was not at rest, and from the time of that going forth into the wilderness, led by that strange, inward drawing, which I have described, I began to take an ever-growing interest in the manifestations of the strangely powerful and singularly varied spirit of modern mysticism as it was displaying itself in America in the forms of Spiritism, New Thought, Christian Science, Mental Healing, Theosophy, Occult Science, etc., etc.

I became an omnivorous reader of the vast, fungoid literature of the subject. I attended seances and meetings. I sought out and interviewed all sorts and conditions of men and women who were leaders or followers of these movements, in New York, Massachusetts, Chicago, Los Angeles, San Francisco, Boston, and elsewhere—from men like William James to roughneck fakers like Schlatter, the "Divine Healer."

5. Ghosts in Helicon Hall

It was my sojourn at Helicon Hall that led me into the path I followed among the new cults and religious movements. That typical colony of the uneasy spirits of the place would be assembled to watch a table arisen to such heights of fantasy and widespread influence in this spiritually distracted country.

Spiritualism, which as I have said, was represented at Helicon Hall by several devotees, suddenly broke out there in a spasm of fantastic activity. Seances began in the rooms of the woman who lived in the next room to mine, and word was passed about, supposedly on the quiet, to "the right people," that there was a chance to see and hear strange things. After a while, however, there was no pretence at secrecy, and sometimes nearly the whole population of the place would be assembled to watch a table frantically galloping about, with Upton Sinclair clinging to its top, his justly famous legs waving in the air.

And there was one highly exciting night when we thought that we were about to improve upon all previously discovered or invented systems of communicating with the other world. One of our sitters was a young man who understood the Morse telegraph code, and the raps on the table all at once began to come in groups which were readable as code messages; a vast improvement over the cumbrous, ordinary methods of asking questions, and getting three raps for yes and one for no, and so forth, and so on. But the invisible telegrapher failed to come any more after two or three seances; nor did his improved method give us anything of importance from the invisible world. He was probably too progressive for the conservative forces, the reactionaries, over there, and they squelched him, or something.

It was at these seances that I first met William James. He heard about the phenomena at Helicon Hall, and came to investigate. Patiently, like a true philosopher, he sat at the table one night when we

hop**e**d to get communications befitting such a famous
man; but, alas, there were plumbers in the cellar, at
work on the boiler, and no spook had the ghost of
a show to make itself heard through the brazen
clangour of the iron pipes leading to the furnace.

6. The Polish Yogi

It was after Helicon Hall had been wiped out that
I next met the Harvard philosopher. He had published in the *American Magazine* a brief version of
his celebrated address before the American Philosophical Association concerning the hidden energies
of man, and the article had attracted national attention. He told a number of exceedingly interesting
stories of men who had accomplished extraordinary
feats of self-suggestion, or performed mighty labours,
under the influence of optimistic ideas which inspired
them with mental and spiritual and even physical
"second wind," or third and fourth wind, after breakdowns or exhaustion had apparently destroyed or im-
paired their forces. And he affirmed his belief that
in each one of us there was "a reservoir of energy,"
which each one of us might "tap," if we only willed it
so.

I asked the editor of *The American* to follow up this
article by a series of articles dealing with men and
women who had accomplished this self-energizing
process, and I was sent to Boston to talk with William
James about the matter, and collect material for
articles along that line.

William James received me most graciously. I
told him how young men throughout the country were

looking toward him for spiritual light and leading, and I shall never forget the sweet, kindly, self-deprecating manner in which he received my somewhat enthusiastic compliments. And he talked with me a long time in the simplest and heartiest fashion, walking up and down from his tall desk, at which he stood to do much of his writing, to the fireplace, and back again; interested, vigorous, kindly.

His chief "case," in the hidden energy article, he told me, was an European philosopher, an authority on Plato, who had cured himself of an extremely bad case of nervous prostration by Hindoo "yogi" methods of self-suggestion. This man happened to be in Boston at the time of my visit, and Professor James gave me a letter to him, suggesting that perhaps the full account of his remarkable experiences would give me material such as I sought.

He was lecturing, before the Lowell Institute, on Poland and its literature. His name was Wincenty Lutoslawski, a Pole, who had been a professor at the University of Cracow until the Austrian Government expelled him because of his patriotic utterances. I heard him lecture that night. Dressed in the conventional evening uniform, Lutoslawski, even so, was an extraordinary personage; a blazing temperament. Professor James, who saw me sitting by myself, and joined me for a while, told me that never in all his experience had he known Boston audiences so stirred, and so willing to betray the fact, as they had been since Lutoslawski had come to lecture them.

Next day I presented my letter, Lutoslawski received me in his room in a Cambridge boarding house. He was now dressed in some collarless, grey flannel "hygienic" garb, and his room was littered with the various kinds of nuts and "breakfast foods" on which, so he informed me, he existed; flesh foods being too gross and material for a modern mystic! He told me about his Yogi researches in India, and how he meant to form a colony of American mystics; composed of men who were willing to work with him in the investigation of occultism, somewhere in California, or Florida, where the colony would receive the benefit of the psychic force of sunshine, and the open air. And, on the spot, he invited me to join him.

But, genuinely as I was interested, I was not ready to follow this Polish Yogi into the wilderness, and Lutoslawski passed on, along his own strange trails, seeking, as I sought, the high romance. I continued to hear from him, now and then; from California, and then from Austria, and Algiers. In the last place he hoped to found a colony to study the conditions requisite for securing the birth of men and women of genius. . . .

His mission in America failed, so far as the colony was concerned. He afterwards sent me a volume written in French—he wrote his books in Polish, or English, or German, or French, with equal facility —on the Human Will; based upon his study of the American new thought movements.

7. A Chicago Occultist

Then there was the "T. K."

In a ranch house in Arizona I discovered a book called the "Great Work," written by "T. K." It was a strangely interesting and powerfully written thing,

purporting to be by a man sent to this country by a
secret centre of mystical "adepts" in India for the
purpose of instructing Americans in the methods for
developing spiritual consciousness and power according to the teachings handed down from the ancient
mystery religions of India, and perpetuated in the
"great school."

I wrote to the "T. K." He said in reply that my
letter interested him, but that if I meant to be his
pupil, the next step would need to be a personal interview. So when next I passed through Chicago, I
sought him out, and spent an evening in his company, and he told me his story—or, anyhow, part
of it.

Many years before he had been an editor in San
Francisco. He gave up journalism for the bar. In
his youth he had abandoned all religious associatons.
In manhood, his interest in religion re-awakened. He
began (as so many of these queer mystics do) with
spiritualism. Becoming convinced of its extreme
danger to those who dabbled in its necromantic
practices, he gave this up and studied other forms of
modern mysticism. One day, as he was crossing
Market Street, in San Francisco (all the singular
things that can happen take place in this romantic
city), he was tapped on the shoulder by a stranger.

"You are Mr. So and So?" this stranger asked.

"Yes."

"I have an important message for you. May I
speak to you in private?"

"Certainly. Come to my office."

He led the way to his law office. There the
man unfolded his extraordinary message. He spoke

correct English, his attire was the ordinary garb of the Occident. But, he continued, he was, nevertheless, a Hindu; and he was also the emissary, or the ambassador, of the secret college of mystical adepts which in India for untold centuries had kept the light of the ancient mystery religion burning. The time had now come, however, when the Orient was to send its message of spiritual power to the Occident, which was threatened with utter destruction because of its rank materialism. The "great school" meant to form centres in the United States. Several Americans had been under observation. My informant was one of them. It now rested with himself to say if he would proceed any further. If he desired to take up the work, he was immediately to go with his Hindu guide to a place in the Colorado mountains, where he would be given his preliminary training. Then he must go to India to complete his education in the great school itself.

This fantastic proposal was immediately accepted. My informant went to Colorado with the Hindu. He stayed alone with him in the high mountains for eighteen months. Then he went to India and for several years studied in the secret school of Hindu adepts. His special work was to learn how to express Hindu occultism in terms understandable by American readers. When it was judged that he was adequately trained, he was sent back to the United States. He was not to accept any money from anybody. He must earn his living by his own work; work quite outside the "great work." And he must attack two things, and uphold one thing. The two things he was to attack were hypnotism and the

Catholic Church, which, he declared, were the two chief expressions, and instruments, of the evil force in the universe; and which were continually in opposition to the progress of the truth, which he was to uphold; this truth being the occultism taught by the Hindu school of "adepts."

He became a druggist in Oak Park, Chicago, and thus made his living. But his real work was to teach American men and women how to develop in themselves a sort of divine relation to the occult force of the universe, so that they could travel, as he did, even to India, on "the astral plane," while their bodies quietly rested. Mystic masonry, he said, was really a part of the "great work" as taught by the Indian school, and the innermost circles of Masonry were devoted to occult researches such as the Rosicrucians of the Middle Ages, the hermetic philosophers, and other organizations of past ages, had passed on to modern times. He carried on his particular branch of the work for the most part by correspondence, and his pupils were scattered in nearly every state of the union.

—But I was still unconvinced (though to this day I feel assured that the "T. K." was starkly honest, according to his lights), and I remained undetached. All this was interesting—but for me it was not the path of attainment.

8. The Living Dead Man

Also there was "Paul Karishka," the Christian Hermetic.

I met him in Los Angeles, where the cults and occult systems fairly jostle each other in competition for public favour.

Here was a man who had been a United States Circuit Court Judge, and who at the time I met him, and for many years before, was a highly respected and successful lawyer, and a wealthy man. He was, he told me, for we had many long conversations, a native of Maine who had come west when young and grown up with the country. He, too, had been without religion, and had begun to long for religion. He, too, like the "T. K." had met a mysterious stranger from the Orient, a man, this time, from Damascus, representing a secret lodge of "Christian Hermetics." He had gone with this man to Alaska, and been instructed, amid the lonely mountains, in the mystic lore of the ancient East. Then under the pen-name of "Paul Karishka" he had written many books, novels and essays, designed to spread the doctrine of self-development of occult powers, and had taught many pupils the way to the secret of the initiates.

—This man died a few years ago. After his death the poet Elsa Barker, published books purporting to be automatic writings received by her from a "living dead man"; who was no other than my old Los Angeles acquaintance, Paul Karishka.

9. The Truth That Makes You Rich

And Burnell, who with splendid simplicity termed himself the "Truth"!

Attired in a magnificent leopard skin dressing gown, with a huge mastiff crouching at his feet, this

man, also a Los Angeles product, told me he would
not take a million dollars for his business. At his
door there would often be a line of limousines, as his
pupils, mostly women, waited their turn to learn the
"truth" at rates averaging about twenty dollars a
lesson. On Sunday nights the large room in his
house where he received the public, at one dollar each
person, would be crowded; while Burnell lectured,
and a stenographer took down his words. Carbon
copies of the lecture would sell for as high as twenty
dollars each. The following paragraph will give, I
think, a fair idea of at least the construction of these
lectures.

*"Fishes would nothing fresh but fire salt refuses
condoles the frenzy sky adventures Dionysus forces
inner revolting from but abysses roaring far visions
depths,"*—and so forth, on and on, for an hour.

His language, in other terms, was absolutely un-
intelligible; but by a species of incantation, as he
talked, and by means of some inner key of which only
his disciples have the secret, this mystical gibberish
apparently thrilled his devotees with profound and
consoling messages.

I knew a college professor who was an advanced
pupil, and who believed that he gained tremendous
personal power and mastery from his instructor. I
know of another man, a celebrated author, who became one of the best known exponents of the extreme
forms of modern art and philosophy, after being
"developed" by Burnell's "truth."

And all these were only a few of the singular
persons and cults with whom and with which I came

into contact. Since that time they have increased more and more—to say nothing about the Theosophists, and the Vedantists, with their "temples" in San Francisco and elsewhere, and the Bahaists, and the other Oriental importations; and leaving out of account the swarming and ever-multiplying forms of New Thought, and Christian Science.

10. The Temple of Vulgarity

From most of these movements of the modern spirit as expressed in the mystical cults, however, I gained nothing but disappointment.

Christian Science, for instance, had no power to move me save to disgust. As a reporter, I was present in the famous Mother Church in Boston when it was opened. As one of the pilgrims to the room where the writing table of Mrs. Eddy is kept I stood in line for an hour or so while the bell rang at intervals and the room was emptied of visitors and filled again with others. At last I reached it: the sanctum sanctorum. One glance at that plush and crimson interior: that bourgeois dream of heavenly luxury and beauty, was enough for me. It revealed the soul of that stupid and hopelessly commonplace delusion which has gained such a strong hold upon the American public simply because soul-hunger and soul-thirst are universal, and affect even the most commonplace and ordinary and negative lives. There is not a spark of real art struck forth from the stupid, otiose cults of Christian Science and the "New Thought" movements in this country. They are appallingly banal. And that fact for me was condem-

nation enough.   Unless a religion can call forth those
great reactions of the soul which manifest in true
poetry and painting and sculpture and architecture
and drama, it surely is not a real religion.

Still, I could see and freely grant that though these
multiplying mystical cults for the greater part lacked
all reality and true power, they nevertheless were
proofs of the breaking down of the materialistic
systems, and of those so-called Christian sects which
denied the supernatural elements of religion and only
accepted moral and ethical elements.   I saw that the
human soul could not rest content with such sapless
creeds.   And I could understand though I could not
share the feelings of those who turned to Christian
Science or to other forms of the multifarious mystical cults, for in them they found some satisfaction
for the imperious desire of the human soul to escape
from the limitations of the visible world, and the
world of mere intellectualism, and the world of time,
and to enter the realms of the invisible, of the spiritual, the immortal and eternal.

11. The Creed of Pantheism

My investigations were two-fold in character; first
of all, they were incited by a personal and insatiable
interest in the subject of the occult; secondly, I considered it would supply me with material for my
work.   After my studies had been under way for
some time, I received a commission to write a series
of articles, dealing with modern mysticism, to be entitled "New America," for a monthly review now ex-
tinct, *Van Vorden's Magazine*.   This task caused me

to attempt the co-ordination of my desultory researches, and to reach some definite point of view in regard to them.

This point of view I came to consider something very important indeed, for it seemed to me that nothing other than a new dispensation of the fundamental Spirit of Life was opening its beneficent reign on earth.

To me it seemed, as I wrote at the time, that we were living amid the joyous throes of a revolution of peace; a revolution of love. The age of materialism, together with all the creaking and fantastic survivals of old ignorances and out-worn habits of thought known as orthodox Christianity—were passing away, and with them would pass the miseries and the slaveries of man. "You put the case, if I may say so, in a megaphone manner," William James wrote to me; "but on the whole I think you are right."

I saw—as I put the matter—that "Love is the true God of humanity's ever-spreading religious sense; and the world is turning gladly to its radiant altar, in the light of which the ideals of the Brotherhood of Man in the Fatherhood of God are purged clean of cant and formalism, and Fear is known as the only devil—a devil that man is learning to treat as such a weak-spined demon deserves to be treated, simply by ignoring it. Love creates—Fear destroys; Love is health, happiness, light; fear is disease and the only death. From man's rapidly-developing sense of his own creative and curative power—from his sense of his own divinity as a part of divine and everlasting life—there is up-springing and flowing in all directions movements which are profoundly affecting the human race. Some of these movements are fantastic distortions of truth; some are the masks of mercenary charlatans; but the world should purge the false from the true and partake of the great good underlying all. And there comes to those who communicate with this new spirit a sense of their own progress from a vague beginning in darkness, on through merely nebulous consciousness, down to the vivid self-consciousness of the present. From being merely specks of insentient life, men and women have developed into life-consciousness; little by little, and now and then by leaps and bounds; and then they passed into self-consciousness; and now we are rapidly entering into the inheritance of the next great step forward in evolution, namely, the entrance into cosmic consciousness. Man, at last, is acquiring positive knowledge of his spiritual existence. This knowledge is coming to him not only through the use of his reasoning powers, but also through the gradual unfolding of new and supra-normal faculties. Phenomena such as are evidenced in hypnotism, clairvoyance, thought-transference, spiritism, and the like, are the outward signs of this growing inner faculty. On all sides these signs of the new times, these tidings and tokens of the unfolding and developing of the new world of sunshine, hope, strength, health, and love, are appearing and multiplying."

And—as I also wrote at that time—I hoped to be "a Voice of this new world, and a Voice of the people, telling the new tales of hope, and singing the new songs of joy, and so be one of many builders, helping to build for the people the crystal house of beauty.

"For at last (I dared to affirm) I knew what I had

long sought to know; I knew—myself; I had found myself. And in finding myself I had found the clue to all other souls, and to all the secrets of life. They merge into one secret, and this secret is that which is at the core of the new religious movements; it is joy, endless joy; strong, sure joy that mounts ever onwards and upwards, to higher regions of life. All is life; death is but the shadow of a gesture of life; a shadow seen only in the minds of men who are not yet awakened; of men still wandering in the darkness of sense illusion and of self-illusion; the illusion of the narrow, personal self which men must transcend as they rise into the consciousness of the great self that is behind, and above, and below, and before, and permeating all things.

"For those who understand the New Spirit, know that the universe is not dead matter, but a living and eternal force of which man is part; and that man's soul is immortal; that the cosmos is so ordered that all things and all events work together for the good that is to be the consummation of all things. And always the search for the higher good will proceed, onwards and ever upwards."

And, obviously enough, the search required a leader—or, rather, many leaders. Should modesty restrain me from claiming a post among them?

Nay, modesty forbid! Get thee behind me, modesty!

12. Antimonies

And at last I boiled it all down—all my adventures and researches in modern mysticism—and extracted the quintessential facts, as follows:—

First, that the force behind all the phenomena of life was a spiritual force, and not merely a material, or chemical, force.

Second, that it was a force that could be controlled and used by man.

Third, that the human will was the instrument by means of which the spiritual force of the universe could be utilized.

Fourth, that the paramount duty of those awake to these facts was to make them known to the world, for these were the truths which when known would make men free indeed.

.   .   .   .

Irrefragible, it seemed to me, were these shining and energetic truths.

But . . . but, unfortunately, there was another fact; a fact which knocked all the others, so far at least as I was concerned, into a cocked hat. This fact was the highly embarrassing circumstance that having reached the point where I had discovered that the power of my own will was the greatest of all human powers, and the key to all good, to all my desires— the key which, as William James had long ago said to me in Boston, was the master-key that unlocked the bottomless reservoir of hidden energy—I had completely lost control of my will.

I was like a man who had locked up the pearl of great price in a safe, and who had forgotten the combination.

I stood at the door of the earthly paradise, but I couldn't get in, for nobody could let me in but myself, and I had lost, or broken, or gambled away, the golden key.

I could make resolutions, but I could not keep them. I had grown quite undependable, untrustworthy; to myself, and all others. For example, there was the matter of drink. All my life from boyhood I had been in the habit of going on wild sprees; seeking and finding mad adventures in Alcoholia. To me drink was an escape; a flight from the sordid and the commonplace aspects of life. It opened a door to excitement, to drama, to romance. And I had always assumed that I could do as I pleased in this respect; that I could leave off drinking whenever I desired. But I did not so desire. And, by and by, though I did desire to stop, I could not. My pose of being the captain of my fate, the master of my soul, in this respect, as in so many others, simply could not be sustained. I was not a master; I was a slave.

As I gradually realized my situation, I made more earnest attempts than in past days to leave off; but I grew worse and worse. My orgies grew ever more ill-timed and desperate. The only concession which I would make to my new-found spiritual interests was to adopt yellow chartreuse for my favourite brew of illusion; because I had somewhere read that the formula of this wine was a monkish secret which science could not penetrate. . . .

And this sardonic antimony extended its impassable gulf between all my ideals and my actual life; between what I wished to do and be, and what I really was, and what I did.

More and more, the humiliating weight of this knowledge of real failure weighed down upon me and crushed my spirit. I was forced to see myself as one who taught, but who could not do what he taught; a living lie. And I was but one of many artists whom I knew to be like me in this respect—writers who called upon others to follow them where they themselves could not go; writers who set themselves up, as I was fain to do, to be prophetic and creative, destroying old creeds and formulating new ones, but who only substituted vain words for reality. All—all without exception—after passing through phases of ebullient exaltation and excitement, became sad or mad or bad—never, never really or permanently glad. There was nothing stable in their volatile and fantastic forms of religion and government and art. Their theories were only meant for other people to carry out. Only here and there could you find one of these modern prophets willing himself to do what he preached, save only when he preached sensual indulgence, under the title of "the larger freedom," or "the higher morality," or "liberty of life." But only now and then did a Tolstoi or a Thoreau, or a Whitman or Whitman's disciple, Edward Carpenter, attempt to carry out any theory of social or religious "reform" which would entail hardship or moral effort. As one typical modern expounder of "advanced ideas" recently stated the case in a letter to the *New York Times: "I put forward the claim that a man must not be judged upon what he is but upon what he writes."* That is the true creed of the modern artist, the modern literary "uplifter." Never mind what I do or what I am, but only what I write!

It is the utter prostitution of the sacred Word!

Well, here it was that I broke away from the art that would be religion without obeying the very first law of religion, which is sacrifice—primarily self-sacrifice.

The deification of self, in these modern times, came to its frightful climax in Nietzsche, on the day when he telegraphed to Georg Brandes: "Write for me the music of my new song! For I have found the new heaven and the new earth!" And then he was led away—poor, shattered soul!—with an asylum nurse wiping the drooling lips that had attempted to sing the psalm of the Apocalypse of Self.

Yet one may admire Nietzsche much more than his swarm of flabby disciples. He in all honesty at least attempted to achieve his own ideal. But most of the swarm of would be saviours of society and liberators of the human soul stick by the fallacious creed expressed so well in the letter I have quoted above. "Never mind what I do or what I say but only what I write."

From this creed I recanted, disgusted by the antimony so visible in myself between my ideals and my practice, and discernible also in nearly all the rest of the writers of the day.

Art was a great power; but the exaltation of Art into religion was idolatry.

Will was a tremendous force; but self-will was essentially suicidal.

What was the power beyond and above the power of art and of self-will; the final power?

What could it be, but God?

And I set my face at last towards Him, Who Is,

and Was, and Is to Be, and the supreme adventure of
the high romance led me forth from my hut among
the pines, and up the trail that led away from it—
the old trail worn by the feet of the Spanish padres
long ago—along the slope of Mount Carmel. . . .

CHAPTER XII

1. On the Road to Monterey

IT is only in looking backward that the omens and portents of the great adventure, which now was dawning, fall into any semblance of order and connection. At the time, things happened, that was all. Not until the most palpably extraordinary occurrences arrived did I give what was happening any special attention, and even then I did not see their relation to each other. But now I can discern the connecting links of cause and effect which led me to the supreme event.

It was at Carmel-by-the-Sea that Junipero Serra founded the central one of all his missions, and there he died and was buried. Though the mission still stands, Carmel is now more celebrated for the fact that it is a colony of artists, poets, fictionists, painters, and their followers, than because it was the cradle of religion in the west. . . . Rather typical, is it not? of an age when Art has endeavoured to assume more and more a consciously religious function in life. . . .

Nowadays it is only once a week that the old mission is anything more than something which tourists motor over from Del Monte to snap-shot or glance at, or which painters sketch because its historic interest appeals to them, or else because its adobe walls against the sapphire sea or the turquoise sky

271

—or the sky of pearly-grey if the ubiquitous sea-fog is about—assumes a heavenly beauty of colour that evokes from them a creative impulse. Once a week the parish priest,—very appropriately, a Spaniard,—drives from Monterey and says Mass. A handful of Catholics worship; tourists come drawn by curiosity. Then the church is locked up again for another week, except when curious visitors or pious pilgrims come.

But in the village hidden among the pines north and west, the writers are at work, and the painters are busy, and the influences of Art go forth constantly in colour, and line, and words. . . . An age, this of ours, as W. B. Yeats has written—"when we are agreed that we 'make our souls' out of some one of the great poets, of ancient times, or out of Shelley or Wordsworth, or Goethe or Balzac or Flaubert or Count Tolstoy, in the books he wrote before he became a prophet and fell into a lesser order, or out of Mr. Whistler's pictures, while we amuse ourselves, or at best make a poorer sort of soul, by listening to sermons or by doing or by not doing certain things. We write of great writers, even of writers whose beauty would once have seemed an unholy beauty, with rapt sentences like those our fathers kept for the beatitudes and mysteries of the Church; and no matter what we believe with our lips, we believe with our hearts that beautiful things, as Browning said, . . . 'Have lain burningly on the Divine Hand.' " . . .

Yes; so, for the most part, we of Carmel believed, as did we of Helicon Hall, and of those radical circles in New York where aforetime I mingled with the

spirits of my time. We would make a few changes
in the creed as proposed by Yeats; among the "soul-
makers" named by him we would admit the experts
in socialism, and "social service," and also, maybe,
nowadays, the leaders of "intellectual anarchy," and
the I.W.W.

I was in company that day, with a new acquaintance, an English music critic, a prose stylist named
Redfern Mason, who had been converted to Catholicism, he told me, by reading Dante, and by the
sight of Cardinal Newman lying in his coffin. My
friend was on his way to Monterey, to assist at Mass,
and I was accompanying him . . . Why? . . . Well,
at that time I would have been hard put to it to
answer definitely; all I can say is that I was attracted.

At Mass, I wondered at my friend, at his great devotion; yet I knew, though vaguely, that Something
was Happening; that the Mass was no empty form;
and it was an Action. But I had so long forgotten all
the little knowledge of my childhood, that I could
not understand what the Mass really meant, and really
was.

As we followed the trail through the odorous pine
woods, the day I have in mind, we talked of
"mysticism" and its relation to life and religion;
he maintaining that when it was true, it was simply
a portion of Catholic religion, and I maintaining that
it stood apart from and above all known creeds and
formal faiths. But on one thing we fully agreed,
namely, that all the signs of the times pointed to a
great revival of interest in the supernatural. The
soul of the world was weary; materialism was futile

to console or guide it; the world invisible was opening many vistas of adventure and affording glimpses to those privileged or courageous souls who boldly and persistently explored its purlieus. To my companion, many of these vistas opened perilously near the Pit, or into regions where the False Light rosily shone upon a region of illusions which hid, as a golden curtain over the mouth of a charnel house, the domains of diabolism; and I, after all, despite my contrary opinion, was forced to remember back to several episodes in my own experience which went to show that there unquestionably were grave dangers in the so-called mystical planes of thought and life. I spoke of some modern mystics of my personal acquaintance. He said: "They are false. They are merely mystagogues. But have you read the life of Sister Teresa?"

"George Moore's novel?" I asked.

"Oh, that!" he said. "No; I don't mean that."

Then he told me of a book by a young French Carmelite nun, who had died a few years before. The book had been translated into all the languages. Thousands of apparently miraculous events had followed prayers addressed to her. She had begged when dying to be allowed to return from the supernatural world to this world after death and do what good she might for us who lived here. In her own words, she had said she would "let fall a shower of roses" after her death, each rose a spiritual favour. And she had more than fulfilled her pledge; for the shower had become a torrent. It now required a monthly magazine of many pages to record the worldwide evidences of Sister Teresa's power. In prosaic

St. Louis, a Catholic newspaper each week printed
several columns of acknowledgments from people
who believed that Sister Teresa had helped them.
Some of these favours were as extraordinary as any
of the miracles recorded at Lourdes, and were as well
supported by scientific testimony. Others, of course,
were unprovable, and many were slight and possibly
negligible things; but they all afforded abundant testimony to the tremendous extent to which tens of
thousands of people believed that their invisible
friend was helping them from the unseen, supernatural world—from a "heaven" of happiness which she
had gained by following the teachings and the counsels
of Jesus Christ in His Church on earth.

I was very much interested in all this, but as my
friend had not read the book himself, only heard
about it, he could not tell me some of the things I
was most anxious to know; yet I very clearly remember the unique sort of impression which the episode
made upon me . . . Sister Teresa! . . . the very
name held something ineffably attractive. It was like
the sort of presage which you feel at times when you
pick up a new book, a glance at which assures you of a
new devotion in your literary life, but which at the
time you cannot, or do not, read at once . . . but
which you come to later on with a gusto of appreciation.

2. The Bishop

It was months later, when all remembrance of Sister Teresa had passed from conscious thought, that I
heard the name again. Once more I was in company
with Redfern Mason; but now it was in the city, in

San Francisco. He had taken me to call upon a
friend who hailed from the same city in the East
where he had lived before coming to California.
This friend was a Bishop of the Catholic Church, and
I felt very interested, curious, rather, in the prospect
of coming into contact, unofficially, away from a
church, with a Catholic prelate.

The occasion was quite exciting. I do not know
just what I expected; but my thoughts pictured vested
figures, and pomp and ceremony.

I entered, as a matter of fact, the office of a man
who impressed me as many a first-rank captain of
industry or leader in one of the professions had impressed me in my reportorial days, when I interviewed
them by the hundred. In short, he was an efficient,
practical, wide-awake personage, with obvious power,
a strong personality. He sat at a roll-top desk, in
an office, working at the business of his diocese. He
wore no robes . . . no lace . . . nothing ecclesiastical, save, of course, the Roman collar and the
pectoral cross—though that was tucked out of the
way as he worked—and the ring which my friend
kissed as he entered the room. I think I was disappointed . . . yes, I am sure I was. I think that
the plain evidences before me that a Catholic Bishop
could be a practical, keen, administrator of business
affairs, up-to-date, and just like any other big American leader of men, blew rather coldly upon my innate romanticism. I would have preferred a Bishop
more in keeping with a dramatic idea of a Bishop,
conceived by a mind still densely ignorant of Catholicism.

As for the talk that followed, I won't go into it

deeply. The Bishop, it struck me, did not seem inclined for abstract or theoretical discussion; he was warmly and humanly interested in meeting his friend, the Englishman, and in talking about mutual acquaintances, and discussing books, and writers. But my friend was bound to get me into the talk; I could see that, and with an Englishman's stubborn persistence he succeeded.

And with that ready command of the powers of attention which is a mark of men who know how to lead other men and who possess great executive ability, the Bishop gave up chatting about friends, and books, and spoke with me about my studies in mysticism. But anything less "mystical," in the usual sense in which people mistakingly confuse the mystical with the mysterious and with the "superstitional"—if I may coin a word—than this occasion, could hardly be supposed. And yet, it was truly mystical. Indeed, the moment had come when something was to happen, something of great importance.

The Bishop looked at me more attentively, and asked a few questions. He is not one of those men who take a long time to understand a situation; his apprehensions are swift and sure. He is also most frank and simple; and makes others simple also in their response to him. He soon was in possession of the essential facts of my case, that is, its spiritual facts. And then when we came to the subject of mystical literature he broke in with precisely what my friend had said in Monterey.

"Why don't you read some of the modern cases of the real mystical life?" he asked. "The modern fads and cults do not have a monopoly of the subject, you know. I'll tell you what I will do for you, some day; I'll take you to see the Prioress of our Carmelite monastery, where the mystical life is cultivated by experts, as it has been from time immemorial. She will take an interest in you because of your interest in this subject, I am sure."

"There is a Carmelite monastery in San Francisco?" I said, surprised. Two of the mystical authors whom I had read (very partially, and mostly at second-hand, through quotations and in articles about them rather than in their own works) were Saint Teresa and Saint John of the Cross. I knew that the Carmelite Order had been one of the great centres for the mystical experiment; but to hear that it was at work in San Francisco, in my own city (for I have come to consider San Francisco my own), this indeed strangely surprised me. That there were people who even today, even in the United States of America, locked themselves up for life in a monastery in order to follow the life of prayer and mystic self-immolation, somehow or other gave all my ideas an unsettling shock. Mysticism as an individual experiment, unshackled by "dogmas" and ecclesiastical restrictions and authority—mysticism as a modern "movement," as part of the revolt of humanity against all the restrictions of "dogmatic" and "mediaeval superstitions," as part of the new "spiritual science," oh, yes! that of course was all right; but "orthodox" mysticism, a mysticism considered simply as one part of a positive, final, authoritative religious system, no, that view was decidedly unacceptable.

All the same, however, I was very curious and interested. I very much wanted to see the Carmelite Prioress. I most emphatically accepted the invitation.

And the Bishop continued, after I had so expressed myself:

"I think you would be interested in two recent books which illustrate the practical results in our own day of Carmelite mysticism. They will show you that we don't regard our Saints of the Middle Ages —which you heretics so mistakenly slander—as the end of the chapter of the supernatural in the Church."

"I would be very glad to read those books," I replied. "Please tell me."

"They are the autobiographies of Sister Teresa, the Little Flower, and of Sister Elizabeth, of the Trinity, two young Carmelite nuns who recently died in France."

I stared at the Bishop, who smiled; the light of his kindly interest in his glowing eyes.

Sister Teresa; again this Sister Teresa, the Carmelite! And again the leap of a strange interior interest.

"Come back when you read them and tell me what you think about them," added the Bishop, and we arose to go.

I went that very day and bought the two books, and read them, one after the other . . . how avidly, how thirstily, it is hard indeed to describe.

.   .   .   .

Once upon a time, when I was a boy, I went to sea with my father in a sailing ship on a voyage among the West Indian isles. We were caught in a

long calm, and our water ran low, so low that at
last we were reduced to a very small amount, and by
the Captain's order were forbidden to drink more than
a very small quantity daily, not nearly enough to
satisfy our thirst in that tropical place. Then one
day the rain came, ah, such a cool and sweet and
copious rain. We loosened the ropes of the poop-
deck awning, and in the awning and in the bags
formed by lowering the sails, we caught enough water
to fill all our casks and buckets. And we drank and
drank and drank our fill.

Well! I could not indeed as yet drink my fill, but
my spiritual drought was broken by those two books,
and I drank and drank and drank out of my reading
and re-reading a refreshment and a satisfaction never
known before.

.   .   .   .

It was the book of Sister Teresa which especially
moved me. Over its pages I did what no other book
ever caused me to do in all my life before, nor any
play, nor any work of even the highest or profoundest
art—except, one, "The Hound of Heaven"—I wept.
Again and again a blinding rush of hot and stinging
tears blurred my sight and stopped my reading. . . .

The other book, the Sister Elizabeth, stirred me
not so strongly, but perhaps even more deeply.

The two books are before me now. The first consists, first of a prologue giving an account of a French
family, the head of which was a jeweller named
Martin, the son of an army officer. Failing in his
efforts as a young man to become a monk of St. Bernard, he married a young woman, Zélie Guérin, who

had also failed in efforts to become a nun. She prayed that she might become the mother of many children all of whom might enter religious life. Nine children were born. Four died in infancy. The other five, daughters all, became nuns.

The youngest of these was Thérese, or Teresa, as she is perhaps more commonly known in English-speaking countries. She became a nun at the age of fifteen, in 1888, at Liseux, and nine years later she died, September 30, 1897. Shortly before her death, at the command of her Prioress, she wrote her autobiography. This was published two years later. Edition after edition was exhausted. Translations appeared in most of the modern languages.

After the prologue, there is the autobiography itself, eleven short chapters in all; followed by reports of her sayings and counsels and a sheaf of her letters, poems, and prayers. Then comes the account of the proceedings set on foot to "beatify" this young nun, that is, to secure the official pronouncement of the authorities at Rome that Sister Teresa is entitled to the honours of sainthood in the minor degree known as "Beatification," which, if accorded, may or may not be eventually increased to the full honour of being pronounced a "Saint."

There are further sections which from our modern point of view are stranger than all the others, containing many accounts well documented in most instances, of "miracles" which have taken place since the death of Sister Teresa. There are cures of diseases (many of which had been pronounced incurable by medical science), like malignant cancer, liver complaint of thirty-five years' standing, tuberculosis, cataract on the eyes, cerebral uremia, elephantiasis, hip disease, and many other things. There are startling instances of sudden or most unexpected "conversions," sometimes accompanied by apparitions of the dead nun; or by manifestations of her presence in the form of inexplicable perfumes. There are marvellous stories of the relief of desperate cases of want. Many thousands of letters have been received at the Carmelite monastery in Liseux relating and gratefully acknowledging all manner of "favours" granted by the Heavenly power through the intercession of Sister Teresa.

The other book, the autobiography of Sister Elizabeth, was much less "sensational," but told a somewhat similar story. Its writer, Marie-Elizabeth Catez, born at Bourges in 1880, the daughter of an army officer, and moving in good society, entered the Carmelite monastery at Dijon in 1901, dying five years later. Her "life" was written and published in 1909, rapidly went through many editions, and was spread abroad in translations. Fewer and less remarkable "miracles" or favours are attributed to her power. Her book and her life invite those who understand their message and their mission to follow this great soul in her progress upward through still, internal regions of spiritual life where remarkable "happenings" have little effect one way or the other upon the soul which knows that these things do not matter when only one thing matters, which is, for the soul to find God and be transformed in Him.

Now, while I was still under the strange influence of these books, I called again to see the Bishop, and

talked them over with him.   And all at once, looking
at me with eyes full of laughter: kindly, sweet-tem-
pered, loving laughter—he said to me: "Do you know
what's the matter with you?   It's only one thing.
The Holy Ghost can't get into a soul when it is full
of that which is not holy.   You need to go to confession.   That's all.   You need to go to confession.
We can talk about 'difficulties,' intellectual enigmas,
and all the rest of it, and we won't ever get very
far; though surely I'll talk with you about such things
as much as you please.   But if you clean the windows of your soul, there won't be any difficulties.
The Holy Ghost will answer everything."

—Well!
I think even then that I knew he was right.   But
I got away from the subject and from the Bishop—
as soon as I could.   I was stricken in the most vulner-
able point of my armour of egoism.
—Confession!   To plunge my memory into the
darkness and the foulness of my life, and expose all
that to somebody else? . . . No.   No.   NO. . . .
Impossible. . . .
Yet, as I turned to the two books again the thought
would not let me go: the thought of what the Bishop
had said.   The Holy Spirit would not, could not enter
my soul, because it was not fit for Him.
How different in the case of the two Carmelite nuns.
They, like me, were writers, that is, they both possessed a certain measure of ability to express themselves in literature.   They, too, believed as I believed
that something could be done through written words to
effect what they held to be good.

Yes, but they first of all lived the words they wrote.

They were not to be judged merely by what they said or wrote, but by what they were, and what they had become, by willing it so. And, therefore, these two simple, young, innocent, worldly-ignorant girls had taken a course the exact opposite to that which I and most of the other modern writers and seekers after happiness pursue. We seek multiplicity and variety of sensuous experiences. They withdrew from them as completely as they could. We seek after the widest and most complete publicity for our opinions and our actions (save those things which in the present "bourgeois" and "conventional" state of society we do not as yet dare to make public). They withdrew from the already limited and restricted sphere of the young French woman and went into monasteries for ever. None save their own families or their associates ever even saw them again. There, in quiet and silence, they prayed and wrought without ceasing to become conscious and ever more conscious of God, to make themselves ever less and less that God might be more and more; and, after a few short years, they died and were buried in their obscure, monastery burial grounds.

And now the whole world feels their power. From their quiet graves they move great men and shape the destinies of millions of souls. For now, men and women who teach, who preach, who write books, who study science, who lead armies, who paint pictures, who make dramas, who give themselves up to be missionaries, or who labour in thousands of humbler yet none the less necessary and essential tasks, feel and acknowledge the power gained by the two young nuns who lived and died a few brief years ago in France. Whether that power is communicated simply through their own writings or the multiplying mass of things written around or because of their books or lives, or whether in all verity that power manifests more directly and immediately in spiritual communications, in prayer and miracle, one thing is indeed most obviously true, namely, that no mere "artist" or "intellectual liber-ator" of our day wields such tremendous practical power as that exerted by Sister Teresa or Sister Elizabeth.

Now, I asked myself, what is this power?

—As the fantastic end of all the fantasies of my life, am I come to the point where I think that to shut one's self up in a monastery and pray from dawn to midnight is the answer to the riddle of existence?

No. I did not think that. But what I did think concerning the nature of the power wielded by those who live such a life (and live it successfully, for there can be failure and disaster in that life as in all other forms of this adventurous and most perilous existence), was made plain to me when, shortly after my last talk with the Bishop, I went to the Carmelite monastery to see the Prioress, as the Bishop had advised.

But I did not go with the Bishop. I rather avoided him, I'm afraid, after his probing lance of a re-mark concerning confession. That remark had in-deed proven a veritable surgical stroke. It plunged into a secret yet obtrusive tumour in my soul. I knew it was there, as many a cowardly person knows

they have some obscure and alarming physical afflic-
tion but will not face the fact, diagnose the condition,
and submit to a dreadful yet absolutely essential
operation. Yes, the Bishop's remark plunged into
that tumour, and cut it open, but did not eliminate
it, simply caused it to bleed and to drain forth the
evil emanations of its corruption and its deadly
nature.

3. Sin

This aching tumour was my newly awakened and
ever-growing consciousness of the pressure of moral
guilt upon my soul. Yet I had long ago decided that
morality was a purely relative thing. Why, then,
was I suffering so?

I tried to get to the bottom of my confused and
wavering mental condition, and, so far as I can express the result of my effort, it might be summarized
as follows:

First, I am positive in my belief that I exist, a
separate, self-conscious, unique individual.

I did not create myself. That is beyond all question true.

Moreover, it is for me unthinkable that I am the
fortuitous result of accidental material forces,
chemical or mechanical.

Therefore, I must accept the belief that I was
created. A force not in any way dependent upon
myself or the world of matter in which I am living,
created me, and created the world of matter and all
other things.

Words like "Life-Force" or "Nature" or "Creative

Principle" do not fully express the nature of this Creator.

Pre-eminently am I persuaded of the Creator's Eternal Personality.

And the name of God opens up for me marvellous and unending vistas of meaning.

Hence, I *must* believe in and acknowledge a God, and that I am His creature.

Now, if God gave me life, He and no other force it is which sustains me in life, and He of course can do what He will with His own. At any moment, then, He may take my life away from me.

But this applies only to my life in this world: the life of my body; not the life of my soul; for concerning this I have the same positive belief that I have in the existence and the supreme power of Almighty God. My soul cannot die. I—the true I—am immortal.

Now, there must be a reason for everything. If there is a God, and if He made me, and made me in essence immortal, and if I find myself despite these facts living as a mortal human being who must inevitably die, there must be some good reason, some truly sufficing explanation. Also there must be some good reason for the fact that I, like most other human beings (in a greater measure than some, and in a lesser measure than the greater number), live a life of sickness and suffering and pain and trouble and disappointment. There must be some good reason for the frightful misery and degradation of the world of men today. And there must be some good reason for the fact that in me was implanted an irresistible urge toward artistic creation and expression, even as in so many other men and women.

What then, was the reason for all these perplexing things?

Of this, at least, I was certain, namely, that indeed the reason was and only could be, Good.

If there was a God—and there is a God—it followed that He must be Good.

Only in a state of madness or of self-willed Evil could any one seriously believe that the ultimate nature of the ultimate Reality could be anything else than perfect Good.

God, therefore, could not contradict Himself. He could not cause that which was evil. All that was truly good must necessarily be due to His power or permission. Impossible for a sane soul even to dream that God could cause evil or will that which was bad or injurious to His creatures! Hence, if we suffered—and if all the world suffered—and if our lives were maimed and crippled and repressed—and if indeed the best possible human life was a poor and limited thing compared to what the life of the soul could be—then there were only two possible solutions of such a mystery.

The first was that *something had happened somehow, somewhere, to man:* something for which man was absolutely responsible, and the consequences of which were disease and pain and death—consequences in which all human beings shared, even as they shared the responsibility for that something in which man had failed or transgressed.

The second, more partial answer was, that if God was good—and He is—and we nevertheless were troubled by sorrow and pain and death, then it must be that much of all this woe and darkness was not evil at all but in reality good.

In short, it was clear that there could be no evil whatsoever save one thing only, which evil thing was to repeat in any form or degree the thing which had first caused all our woe and loss, which thing, no matter what form it may have assumed, could in its essential nature have been one thing only, namely, Disobedience to God. . . .

In a word, it must be Sin.

Thus, without theological training, reading, or instruction, I arrived at the full, free acceptance of the dogma of Original Sin.

And by its light, I could see what a poor, blundering, blinded, mistaken fool I had been, and what millions of words I had wasted or misused in complaining about my bad luck, and the wretched conditions of the world which so hampered my mission to lead and mould my fellow men!

What stupidity! What vain arrogance!

For that which was really bad, truly evil, in my life, I alone was responsible, through my disobedience to God.

Sin explained all that was evil in my life.

And all other matters: trouble, pain, hardships, which could not be traced back to wilful transgressions against what I knew to be good, were, of course, not essentially evil but in themselves opportunities for good . . . they were disciplinary; they were purgative; they were illuminative; they could indeed, if I but truly willed it so, and God consented, be the means that finally would unite me to the will of God. . . . My will freely and joyfully saying: Thy will be done!

4. The Coming of the Comforter

So do my thoughts now arrange the sequence of the progress of my soul. . . .

But (I thank God again and again) He did not permit me to rest content with mental searchings and mental conviction and statement.

I tried indeed to have it so. I tried to fill up the void in my soul with reading and with dreams. I devoured "mystical" books without cessation—but nothing could keep back the flood that was coming; nothing could avert the necessity of looking into the depths of my own soul, and of then turning to God. . . . Who is the Judge: but Who is also the Good Physician; the eternal Comforter. . . .

. . . .

And now I entered a most dark valley, through which I journeyed in strange pain and desolation, before I came at last to find footing upon the lowermost slope of Mount Carmel, and saw far above and beyond me the white lightnings of the eternal sunshine gleam for a moment upon the far invitation of glorious upland vineyards, and the peaks that touched the shimmering garments of the adoring stars. . . .

—But how may I describe the valley of pain through which I journeyed?

How may I lift the veil upon the days and nights of anguish so piercing yet so welcome, so singularly bitter-sweet, in which I came to see myself not as

the proud master of life, or the unfortunate victim
of society—but as the stained and wounded wanderer
from my Father's House? . . .

. . . .

—Suffice it to say that as in all its revealing
light and purgative power, this conviction came, pain
and sorrow swept over me, and grew; and, though
at first I knew it not, the Comforter also drew near,
and nearer.

For there came a day when I became conscious
that there was a Presence in the world; a Personality
vast enough to fill all the world, and yet also dwelling
in my heart; and little by little, gently and per-
suasively, yet irresistibly, the Name of the Presence
was made known to me; the Name above all other
names; the Name of Christ.

Yes, it was Christ who sought me out,—O mystery
of ineffable condescension!—

Nor would He let me alone; this Christ Who became Man so that men might become partakers of
God; and, once I had recognized Who it was Who had
come, the rest of my journey was not long.

So silent and still and secret was His approach
to my soul that it is impossible for me now to say
when and where He just appeared.

I became aware of Him as One Who could not be
left out of the accounting by any (at least) of those
who studied mysticism even superficially.

The true mysticism exalted Him as God.

The false or mistaken or groping forms of
mysticism all claimed Him either as supreme example
of man's ability to unite with the divine, or as chief

among mystical "masters" or "adepts" or "prophets."

To be sure, I did not in those days distinguish between that which was the true mysticism and that which was false or partial or mistaken or merely groping in a mist.

How could I, lacking the true criterion?

But there was something, I think, in my artistic sense, which helped me to find my way through the dubious places in which so often I wandered. There was so much sheer nonsense in so much of this stuff; there was so much bad taste, and shoddy and pinchbeck craftsmanship in the literary handling of the material!

On the other hand, the more the writer approached the true Centre of his subject, the better his handling of it became; not necessarily in the mere technical part, but in his ability (or perhaps it is better to say, in the gift granted him) to let the Light and Life shine through, making his matter to glow and grow warm and pulsatory with the presence of Love.

I do not refer to the poets or artists who attempt mystical subjects; whose intuitions, or sympathies with mystical truths, incline them to express such high matters as Francis Thompson (for example) touches upon in his Hound of Heaven. No; for even at its highest and greatest, all literary or other artistic expression of mystical matters lacks force, the effective, real force, which is possessed by the much less beautiful or exalted expressions of *those who have gained the doctrine by living the life.*

. . . .

—For the secret of power, I recognized, consisted in personal action.

The most beautiful artistic expression of a truth had no such energy as the doing or living of the truth.

Therefore, the words of Christ have transcendent and unapproachable power because He was His words; He lived them; His life was in them, and remains in them for ever. . . . "I am the Way; the Truth; the Life," He says, not, "I write a book about the way." And the words of those who do not live, because they do not Will, what they say, are without real power.

Now, those who actively and consciously will that which is evil are few indeed—although such perverted souls there have been and there are today, especially in the region of the false mysticism—but the harm they do is frightful. They are priests of the Anti-Church, ministers of the Spirit of Denial. And they are served in turn by a host of followers, mystagogues, charlatans and deceivers, many of whom are great artists, and the leaders of intellectual modernity and of Godless science.

They are those who would identify themselves with divinity and throw down all final distinctions between good and evil.

They are the evangels of the New Paganism.

The soul-hunger of humanity must find food; and if the true food, the Living Bread, is kept from humanity it will turn perforce to the strange foods of idolatry.

—But the Grace of God—there is no other explanation—preserved me from the dangers amid which I adventured. More and more in my reading

I turned from the false lights of fantasy toward the
fixed stars and the everlasting Sun.   That is, I turned
more and more from Blake, and Swedenborg, and
Maeterlinck and Yeats, and Whitman, and Nietzsche,
and Wells, and William James, and Vedanta, and
New Thought, and Spiritualism, and Mystic
Masonry, and Mental Science, and the swarming confusion of egotistical and idolatrous voices and cults
and movements of the day, and more and more I
turned toward poets like Crashaw and Traherne and
Herbert and Thompson, and writers—especially these
latter—*who had lived the life of devotion,* the
Christian Catholic mystics: Saint Teresa, and John
of the Cross, and many, many others.

—Too many others, in fact.   Also too many
writers who were not mystics but who wrote about
mysticism.   I read too much, and prayed too little;
though I had indeed at last began consciously to pray,
petitioning (vaguely at first) the Power above all
other powers, the One Supreme and Central Light,
for help and light and strength.   And by and by
my prayers became more definite, and (thanks be to
Him) at last I turned to Christ in my prayers. . . .

—But, just the same, my life was almost as
confused, nearly as whirling and as unfixed in principle, as before.   My soul was glutted with reading;
gorged and stuffed with mystical books; but it had
assimilated little or nothing; it was in the throes of
a spiritual dyspepsia.

Only the fact that I had formed a habit of prayer,
and that my will was turned in part toward its
Object, saved me, I feel sure, from succumbing

to a fixed fantasy of the spirit, a kind of mad
pantheism in which Christ and His Holy Church
would have been merely part and parcel of a system
including all the gods and idols, all the masquerading
spirits of the abyss, all the welter of modern fads
and follies, vanities and insanities, the ecstasies of
evil, and the vertigoes of vice.

And ever more and ever more the pressure of the inward conviction of sin increased. There grew upon
me a never-lifting distress. I could not turn away
from my as yet undeclared yet positive knowledge
that all my life I had been doing wrong, and that to
commit wrong wilfully was in very truth the only
absolutely evil thing in all the world.

Confess it, then! Confess the fact, my soul tried,
and tried again and again, to tell me. I stifled the
voice. But the voice would not let me be. I plunged
into work, into reading, into dissipation; but I could
not forget; I could not escape.

Well, I said to myself, at least it can do no harm
to see this Prioress. Probably I will find that she
does not share the rather old-fashioned and "superstitional" views of the Bishop.

As for me, of course, I *cannot* accept the formal
authority and creeds and dogmas of any church;
least of all this outworn Catholic Church, with its
notorious tyranny over the mind and the soul. It
locks up individual liberty with that boasted key of
Peter; it is a huge machine that may be suitable
for the multitude, but not for thinkers or for
artists.

—For I was now ready to acknowledge the necessity for a religion that will teach morality and keep the people in touch with supernatural life. Poetry and literature and all the arts, and life itself, lose colour, vitality, and beauty when people cease to believe in the Supernatural. A purely natural scheme of things is bound inevitably to issue in miserable mediocrity in art and literature and social systems. And, no doubt, popular religious government requires a mechanism for its operation, just as popular political government does. As we progress more and more toward the future stature of the race, the necessity for the mechanisms will cease; the perfected individual will require no other authority than his own will in all his works and ways; his will no evil working because it will be good. . . . But that time is far distant from us now; that at least is a fact there can be no disputing save by utterly impracticable idealists, or, rather, impossibilists. Government is necessary, man being as he is; and authoritative religion as well. But, of course, there are circles within circles, and the restraints and the rules requisite for the great crowd do not apply to the superior souls of today who are examples of what all will be in the future and where, if not among the artists, will these emancipated spirits be found? Yes, I concluded, although religious systems are useless so far as I am concerned, still, it will be interesting to study this quaint survival of mediaevalism, and some day I will go to this Carmelite monastery. . . .

But, at last, when indeed I did go, it was not because of the reasoning given above. It was because of my hunger and my thirst, because of my incessant craving for spiritual *food and drink.* The debates and the enquiries of my mind settled nothing, and discovered nothing. It was my secret soul that was urging me forward. It was my soul that could not rest content, that could not be satisfied until it had set its face away from the shadows and the shams, the false gleams and all the illusions, toward Reality.

CHAPTER XIII

AT THE GATE OF MOUNT CARMEL

A ND so there came a day when I set out for Mount
Carmel.

It was a sombre day. It was a day of misery.
Things had happened—things too private for me to
reveal—things which had most bitterly humiliated
me, and shamed me, and cast me down.

Not only so, but in upon my storm-tossed mind and
soul there had swept a flood of pain and deepest
despondency, a flood of confused introspection, which
like some powerful solvent extracted bitter, poisonous
juice out of a mass of memories writhing and seething in the alembic of my heart, and forced it upon
my shuddering soul to drink.

All my misfortunes, failures, miserable mistakes;
my frustrated purposes; my mad adventures and
excesses; my ruined plans; my lost work; my sickness
and disappointments and defeats—all, all were there,
commingling their acrid emotions and sickening
toxins in that frightful chalice of recollection.

Such was the quintessence of my past.

What of the future? The future; ah, that I could
not face. . . .

I walked slowly through the streets, dragging my
nauseated and crippled soul, like a half-repentant
suicide dragging himself to a hospital after swallow-
ing his dose of poison, forced by his still existing

will-to-live, but wavering in spirit on the verge of that abyss where the will dies and the soul seeks destruction as a falling stone seeks the earth. . . .

The monastery was situated in the house where Robert Louis Stevenson's widow had lived after Stevenson's death in Samoa, a house in which the great romancer, I am sure, would have delighted to dwell. It was perched on the steep side of Russian Hill, overlooking San Francisco Bay toward Mount Tamalpais, with Alcatraz Island lying at the foot of the hill, reminding you of a sympathetic picture for one of Stevenson's own stories—a picture drawn by Maxfield Parrish, let us say. And this fact of the monastery being in a house so closely associated with literature possessed for me I know not what half-serious, half-fanciful meaning. I had failed to find that which I was searching after in literature—or in the roving and adventurous life I had led in even more pronounced a fashion, perhaps, than R. L. S. himself. Was my house of art, my quest for adventure, to become a house of religion, a quest after greater adventures than those of the open road, and the ways of the sea, and the deserts and cities of this passing world?

But on the afternoon when at last I dragged myself to this house, these thoughts were not in my mind; literary parallels and associations did not interest me. Nor did the unusual beauty and artistic quality of the house impress me, then, as later it most strongly did. I was far too bruised and sore and heavily laden to notice the superficial aspects of my adventure.

Passing up a short flight of stairs protected by an iron railing of peculiar beauty, I entered the door where a sign said: "Enter without knocking," and found myself in a small room with one or two book-cases, and a bell-pull hanging against the wall. I was about to ring the bell when I saw a slip of paper pinned under it saying: "Community in retreat: do not ring the bell. Leave messages and petitions at the turn."

Retreat? What was that? And "turn," what could that be? I did not know; but what I did know was that my usual bad luck had followed me to the door of Mount Carmel. I had at last dragged my-self there, ready to knock—and now I was forbidden to knock. I must go away. Would I ever try again? It was most unlikely. A mood, a day, had come in which I had experimented; but the experiment had failed; I would go away; probably not to try again. . . .

But there was a large picture of Sister Teresa on the dusky wall of the little room. And in the book-cases were a number of booklets concerning her. There was a copy of a periodical devoted to chron-icling the "favours" attributed to her intercessory power. I stopped to look these over, and wished that I could buy some of them. Then I thought: "I have come, and I am turned away; but why not leave a message?" And I drew a sheaf of news-paper "copy" paper from my pockets, and a pencil and scribbled a few words.

"To the Mother Prioress:

"I have just finished reading, at the recommenda-tion of Bishop Hanna, the books concerning 'Sister Teresa; The Little Flower of Jesus,' and 'Sister

Elizabeth: The Praise of Glory.' I am a writer, 36 years old, married with two children. I am trying to reach Jesus Christ. I am a great sinner. I was born into the Church but have fallen away during twenty years.

"Will you pray for my conversion to Christ, dear mother, asking Sisters Elizabeth and Teresa also to pray for me? Sister Teresa has brought about many conversions. Please pray that she may intercede for me. Surely God will grant her prayer."

As I folded the scrap of paper, all at once in the dark doorway that led to the interior, a nun appeared, and advanced into the room saying: "Is there anything I can do for you?" She was an out-sister, as I learned afterward. I said, I had come to see the Prioress, if it were possible. "No; the community is in retreat," the sister said; "no visitors are received." But it was permissible to buy books and these were selected. I gave a coin in payment. The nun said she must go inside for change. I gave her the note, then, asking her if she would deliver it to the Prioress. She bowed, and withdrew.

She was gone for quite some time, and when she returned, she said to me: "Reverend Mother says if you will come to the speak room, she will see you. Please come this way."

I followed her down a little dark passageway into a little dark room. She immediately left me and shut the door. In the wall, high up, a barred window admitted a dim light. There was a crucifix on the wall, a picture or two, a holy water font. Two chairs stood on the bare floor in front of a grating that reached from the ceiling to within two or three feet from the floor. Behind this grating, some two feet distant, was another grating, covered on the inside with a black curtain. And save for the passing of a cable car outside, now and then, there was no sound to break a silence that seemed not merely to be brooding in the room, like a presence, but which also seemed to emanate from the depths of the atmosphere, like a power.

Then I heard a voice: a clear-toned, energetic woman's voice out of the silence, that said:

"Praised be Jesus Christ!"

Astonished, I said nothing in reply. What could I say? This Jesus whom I had denied . . . how could I praise Him?

Then the voice went on: "Is there somebody in the room?"

I divined that the speaker was behind the black curtain, within the second screen.

"Yes," I answered, "yes, Reverend Mother."

"Oh, yes! I am so glad. I read your note. We are in retreat, you know. We don't receive visitors while we are in retreat; but I felt I must make an exception. So you have read Sister Teresa?"

I replied—I know not what—but soon my lips were unsealed, and my heart and soul, as well.

Now it is not for nothing, on the contrary there are very good reasons, why there are veils drawn between those who live in Carmel and those who live in the world. And veils of reticence are no less essential, when it is a question of discussing certain matters concerning the soul. I must draw such a veil between my readers and the remainder of the interview.

What I said and what was said to me must remain unwritten.

Only this I feel I should say, namely, that I was frank. I did not hang back. I told the invisible listener how unhappy I was, and why, and how I had been searching after God in strange places, and how Sister Teresa had led me to this place, where out of the surrounding darkness and out of the brooding depths of silence and mystery, the voice had spoken, which said: "Praised be Jesus Christ!"

By and by, I rose to go.

"You will please wait for a minute, while I give Sister Gertrude a relic of Sister Teresa for you," said the voice. "And the prayers will begin at once. We will storm Heaven for you. And you will come again?"

"I will."

And presently I was out in the street, walking homewards, the little packet of books in my hand. The out-sister had said she had placed the relic of Sister Teresa in the packet.

The sun was shining as I went along, a golden, reddish sunshine of the late afternoon. I passed a little open space of greenery, a hill-side park, walking like a man in a dream for whom, as the dream slowly fades, the distant horizon shines like silver, and secret stars drop down the sky, slowly, one by one, like big drops of violet rain.

And, just then, as I walked past the little green hill, feeling as if the golden-reddish sunshine were inside me as well as shining all about me, and upon me, there fell about me a breath from Heaven. . . . I inhaled a potent, penetrating perfume, stronger and stranger by far than rich and subtle incense, simpler by far than the odour of yerba buena or of mint or violets; sweet, most rare, and wonderful.

I remember how I lifted the bundle of books to my face, thinking, with an inward smile: "The good nuns are women still. These books have been lying too near the scent bottle or the powder box." But soon, in fact almost instantly, the perfume was gone. There was no odour, none at all, emanating from the bundle of books.

"Perhaps it was a whiff from some flower or herb in the grass of the little park," and then I thought no more about it; but walked on, trying to retain my strange new sense of the other-world, striving not to lose it, and not to find myself back again in the grey and chilly world outside that world of warmth and light and gladness. I was like a little child sent away from its first Christmas or birthday party, shutting its eyes to see again the shining things, and to hear the music.

Then I reached the door of my apartment house, down in the heart of the city, and, as I entered it, all at once, instantaneously the breath from Heaven breathed once more upon me. . . . I was in the midst of a pulsation of perfume, more exotic than the richest incense, yet simpler and more familiar than the homeliest scents that are distilled by all sweet flowers, and rare and wonderful.

Whereupon, I remembered, and I knew. I remembered that the account of Sister Teresa's manifestations are full of such instances of psychic odours. She is the Little Flower. She said just before her death: "I will let fall a shower of roses." After her death she came back to earth in vision, and said: "I will make the shower of roses a torrent." She asked God, before she died, to let her soul stay till time is over near the earth in order to do good for poor souls in this world.

And at my feet, even at mine, at the feet of the stained, broken, wandering writer, she had thrown a secret rose: a mystical rose, the rose of my desire.

—That night I wrote to the Prioress, and related the incident, saying, as I have said above, that perhaps it was only a fancy, or an illusion, the curious product of mental and spiritual excitement; but that I could not credit any such explanation, although I knew that to believe such a wonderful thing could have happened to me was perhaps the worst form of illusion. How could I dare to believe that the Little Flower would give to one exiled so far from her purity even a single inhalation of her fragrance in Heaven?

But I begged the Prioress not to cease praying for me. I implored her not to forget her promise to beg Sister Teresa to pray for me. I begged the prayers of the community. Frankly, and with no reservation of pride, I stood in the dust at the door of Carmel, a poor, a wretched, a suffering beggar. I wrote the letter with tears streaming; such tears as I had begun to know; tears that burned and tore me, yet which in their passing left me lighter and stronger, and more determined to beg harder and harder.

And even in the midst of all this disturbance, of this storm in my soul, my poor soul tried to sing, tried, as ever it tries, to find living words to express its desires. Poor were those words, and awkward and harsh the sound of them; but I remembered that on Mount Carmel there have always been poets. Saint Teresa and John of the Cross were great writers, marvellous poets, as well as seekers after sanctity. So I felt that my beggar's song at the gate of Mount Carmel would be understood, despite its wounded rhythm. They who were on the mountain would understand that, in all forms possible, I was begging my way along the road of my quest—that the follower of the high romance had put aside some of his more cumbrous garments of egotism, of spiritual pride, and was humbly asking for help. So I put this in my letter:—

TO THE CARMELITE NUNS OF SAN FRANCISCO

By the deep wells of Love they stand
 In God's most mystic garden close.
A crystal cup is in each hand,
 Sealed with the Cross that bears the Rose.
And when my thirsting soul did pray
For waters pure of life, 't was they
 Who gave one little drop—
One little drop of love and light,
Yet sweet with life, and charged with might.
 O Mother, Sisters, pray with me
 That never may my thirsting stop
Until my soul and Christ unite!

Carmel understood. From Carmel, the next day, this came to me:

AN ANSWER

A breath from Heaven hath thrilled my soul,
   And earth is fading fast away.
How faint the floods of anguish roll
   Upon the strand of yesterday!
The far horizon holds for me
A silver line of life to be.

A breath from Heaven! turn not in scorn,
   Nor say such gift I may not claim;
A Saint was in one moment born
   On Calvary's darkened hill of shame.
He turned to Christ, nor turned in vain,
To Him who for his sake was slain.

There, soul to Soul upon the Cross,
   There, eye to Eye in tears, in love—
O Blessed gain! Earth knows no loss
   Save losing Thee, O God above!
Thou art not lost, save to the heart,
That will not in Thy love have part.

A breath from Heaven! I ask no more;
   One breath is deathless life divine.
The fragrance of the farther shore
   Floats o'er this seeking soul of mine,
To bear Thy love, O Christ to me.
Today is Paradise with Thee!

It was my own inward conviction expressed for me. Why should I for an instant let my doubts obscure what had shone for me in such clear light?

I doubted no longer; in fact, I knew I had not doubted at all; I had only tried to doubt. Sister Teresa had cast at the feet of the poor beggar at the gate of Carmel, a rose of Paradise.

Now, most freely, I admit that there are natural explanations of this occurrence.

It is obvious from all that I have told you that there is much of the fanciful in my temperament. I had read Sister Teresa's book and been keenly impressed by it. I had read of a dozen instances of this supposedly supernatural phenomenon of the perfume. Then I had gone through a strenuous psychological experience. I was in the midst of it, indeed, when the perfumes came. What wonder if the suggestions implanted by my brooding, at such a favourable time for suggestions, had resulted in my jangled nerves and excited imagination conspiring to cheat my senses?

I do not say no. Perhaps this is the explanation. . . Only, you see, it is not the true explanation.

The very springs and sources of all good things, that delight us here upon earth: music and colour, and harmonious form, and fragrance, and all beautiful things whatsoever, are fixed, not in time, but in the region of the eternal. In this world, all such things are "real" enough, "objective" enough, most surely, but at the same time only evanescent symbols of the realities at which they hint. In that sphere to which the perfected soul attains, the deep wells of beauty pour forth delights and ravishments which the keenest of sense-muffled, sense-stained, sense-dulled joys are poor indeed.

Free souls, the intimates of the House of God, the undaunted sons and daughters of desire, children of the liberty of God, live among these joys, and they control the forces thereof, and, by God's consenting will, the miracles of His Saints are the operations of these forces by or through the souls of the just, for the purpose of furthering the work of God.

The "Saint": the man or woman who is granted or who attains on earth the "sanctification" of his or her soul: that is, who turns from all perversions of the powers and the proper uses of the soul—which has only one end: one permanent purpose, namely, to serve and glorify the Creator and be in fine united to Him—such a one compared to ordinary "good people," is like the great genius among commonplace, average people.

He has access to powers which are impossible to others. He does at a stroke what others could not do in centuries of labour. And, surely, his mission is also comparable to that of the artist: it is to reveal the hidden joy and beauty and power and liberty to which the soul may attain, as the artist reveals the wonder and beauty and power of controlled and harmonized sound, colour, form and thought. And these things when they are worthy and true, all the achievements and aspirations of art, are shadows and signs, evanescent and partial at their very best, of the higher and permanent things; they are forecasts of the joy of the soul when it is united to God.

Even those great poets and artists who draw the closest to the truth fall far below the plane of the saint.

The saint is the most necessary and the most practical person in the world. To fall short of the highest accomplishment, namely, the attainment of immortal life and liberty and joy, is to fail absolutely, no matter what measure of "success" one may win in any temporal and impermanent thing.

Saints are the masters and the exemplars at once of the art, the science, the rule, the way, the truth, of eternal life.

The mystics among them are the very flowers of the flock, and are of all the most necessary and practical.

God is a spirit.

He moves all things by spiritual forces.

The mystics, the saints, are the communicating mediums whereby His power, His truth, and His love are spread among men. They supplement and co-operate with the more immediate and direct agencies of grace: which are the sacraments instituted by Christ, and besides these, His free grace, given where, and when, and why, and how, He alone knows, as He alone should know.

But the saints, and mystics, being after all, eminently human, and knowing as none others know what human beings suffer and how they aspire and act and fail, accomplish, under God, work which they alone may do.

They are the power-houses of the Church. They generate spiritual force which diffuses itself throughout the world. They are closer to the hidden power of the Most High than all other souls.

Which of course is why they are so practically useful.

For God is Love, and the mystics are the lovers of God, through whom His love is spread upon earth.

It is the function of love to give itself, to communicate itself, to unite itself to all things not contrary to its nature. Therefore, God, being love, seeks without cessation to enter all souls and unite them with each other in Him, for souls are the units of the organism of love. When they are dispersed and torn asunder, there can be no complete happiness and satisfaction. They yearn toward each other always —unless they turn from love to hate and reach that awful, that unwordable point where of their own will they seek separation instead of unity, and, of their own volition, plunge into the abyss of denial and of everlasting death, the abyss of endless egotism.

God being love, it is love that flows from His daily coming in the Sacrifice of the Mass. It is by love, and through love, and because of love, that His saints are given the largest measure of the love that flows out from His sacraments. And this overflowing love, they, imitating God, dispense to others. That is their work. They are specialists in the Science of Love. They are experts in Prayer. They are the real reformers. They are the poets who live poetry, being saturated with beauty and grace. They put pleasures aside for the sake of happiness.

It is known now that just before the war there was a great flight of souls out of the ways of the world into the ways of God, not only into the cloisters, but also to live the personal effort at sanctification in the world.

There was a new outpouring of mystical literature from the presses all over the earth. There was concurrently a new quickening of religious life.

The powers of good were mounting and multiplying for the struggle with the powers of evil. Do you say, the latter, then, must be the stronger, for look at what has happened: see the desolated and shattered world, stricken by the horrors of the worst of all great wars? But in answer I say that the spiritual warfare of good against evil is a greater and more awful struggle than the one that has ravaged this world: the latter, at its worst, is but a grim and frightful pantomime, a gruesome shadow, cast from the world of spirit in which the warfare of the forces of evil against the everlasting God goes on: a warfare of which the end is certain, though not the duration. For the results of the warfare of time are impermanent, save as they conjoin with the spiritual struggle whose results are for all eternity.

And when the war is over, it will be seen by many who now do not see that religion must be recognized as the only force that can keep the world sane and endurable. Its power will be bitterly contested. Let none of us fail to remember that fact. The anti-religion of the new paganism will appeal not without tremendous glamour and apparent power to hungering and thirsting souls. But Christ must and will prevail.

. . . Of course! For, even if this world should pass utterly into the hands of that most evil one who denies God, his prize would be temporary, his victory a chimera. For to Christ belongs eternity, and nothing short of eternal success comports with the power and majesty of Jesus Christ.

As mediums for the communication of love from God to man, the ever-growing number of those who seek personal sanctification, whether in the world or the cloister or in the direct service of the church in priestly offices, or as teachers, and in all the branches of social service—in which the Church from the beginning has led the way, and will continue to lead—will inevitably increase. Such souls are the hidden centres of energy in all Christian works and movements which amount to anything.

They keep alive and active the supernatural motives without which all good works grow sapless and rigid and decadent. They invisibly join hands with the heavenly spirits who are appointed to assist humanity. And, as the Catholic Church is the centre of all true progress, the signs of the coming advance of spiritual concerns (the only concerns that are of permanent value) may be discerned in the growing up of many centres of the contemplative life throughout this country, and in the lives of many individuals who are living in the world, married or unmarried, doing this thing or that thing, whatever they are called to do, but making all things subserve the progress of the one only thing that matters, namely, the love and the service of God.

But how reluctantly self-love and pride surrender, even when they know they have been conquered! How stubbornly they hold back the soul when the door has opened to its knocking.

My pride and self-will said to me:— "Well, yes, of course, this is a perfectly charming adventure; make the most of it. You have known that mysticism was a road of romance and wonder. All your life you have sought to escape from the humdrum and the tedious and commonplace ways of ordinary life. You have discovered that the soul is not happy in a materialistic world. You know that materialistic science is a stupid blunder. There is, in all verity, a God who will reward those who seek Him out. He is the Creator of souls, and souls are immortally self-conscious and personal beings.

"And, no doubt, your soul, searching so passionately for the life and light of God, has communicated with the soul of one who has found and who possesses what you are looking for, and a gleam of the pearl of great price has shone for an instant from an interstice between the visible and the invisible worlds. But, granting all this, there really is no valid reason for you to suppose that because this particular soul happens to belong to one of the innumerable households of faith that you are necessitated to rush into that household, where you may simply chafe and rebel against all its formalism, its narrow tryanny over free and independent souls. No, no, no; read and profit and communicate with Sister Teresa, or any other Catholic mystic, living or dead; but preserve your own independence; be content as a member of the great church not made with hands in which not only Catholic Saints, but the poets and the artists and the intellectual revolutionaries are the ministers of that limitless Truth which no dogmas or creeds can ever confine."

Which argument I really for some time could not answer. Vacillating and distressed after the first glowing rush of conviction had ebbed, as all things ebb, I beat about the open door as I have seen birds beat about a window, the light of which had blinded them; only I was not blinded by the light, I was still blinded by the darkness of my own conceit.

I called on the Bishop.

He lifted his eyebrows in surprise when I told him I had visited the Carmelite Prioress.

"A very able woman," he remarked; "a member of an old and distinguished Boston family. I daresay you think it a very queer thing for a woman of cultivation and great gifts to shut herself away from society like this."

"No; I think I partly understand it," I replied.

"They are experts in prayer," he said, "They call down power for us who work."

He looked at me, smiling; his eyes full of vigorous life; sparks of colour touching the amethyst ring, the golden cross peeping from between the buttons of his black coat, the purple below his collar.

"You seem, strangely enough, to understand the work they are called to do," he said; "but you do not understand the Church of which that work is but a part."

"That is the case," I answered, "there are so many things that the Church tells me I must believe, which I can't believe."

The Bishop busily turned to his desk.

"Well, come around again some day, and tell me what your difficulties are, and we'll talk them over," said he. "Telephone, or drop in, just as you like."

This wise, enlightened Bishop! This Bishop who is a great theologian, but who knew it was not theology that troubled me; but only the sickness of sin!

A few weeks later, I called on him again.

"Sit down, sit down!" he cried. "And what's the news?"

At that time, I was connected with a daily newspaper, and the Bishop's keen interest in all that concerned the welfare of his city or nation led him to have many a talk with one who knew something of the inner workings of public affairs from viewing them as a journalist. Indeed, nothing human is without interest to him; interest and keen concern— even as is the case with the ancient Church, ancient and ever new, of which he is such a distinguished servant. For the Church knows how all things human may be made good where they are not good by one power only—not vast philosophical schemes of reform, or legislation, or by word, but by the power of goodness; and the Church is the channel for that goodness, ever flowing from God toward man, and only diverted or wasted or perverted by man's own fault. . . .

But I think the Bishop knew as soon as he glanced

at my face, that day, that I had come to talk business; for his own face grew alert and serious.

"I have come," I said, "to give in."

"But your doubts," he said. "There are things you desire to see more clearly—"

Then, in his quick impulsive manner the Bishop jumped to his feet, and made a little gesture which I'll never forget; a gesture which brushed all minor matters aside. He knew that all further talk and beating about the bush were useless, purely a waste of energy. For I no longer had any doubts. They had all gone away. Faith had come. And faith told me all and more than any theologian could do; for theology is merely the intellectual and verbal expression of faith, and therefore at best only a partial expression; because Faith holds that which is too deep and transcendent for the unaided mind to understand, or for words to say. Faith can only be fully expressed in action, in terms of life, in sanctity above all. . . .

So the Bishop brushed all idle talk aside, and he said: "My son!" And the love which his Church exists to communicate from God to man, shone from him, and was in the touch of his hand.

Next morning, I confessed. It was not, this sacrament, at all what I feared; it was not a surgical operation, but a bath of balm for my bruised and aching heart. The following morning, in the little chapel of the Carmelites, on the Feast of the Assumption of the Blessed Virgin Mary, Queen of Carmel, I communicated, and God returned to my soul. . . . Truly He is, and He rewards those who will seek Him out. . . .

1. How Faith Returned

It was long afterward, that I asked myself, How, and Why, did my doubts disappear and my Faith return?

All I can answer is, that the Carmelites, the Bishop, and other friends had been praying for me. There was, in especial, dear Katie Lynch, who for years, I know, had prayed for me, as she did—and still, God bless her, she does—for all the men, "Her boys," of the newspaper where she sits at the telephone exchange. Shall I ever forget the joy in Katie's face when I stopped at her switch-board, one day, and whispered that I was being received into the Church? And Katie was in the little Carmelite church, next morning, to be sure, and said a prayer for me. It was Katie, and the likes of her, who taught me where true religion is mostly to be found, and true mysticism,—among the poor of God, the faithful souls, who live lives of goodness; the priests, and the nuns, and the men and women you may see in the grey wan light of early morning, going to early Mass. . . . Ah, when I think of this vast net of prayer and self-sacrifice which is woven from Atlantic to Pacific, from north to south, in every town and city in our great country, this tidal ebb and flow of sacramental spiritual power, then I know what a force for good this Catholic Church is in our land of over-much materialism, of too much fret and worry about the things that do not matter. . . .

Secondly, I, too, had been praying for light. More to the purpose, I am sure that Sister Teresa and Sister Elizabeth, prayed also, on the other side of the veil.

And now that my will—which I had falsely thought to be so powerful, but which in fact had become so weak that I could keep no pledge, could maintain no determination, but on the contrary had become a prey of every mood and impulse that swept over me —now, I say, that at last my will was even feebly trying to will the will of God, it was assisted. Its impeded power (impeded because of its wounded, crippled, poisoned condition) was being supported by the purified wills of my friends on earth, and my friends in heaven. . . .

And, therefore, faith returned; first dimly, and uncertainly, then stronger and stronger, and steadier, and steadier, like the sure sun rising. And, like sun shining on ice, faith melted the frosty egotism that had congealed the inmost springs of good action in my soul; and the tides of faith now burst forth, they streamed through my being; they broke down all obstacles; they swept away the worst of the rubbish and waste and filth, and carried my soul, as on a raft of hope, over the flood and the wreck of my old life, to the shore of certitude.

Now, I am aware, that there is what would seem to many minds a very plausible explanation of this return of faith, its smouldering approach and then, as it were, its spontaneous combustion, in my soul. This explanation has been made by many of my friends, who say: "It's all quite simple. The Church had him under its influence in his childhood, and the power which moulds the child will usually prevail with the man, even if for a time he throws off the influence."

But, as a matter of fact, the only hold which the Church had upon me when I was a child was precisely of that sort which critics of the rational kind will not recognize—it was almost solely supernatural. That is to say, I did not go to a Catholic school, but received what little education I did receive in a non-religious public school. My home atmosphere was far removed from being strongly Catholic; it was only superficially Catholic. And from the age of fourteen even this slight connection with the Church was broken off. On the other hand, I did receive the sacramental seals of the Faith; I was baptized; I was confirmed; I became a communicant. So, for my part, I am satisfied, that deeper than the evanescent impressions which my mind took from the few catechism lessons and instructions given me, were the spiritual marks of the sacraments; and that the sacraments left channels, as it were, in my soul, which channels became lost beneath debris and rot, yet were nevertheless indestructible, and when the flood of faith again entered my being the debris was swept away, and the sacramental channels of grace resumed their functions. . . .

But, even as I examine and search into the mysteries of this re-birth, I know that to the mind without faith, I talk Chinese or gibberish. For without the illumination of faith (which is not credulity, though many critics of Christianity confound the two things), the mind is unable to understand and act upon the truths of religion. Faith is a mystical power which enables the mind to recognize religious truth. I do not mean that faith brings the vision of truth; for the vision of truth belongs to eternity, though certain highly privileged souls gain glimpses even in time; but faith supplies a certitude of truth, a conviction, which is a power in itself to the soul as it struggles forward upon its mission: its mission of proving itself, in this evanescent life, worthy of the life more abundant of eternity.

So, faith itself it was that taught me the truth, and showed me that Christ in all verity was God; that He had become man that we might follow Him to God; and that Christ was still with us, here upon earth, in His mystical body, the Church; into which He would have all souls incorporated, in the union of will and of faith, in the life of love—brothers all, in the Fatherhood of God. Therefore, no longer was there any question, for me, of would I or should I enter the Church. I now found myself in the Church; and that was the end of my bitter struggles. . . .

And week by week, and month by month, and year by year, thereafter, God let His light shine clear and still more clear, and I knew that faith illuminates the mind, and that only in the light of faith can truth be known. With faith, one may truly see; not all, not everything; still as in a glass darkly; yet, it is seeing, it is assuredly seeing that part by which the whole is fully believed in; and so, my mind, attempting to deal with its changed relations, and feeling it necessary to do so, though well aware that to those without faith its processes are perhaps even more unconvincing than the lyric cry of pure, instinctive faith, arranged its attitude toward the Church, as follows:

Since there is a God (I said) Who is Good; the creator of all men and of all things, and their sustaining principle, it is inconceivable for me to suppose that He would not communicate this truth to His children.

Nor would He entrust such a work of love to any other than Himself.

God alone could be the Authority for the communication of Eternal Truth.

But mortal man could never understand the divinity of God.

Humanity could not face on equal terms the absolute Spirit. If it could do so it would be equal to God; which is impossible: which to believe is to sin the sin of absolute pride: for God is the Creator of man.

Hence, God in His goodness must will to accommodate Himself to man.

How else would He do so than by becoming man Himself?

This was the turning point.

I saw, and fully acknowledged, the necessity of Jesus Christ.

He was a man; and He was also the Eternal and Omnipotent, Absolute Divine.

And, this being so, how unquestionable the fact that Christ would create and perpetuate an infallible Guide and Authority to spread His teaching and maintain it pure and permanently immutable! For He knew the nature of Man; He better than any knew the injury which had been caused by man's Fall from uprightness and truth—a fall due to Pride and Disobedience: a fall which all men go on repeating in greater or lesser degree. Left to themselves, cut loose from the restraint of obedience to lawful Authority, was it not the ineluctable tendency of human beings to set up and worship each for himself an idol made in his own likeness, or in the likeness of that Evil Spirit who became Evil by the first act of self-will and disobedience?   Hence, would Christ not set up a Church: infallible, perdurable, speaking and acting with absolute and immutable Authority?

Every fibre of my being answered, Yes.

There must be a Church established and maintained by Jesus Christ, acting with His authority, and that Church I must find.

And find it I did—the Church of my childhood: the Church of the Holy Child; the Body of Jesus Christ.

CHAPTER XIV

HOW SISTER TERESA CONFIRMED HER FAVOUR

1. I Sail Away to War

I TOLD the Bishop about Sister Teresa's gift of a rose, or rather the perfume of a rose; a mystical rose of Paradise.

"Of course," I acknowledged; "there is a perfectly reasonable case to be made out for the view that there was nothing at all supernatural in the episode, and that it was merely an instance of auto-suggestion. . . ."

The Bishop shrugged his shoulders. "Yes, of course," he said. "But supernatural things happen, you know; yes, they happen."

He was right. For such a things not only happened to me, but it happened again, in confirmation of the first visitation.

Just one year from the day when the little breath from Heaven blew across my dreary path, and made it break out in blossoming beauty, the true road of the High Romance, found at last, once again Sister Teresa manifested her interest in her brother who was wandering amid the illusions and the mists of time.

It happened in Mexico.

I had persuaded my managing editor to let me alleviate the drudgery of a reporter's task by writing art criticism. One day I came in from my rounds of the picture galleries, and was told to pack up and go aboard a warship in the harbour that was to sail in the morning for Mexico. Huerta had insulted the American flag. The United States marines were ashore at Vera Cruz. The Mexican crisis had arrived at last. It was War! Or, so we thought. . . .

I did not know any good reason why I should be going, but I soon was on my way. It was an assignment; handed out in that amazingly haphazard fashion in which so many of our big newspapers transact their affairs. I knew no Spanish. I had given no more than the most cursory attention to the messy situation in Mexico. I had no experience in naval or military matters, and knew next to nothing about international politics; but, as usual, such considerations did not get themselves reckoned with; what my paper wanted was lively reading matter; I was supposed to be a pretty good reporter—and a pretty good reporter is expected to be competent to handle any subject in the entire encyclopedia of human events.

Such a view, which is the working policy of many an influential paper, is part and parcel of the frightful fallacy which gives to private, personal judgment such devastating power in human affairs. It explains a great deal of the trouble of our reckless, ignorant, superficial modern world. It is the fallacy which permits irresponsible, ignorant, reckless, egotistical scribblers to hypnotize whole populations with their editorials, and sway them this way and that way to suit their own views or the views of their financial and political masters. It is the same philosophy which underlies the preaching and the prophetizing of modern artists and revolutionary intellectualists, only it is seen at its crude and vulgar worst in the yellow newspaper.

However, I did not indulge myself in such reflections. This, after all, was an adventure! So I bought a pair of binoculars, a fountain pen, (a leaky nuisance which I heaved overboard a few days later), khaki clothes and such like contraptions, and duly became a War Correspondent.

The thrill of it lasted for quite a time. We steamed forth from San Francisco Bay, convoyed by tugs full of motion picture operators and newspaper photographers (I did my best not to look self-conscious when the cameras clicked), outward bound to War!

The ferry boats went past, careening by the battleship on which I was stationed, tip-tilting with the weight of wildly cheering commuters, and from a press tugboat one of my fellow reporters howled at me through a megaphone: "Put a punch in your stuff, remember!   Don't forget, now, put a punch in your stuff!"   He was giving me a friendly yet warning tip; for I was rather suspiciously tainted with high-browism, I am afraid, in the opinion of my local room.

The Golden Gate opened before us; the tugs fell back; the cheering died away; the city became a vague strip of mottled colour on the shore, the land itself grew faint, and the sea received us into its silence and its peace.

But we did not heed the message of the sea.   It was only a sort of street or passageway down which we steamed on the grim business of war.   Southward we thrust steadily on through the sun-drenched, slowly rolling waters. The great ship was like a moving city of steel, rigid and trim as an office building. Sweet pure winds blew their bland breath upon us, full of mystical whispers that came across thousands of leagues of sea, from far islands of romance and the yellow countries of Khans, Sultans and Mikados. At night, in a soft, hazy, purple sky the stars were incredibly multitudinous. I had forgotten that there were so many stars.

Once, late at night, the officer on the bridge consenting, I climbed the forward mast, high up, to the armoured machine gun platform.

Seen from there, the ship that I had considered immense, like a great city of steel (we carried more than a thousand souls), and rigid like an office building, was a slender, frail, tenuous thing, and the foam-streaked black abyss of the ocean was no longer merely a street; it had become mysterious and mighty. Looking upward, the starry sky seemed close; it seemed all about us, yet also remote beyond conjecture. . . .

When I reached the deck again I avoided everybody, wishful to go to sleep with the impression of the sky fresh in my heart. But a friendly marine, doing sentry duty, stopped me with a question:

"Do you reckon we'll sure enough fight the Spiggoties this time, Mr. Reporter?"

"It looks that way," I answered.

"Gee! It's kind of queer, ain't it?"

"Why?" I asked.

"Oh, I dunno—but it's queer. I was goin' to take a job with the Forest Rangers in my home state, Idaho, and then a guy who's a friend of mine, says, 'Oh, come on—let's join the marines, and get a trip to the Philippines, or somewhere.' So we did, and now here we are, off to fight the Spiggoties. Gee, I never reckoned we'd sure enough get into any scrapping on our trip, no sirree."

"Well, how do you like it?"

"Doggone if I know yet—I ain't got nothin' against them Spiggoties, except I guess they are a mean gang, by what I hear—but if they got to be whipped, why I reckon we got to do it—but it's queer, that's what I think—it's queer."

I agreed with him. Queer it was. The whole business. Especially at night, when one had just descended from the silence above the deck, up under the quiet stars that were so irrefragibly remote, so mystically strange.

But it was not strange by day, when we could plainly see the long black torpedo boats hanging about us like some new breed of porpoise, and the huge electrical collier wallowing behind us, and the band played, and the marines were drilling, and the jackies were stowing away the supplies hurried aboard so profusely in San Francisco. Then everything was a stirring and fascinating piece of business. The busy wireless brought us scraps of ominous news from Vera Cruz, and bulletins from the flaming press of our excited land. And I studied maps of Mexico, and talked by the hour with various marine and naval officers, and sent home wireless stuff in which I hoped there was the "punch" that the reporter implored, so that my fellow citizens should not fail to be thrilled in the space between coffee and work, as they crowded into trolley cars, railroad trains and ferries, from New York to San Francisco, from Portland to Galveston.

Presently, the long, dim line of jagged coast became Mexico instead of California, with no change of appearance, except that it grew more barren. Then we sped across the hot, hazy Gulf of California and reached the mainland, and the fleet scattered its units up and down a thousand miles of torrid, steaming, sweltering coast line, with queer, little coloured towns stuck upon the edges of palm groves and blazing desert, every five hundred miles or so, and swarms of alligators crawling on the bars of the few marshy rivers, and buzzards sailing enigmatically overhead.

There for the next five months or so—each month hotter than the one before—we swashed to and fro upon the never-ceasing, liver-churning swell, from Guaymas to Acapulco, and watchfully waited, and waited watchfully, while nothing happened, nothing happened, nothing at all.

Then it grew hotter. After that it grew hotter. Presently it grew hotter. Then hotter. The men could not go ashore. They could only look at the shore and long. The staff officers, however, daily visited the town before which my ship was stationed, and I could do as I pleased—it being understood, oh, distinctly understood, that No Responsibility was incurred for me. The Admiral pointed this out. So did the Captain. The Executive Officer—as became that zealous man—renewed the compact daily.

And the sailormen grew soft, and dull, and pasty of face, and in the hot dank nights the mean, feverish

Mexican devils crawled aboard from the festering city and the hot, sickly swell, and things happened that made the Chaplain look white-lipped and drawn, and made the surgeons swear at whoever was responsible for keeping the fleet in this putrescent pickle. We buried a suicide or two, in the sea, and we shipped home by the colliers many muttering melancholiacs, and at night we languidly looked at stale motion pictures and made the band play till the men were ready to bite their mouthpieces in two.

So I went ashore a good deal, not only to escape from the stuffy, irritable atmosphere of the battleship, but also because I grew fond of that sad, wounded, beautiful, desolated little city of Mazatlan. For nearly two years the revolutionaries had been encamped about it. All its wealthier citizens had long ago gone away, leaving only those whose financial interest compelled their staying on, and, of course, the poor folk—the eternal sufferers, the dumb, the driven poor, that we have always with us. A handful of foreigners, German, British, American, French, Spanish, still lingered. Day by day the revolutionaries attacked the outposts and advanced trenches of the garrison. Anywhere from three to twenty men, women, and children were wounded or slain each day by snipers firing into town from the jungles and hills. The place was quite too strong for the revolutionaries to carry by storm, with their inadequate artillery, but they were slowly, very slowly, yet surely, starving it into surrender. The garrison, of course, maintained a grip on the bulk of the food supply, so, necessarily, the poor folk suffered the brunt of this slow torture. The death rate was frightful. Weakened by malnutrition, the people, especially the children, languidly yielded to whatever sickness cared to take the trouble of attacking such tame and tired victims. They simply lay down, rather willingly, I believe, and drowsed away into the dusky end of all.

In the shade of the dusty trees in the plazas, or in doorways and shops, amid streets scarred with rifle shots and torn by shell explosions, and dirty and malodorous as only a neglected tropical town can be, the dull-eyed, listless, emaciated men stood about in little groups, talking in low voices, or else they prowled about looking for shell-fish on the shore. One day some of them discovered the carcass of a cow, which after starving a long time, had died and been cast forth on the shore for the next tide to carry out to the fish (for the buzzards disdained it). They cut that shrunken, tough piece of skin and bones to pieces so bloodless that they left no stain where the cutting was done, and went off to their poor families, thanking God, saying earnestly: *"Dios gracias."* Now and then some of them mustered enough energy to raid a Chinese shop, looting the corn and canned goods. The frail children begged from door to door, or hunted for cactus fruit in the rocks near the beautiful carriage drive along the shore, and for the rest of my life I shall be haunted by their pleading, mournful eyes. The women also begged, also, being devout, they gathered in the churches. I used to step in to watch and wonder as they knelt before the gaudy altars, or the grotesque stations of the cross, some of them with their skinny arms stretched out in the terrific cruciform symbol; others beating upon their lean breasts, accusing themselves, no doubt—as the good, the best souls do,—of the sins which had drawn down such woe upon the land.

"They are wonderful, these people," said the Englishman who had lived in Mexico for a quarter of a century, one day when we were dining together on the curious scraps served in the hotel which catered to foreigners. "Preyed upon by adventurers and demagogues who possess not a scrap of real patriotism, but who simply tear the country apart to feast on the fragments, the greater number of the Mexican people still retain a wonderful goodness. I have watched them for twenty-five years and my admiration grows deeper. They have never been given a fair chance by their various governments; never educated properly, never really helped; yet they help each other. The poorest are marvellously charitable to each other. They are miraculously patient. In the midst of all the frightful disorders and troubles, they say, 'Well, it is the will of God.' And they wait for better days. When I read the American papers which glibly talk about the great popular revolutions in Mexico, I'm utterly disgusted. Why don't they try to get at the facts? Why don't they show that the facts are that the Mexican people are victimized by a handful of professional politicians and professional revolutionaries, more than they were by the most despotic of their former governments. Why do the people stand it? Well, all the arms are owned by the paid revolutionary fighters; and the people themselves are not united. Those of one state are more isolated from those of another state than nation is from nation, in Europe."

So, believe me, all notions which first I might

have entertained concerning the purple pomp of War, and the romantic interest of writing War news, quickly faded away. This was not a War, but a mournful misfortune, and I hoped that if our arms did go ashore they would go there not to back up the dirty game of the revolutionists, but to police the land for a time, and give the stable elements—if such there were—a chance to set up a decent government, and then withdraw.

2. The Bomb

There was little news for me to send to my paper, even though I risked my neck landing through the surf to the south of the city, and joined the headquarters of General Obregon, staying with him for some days, looking for good stuff. And I went with an agent of the United States State Department, on a hand-car on the dismantled railroad, forty miles farther south, to Rosario, and remained there a fortnight. I gathered heaps of gorgeous local colour; but mighty little news.

Yet I did witness an event which was, in its way, historical; an event which cast a queer shadow before the vast Catastrophe which was even then, though we knew it not at Mazatlan, darkling over Europe.

Attached to Obregon's forces was an aviator with an American aeroplane who almost daily made flights above the city and dropped down proclamations, calling upon the people to join the revolution. So accustomed did they become to him that they would run into the streets when he appeared and shout: " *Buenas dias, señor!*" The Federal forces possessed no anti-air-craft guns, so the aviator was never disturbed.

One morning, just after breakfast, I came upon the quarter deck, and Admiral Howard, pacing up and down his sacrosanct side of the deck, courteously called me over, and we paced up and down, chatting together. As we made a turn, we both saw the bursting black cloud of a bomb explosion arising from near the church in the main plaza of the city.

This had never happened before, and Admiral Howard, and the other naval officers who came running up to the spotting glasses, were frankly astonished; because they thought they knew the location and range of all the few guns possessed by Obregon, and they knew of none so situated that it could throw a shell to this particular spot.

None of us even thought about the aeroplane.

Yet, far over our heads, in the stainless blue sky, where a flock of buzzards soared, was the aeroplane, and from the aeroplane the bomb had been hurled, in an effort to hit a fort which we called Round Top, a hill fortress, on the seaward edge of the city. The bomb had missed the hill by half a mile, and struck in a street called the Street of the Carnival, dashing to pieces, or badly smashing up, sixteen or eighteen of the poor people of Mazatlan, mostly women and children.

This, I believe, was the first occasion a bomb was ever hurled from an airship into a city killing or maiming non-combatants.

Later in the day, we discovered what had caused this explosion, and there was an immediate council of the commanders of the various ships in Mazatlan; an Englishman, commanding a little gun-boat, a German, commanding an armoured cruiser, the *Leipzig,* afterwards sent to the bottom in the battle off the Falklands, and a Japanese captain, besides Admiral Howard.

It then came out that Mexico had not signed The Hague agreement which prevented such outrages. Nevertheless, all agreed, German, English, Japanese, American, that treaty or no treaty, such outrages must be prevented, and notice to that effect was served upon Obregon. He explained that the bomb had been meant for the fort, but promised that for the future no attempts would be made to hit a fort on the very edge of a populous city from an aeroplane a mile or so up in the air.

3. The Carmelite Church

I got to know Mazatlan rather well, and its exotic beauty is impressed upon my memory with a seal of sorrowful and tragic charm.

I discovered, in a small plaza, remote from the more prosperous quarter of the city, a little Carmelite church, a gem of simple architectural beauty, and with a really first-class statue of Saint Teresa. In this little chapel, among the humble people, I spent long hours, trying to make myself understand with practical force that if a man has friends in the other world—as I knew I had—he could only maintain that friendship on condition that he was a friend to people in this world; also, that unless the wells of mystical beauty gave the one that found them strength and courage for practical work in this material world, and for the doing of his duty, he had wandered from the true road and in a desert of shifting mirages had come to the fountains of illusion, and the oasis of vain dreams.

And I would repeat over and over again, in various words and forms, the cry my spirit had so often uttered in the wandering, passionate days of other years:

"If ever I forget my brothers and sisters who are in the dark places, and in want, and ignorance, and misery, O God punish me!"

4. Antonio's Baby

But I did not spend all my time in the golden silence and serene beauty of that Carmelite church. I made acquaintances among the Mexican people, and tried to understand them. Also, I would often go to the chief hotel, and sit down in the huge, still patio (still except when the guns of Round-Top thundered, and the shells went hurtling overhead), and talk with Louis, the German-Jew from Chicago, who managed its sadly diminished business for some absent proprietor.

Louis was very fat, and exceedingly pimpled, and suffered much from prickly heat, and the loss of business. Nevertheless, he was a philosopher who had managed to construct a system of thought by which he maintained his mental peace even in melancholy Mexico. He explained his system to me several times in the long, desultory talks we had in the dusky patio, amid the potted palms, with the stone floor moistened to keep things cool, and from time to time the whole place shaking violently as a shrapnel shell crashed over our heads from the fort.

"Each morning, when I wake up," said Louis, in his husky, fat voice, "I say to myself, I say, 'You can stick it out till bedtime.' Und at bedtime I say, 'Vell, I haf passed anoder day. Now I vill haf mine sleep again.' So der time goes by, und I should worry? My pay, it keeps on—und nod in Mexican money, either, no siree! A check goes each month to mine bank in Los Angeles, Cal. Ven I can't stick it out no longer, I vill go back—unless things get quiet here."

One day when I was talking with Louis a poor woman, young and hollow-eyed and wanly pretty, entered the patio, carrying the most emaciated little bundle of bones and rag that ever was called a baby. Antonio, the bartender, came out from behind the little bar where he concocted American mixed drinks when a rare customer would come, and joined the woman.

"Antonio's wife and baby boy," said Louis.

"What's the matter with the baby?" I asked.

"What's the matter with all der liddle children in Mazatlan?" Louis replied. "They are starving, and der weak women cannot nurse them, und der sickness comes—so they die like—like flies."

I could not stand the sight, and rose to go.

Then the impulse came.

I drew from my pocket a picture of the Little Flower.

"Translate for me, Louis," I said. "Please tell the woman that this is the picture of a Saint, who is doing much to help poor people. Tell her to put the picture under the baby's pillow—and maybe the baby will get better."

So the kindly German-Jew told the woman what I said. She grabbed the picture eagerly. She kissed it. "Ah, *Santa, Santa!*" she cried. She touched the bundle of bones and rag with the picture. Antonio, the husband, grinned sheepishly.

And I went away—and soon forgot it all. For I was concerned with an affair of my own which was deeply troubling me.

5. My Anniversary

It was drawing near the first anniversary of my visit to the Carmelite monastery, and there had come into my mind a haunting, irresistible persuasion that on that day, once more, something was going to happen—something supernatural—something of the kind that had marked the day when I first reached the foot of Mount Carmel.

I could not shake off this feeling. Yet I tried hard to do so. For I knew very well that it is wrong and dangerous to seek for or to invite or to welcome signs, omens, or wonders from the world behind the veil.

If these happen spontaneously—that is different: yet even then we must be cautious, we must refuse to be credulous and eager. For unless such things lead to good works, and improvement of moral life, and increase of faith, they lead to evil and not to good. Faith in God is the only safe guide for the questing soul. No true mystic looks for signs and wonders or strives to open the door of the soul to psychic manifestations.

There are such things as spiritual vanity and glut-

tony and selfishness, and these are most actively at
work in the cases of those who go seeking after supernatural wonders for the sake of spiritual thrills, ex-
citements, and adventures.

Here is where Catholic mysticism differs profoundly from the various so-called mystical cults of
the age.   No saint may be canonized by the Church
if the evidence in the case does not prove that the
miracles and wonders of his life produced good results, led to increased faith, and hope, and charity:
and humility, and temperance, justice, and fortitude.

By their fruits ye shall know them!   The saints
of God are good: they don't just talk about good.
They are not magicians, soothsayers, necromancers,
or sorcerers; they are seekers after God who in their
journey through this life are sometimes granted extraordinary gifts or powers or experiences in order
to confirm the power of God and of the laws of God:
laws which are not the laws of men.   God is Law,
and all that He does is lawful, and never more so
than in those manifestations of His will which
transcend the processes of nature, and are termed
miraculous.

This I knew as soon as Faith came to me; and
with all my will I essayed to put away from my mind
this thought, this presentiment, that on the anniversary
of my visit to Carmel I should once more know that
Sister Teresa was near me.   But I could not do
so. . . .

On the evening before the day I went ashore, and
found a Spanish priest at the little Carmelite church
who confessed me.   I stayed that night at the home
of an American acquaintance.   At dawn I went to

the little church, and communicated in honour of the day and all it meant to me.

After Mass I returned to the house of my acquaintance, my mind still full of the presentiment. Breakfast over, my acquaintance and I sat on the veranda of his house, chatting idly, when all at once a couple of bullets went snapping by us, followed almost instantaneously by the *crack! crack!* of the rifle shots.

Somebody had opened fire upon us from the direction of the fort. We ran behind the house as three more shots spat viciously at us.

However, that was all. There was no attack. Some soldiers, apparently, had opened fire from the distance, but did not mean to follow up the bullets. Yet it was obvious that the exposed position of the house would keep us in a dangerous state if we remained; so, by and by, we cautiously evacuated the premises, and made our way into the city. For several hours after that we were busy going about warning the members of the foreign colony of the episode, which might, we feared, be the prelude to a general attack upon Americans.

6. Another Rose From Heaven

Naturally, the bullets, and the excitement, and the menace, had driven all memory of my thoughts about Sister Teresa out of my mind.

But Sister Teresa did not forget. The bullets did not upset her plans one bit. In fact, they helped her, inasmuch as they drove my consciousness quite away from all brooding over my presentiment, and made what happened all the more objective.

For when I entered the patio of the hotel that afternoon about four o'clock, all recollection of my psychic warning, and of the meaning of the day, had vanished.

I had also forgotten all about Antonio's baby; for when the bartender rushed out into the patio as I entered, and jumped at me and grabbed my hands, wringing them violently, and pouring forth a babble of Spanish-Mexican jargon, I was utterly bewildered.

"What's the matter with him, Louis?" I asked.

The German-Jew said: "Why he's thanking you for the picture of that little Saint. His baby got vell and strong, all at once, when the picture was put under its pillow. Dot iss so. I haf seen the baby mineself. It voss going to die, and now it iss all quite vell again."

Which was exactly true. I afterward looked into the matter more closely. Sister Teresa remembered my anniversary. She did not throw me a rose from her mystical garden. There was no odour as of incense; there was no touch of the poetry of spiritual romance; there was no delectation of my personal sense of delight in the high adventures of the soul.

No.

But, through my little sister in heaven, I learned one of the primary lessons of life and love, namely, the fact that if God gives us roses, or gives us faith, or gives us gifts or powers, little or great, He does not mean us to keep them for ourselves; we must communicate them all to others.

Thus the Little Flower remembered and marked the first anniversary of my coming to Carmel.

CHAPTER XV

CONCLUSION

NEARLY five years have gone by since I found my way to Carmel. After returning from Mexico, when the Great War had cast Mexico into the shadow of newspaper oblivion, my paths of quest ran through less obviously romantic places and circumstances. The prosaic toil of daily duty claimed me more and more—that toil which in other years of the pilgrimage I had either evaded or ignored.

But, now, all life has become a romance.

Never shall I forget the exhilarating, marvellous sense of an expansion of interest, of a deepening of zest, of a lifting up, as it were, of the horizon line, which more and more was mine as I went on farther and farther in my new life. This, too, despite the fact that these latter years held keener and more afflicting misfortunes, graver and more difficult problems, harder and more bitter troubles, than any I had known before—though I had thought myself so singularly the buffet of fate, the plaything of apparently malicious circumstances. But over these matters, I drop the curtain. In the deeper sense of the word, they do not matter—yet in even a greater sense, they matter profoundly: for by them I tested this new life, this sword and armour of Faith, and I found them invulnerable.

The path of the high romance led me beyond the

valleys of illusion, and the roadside inns of the enchanters could no longer tempt me with drugged wines.

I set my face toward the real adventure, the true romance.

The coloured mists and make-believe of my previous essays in the "mystical" sufficed me not when the real thing began. Now I know that it is not what I write but what I am that matters. God forbid that I should claim that what I am is of any particular value, save to God, who loves all human souls, great and small, alike; but God Himself implants the hope that even I may so live as to merit life: that I may use my art not for art's sake, but for God's sake; and thus play a part, even if a most minor one, in the war of wills which is destined to follow the war of shot and shell. For I believe that this country, under God, will know a new birth of freedom, and that in the almost universal overthrowing of the pillars of government and society which must follow the war, government of the people, by the people, for the people, will indeed not perish from the earth but will rather kindle a new fire on the altar of the new nation of the West; a fire which so long, and so long only, as it burns first of all as an offering to God, will light and warm the hearts and homes of untold millions of human beings.

But there is a great and growing peril to be overcome, else not liberty but slavery will be our portion —a slavery more abject and degrading than any that has ever come upon us.

In our country we are face to face with the menace of paganism; a new paganism which sets up the worst of all idols—that monstrous thing, the godless "State" which in Prussia became incarnate in Kaiserism, but which in America threatens to become a bureaucracy, dominated by a plutocracy, served by a priesthood of false mystics, and glorified by an art that idolizes the senses, and drugs the soul with visions of an impossible earthly Paradise. . . .

Against this, only Christianity can hope to prevail.

Christian Democracy is the only perfect democracy, and nothing but perfect democracy will be finally accepted by men, whose kings have failed them, and whose tyrants are being overthrown, whether these tyrants wear imperial purple, or come disguised in the demagoguery of the godless press, or as an oligarchy of materialistic interests, or as self-chosen champions of mob-rule.

The spirit of Christ is the dissolvent of all tyrannies and the very life of liberty, and of the happiness which men have the right, nay, the command of God, to possess. "Follow Me, for I am the Way, the Truth, and the Life." So said Christ, the God-man, the Divine Artist, the living Poem of the Purpose of God, the Liberator of the soul, the Guide to Beauty and to Joy. And in the Prayer of Prayers He gave us the permanent platform of the only political party that can truly succeed: that great party which is made up of all those who consciously follow the standard of Christ, or who, led by His Spirit, belong to the soul if not always to the body of His Church.

Our Father:
(*Oh, words which bind all men together in a com-*

mon bond of dependence, of brotherhood, under one Creator.)

Who art—

(*Oh, everlasting affirmation of the One Reality, Thou art indeed!*)

In Heaven—

(*As St. Francis said: "In heaven, that is, in the angels and in the Saints, illuminating them with Light, for Thou art Truth, inflaming them with Love, for Thou art Love Itself." And from Heaven, through Thy Angels and Saints, Thou givest light and life and love to thy servants of all ranks and station: to poets, artists, teachers, statesmen, rulers, workmen, craftsmen, and men of business; men of the law, men of trade; tillers of the soil; fishers in the sea—but most of all to those who, like Mary, the sister of busy Martha, are content to love Thee and to look upon Thee.*)

Hallowed be Thy Name—

(*Here is the Object and the Purpose of all life and labour and art—the glory of God: for He, being God, therefore Good, hence our Lover, knows that in glorifying God man finds his true life, his real liberty, his only lasting happiness.*)

Thy Kingdom come—

(*Oh, quickly come!*)

Thy Will be done—

(*Which are the words that in all finality express the central and fundamental essential of human life, art, government, science and religion. God is. His will be done. How could it be possible for aught but good to come of that Will, which is the Will-to-Love?*)

Forgive us our trespasses as we forgive those who trespass against us. Lead us not into temptation, and deliver us from evil. Amen.

The Colophon

I have many good friends, I know, to whom I appear a turn-coat to great causes: the causes of "progress," "enlightenment," "humanity," to which I was once so passionately devoted. They cannot understand my "reactionary step." But they believe the reasons for my action to be rooted in what they feel to be an excess of emotionalism in my temperament, combined with a strain of atavistic romanticism. . . . The odour and the misty coils of incense fuming before the candle-lighted altar, the ritualistic beauty of sacerdotal ceremonies, the glamorous enchantment of occult interests, these, together with music, and, no doubt, the relief which adhesion to fixed points of conduct and belief gave to a nature unfitted for the cold, hard, steady labour of intellectual and moral pursuits, explain to their minds my surprising and saddening act. . . . Well, possibly, nay, probably, my own explanation will leave these friends unconvinced; nevertheless I take the chance. I owe it to myself as well as to these friends to give my own account of the matter.

I fear I am indeed almost fanatical in my devotion to art, and that my cravings for its manifestations are almost too intense—but as for finding Catholicism a luxurious revel of aestheticism and romanticism— Ah, but no! It is true that there is great art in the Church; but it does not show itself in any marked degree at present in these modern times, certainly not in the United States. It will come by and by, yes, but now there is little or none. Our church music generally is atrocious; no condemnation can be too strong. Our architecture is not much better. Our statues and our pictures, and our books and our periodical press (save for a few and now happily increasing number of writers and journals) are frightfully banal. The level of culture and art, at present, is deplorably low. If I had joined the Catholic Church for the sake of satisfying my aesthetic desires, no mistake of my life would have been greater. . . .

But I joined it to satisfy the hunger of my soul for God. For I would rather, a hundred million times over, be the crudest, most ignorant, humblest man who ever came out of Catholic France or Ireland, or Poland, or Silesia; I would rather be an African jungle dweller, or a Digger Indian, and have true Catholic faith than to be the greatest and most cultured artist in the world, and devoid of faith.

For it is by faith that we live the only life worth while, the life of the true romance.

And God who is no niggard with His bounty added to His gift of faith two minor yet great favours, by means of which it was more practicable for me to make my faith work, in the pragmatic sense of the word—that is, to render it in terms of art, and terms of life. Faith's deeper and truest work has little direct relation, oftentimes, to outward and visible results; but for me the exterior results were permitted.

For on the day when I knelt before His altar, on the feast day of Mary, Queen of Carmel, God took away from me, instantly, and fully, all temptation to fall into that degrading and crippling vice to which I have been obliged to refer too often for my own comfort—I mean, the evil habit of drinking to excess. It was banished; it never returned. What my own will could not do, God's will accomplished.

Also, He restored me to health; He gave me back my energy and bodily strength.

Therefore, when there came another day upon which I once more knelt before God's altar, and was admitted to membership in the Third Order of Most Holy Mary of Mount Carmel, I assumed—in accordance with the ancient custom—a title, and became Michael of the Will of God. For now I knew that indeed the will of man is a greater and vaster and more awful force than I had ever dreamed of it being in the days of my most exalted self-deification. I also realized that there is only one employment worthy of such a power, namely, to work the will of God. Far be it from me to dare to affirm that I have succeeded—or that I may ever wholly succeed—in this great work; but I know that this work is the only thing which is commensurate with man's dignity, and his imperial destiny, and I know that it is the high secret of the Holy Grail, the Cup of Quest—that Grail which I sought all my life, and which all men seek in their hearts, and which so long baffled my search, but which in a million places throughout the world, every minute of the day and night, is held up, shining and marvellous, in the plain sight of all men, while the appointed Servant of the Sacrifice says above it:

"O God, who in creating human nature, didst wonderfully dignify it, and hast still more wonderfully renewed it; grant that, by the mystery of this water and wine, we may be made partakers of his divinity who vouchsafed to become partaker of our humanity."

So I came back from far places to my poor, shattered Book. Returning to the hut in the pine wood of Carmel, for a space, I put together the fragments of all I had written—such a huge mass!—during some twenty years. I left out a great deal. There were certain chapters and episodes which made literary capital of what, later on, I dealt with in the only right way: in the confessional—and all such morbidities I threw into the fire, where they belonged. Into the same clean purging flame, also, went heaps of similar stuff; all the tortuous efforts to express my baffled questing; the huge, crazy novel written during that frenetic period in New York when I shut myself up in my garret; the self-willed rules of life which I could not follow; the creeds and confessions. So I burned my bridges, my dangerous and fantastic bridges. And because I had learned that not shouting from the housetops, but silence, and reticence, were the true friends of the soul, I considered whether I should not let this book also perish; but because my story has such a happy ending, I kept it from the fire, and I send it forth as an act of faith.

And now, as the colophon to my story, I wish and pray for all who may be good and patient enough to

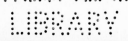

read my words, success in their own adventures, the gaining of the quest of their high romance, and joy and peace at the end of all, the joy of Jesus Christ.

THE END

PRINTED IN THE UNITED STATES OF AMERICA

THE following pages contain advertisements of a few of the Macmillan novels.

The Tree of Heaven

By MAY SINCLAIR

Cloth, $1.60

" Thoughtful, dramatic, vivid, always well and at times beautifully written, full of real people skilfully analyzed and presented, 'The Tree of Heaven' is one of the few great books which have as yet come out of the war."— *New York Times.*

" Miss Sinclair's genius consists in being able to combine great art with a popular story-telling gift. All her detail, the many little miracles of observation and understanding, are not dead nor catalogued, but are merged into the living body of her continuously interesting narrative."— *New York Globe.*

" Genius illumines every page of one of the most impressive works of fiction of today. It is a novel of extraordinary power and worth ranking assuredly among the novels of our time which will make a lasting mark on literature and upon human thought and life."— *New York Tribune.*

" Miss Sinclair has written nothing that so perfectly represents the chaotic spirit of England during the past twenty years. The story contains much of matters that have nothing to do with the war and in all of them she has portrayed the English character to the life."— *Boston Transcript.*

" The Book of the day is 'The Tree of Heaven.' It is a war novel — a gripping one. The story does not take us out of England except in a few letters written from the battlefields towards the close of the book, but it shows powerfully the effect of war on England, as represented by a typical group of people, a most loveable family, and their varied connections and friends."— *Philadelphia Telegraph.*

" Stands out at once, and emphatically, from the common run of books because it is a work of art. . . . A work of sheer artistry, well worth the doing, and done at the full strength and compass of skilled workmanship, it ranks fairly among the best work of its kind in modern fiction; among the very best."— *New York Sun.*

THE MACMILLAN COMPANY
Publishers   64–66 Fifth Avenue   New York

First the Blade:
A Comedy of Growth

By CLEMENCE DANE

Author of " Regiment of Women."

Cloth, 12mo.

With the publication of " Regiment of Women " Miss Dane at once took her place among the modern novelists who are doing important and interesting work. The publication of this new story is sure to confirm the favorable impression which her first work made. It may be described as the story of two young people in love and their development under the influence of their emotions. " A Comedy Of Growth," the author calls it, and the sub-title is completely realized. It is comedy in the true Meredithian sense. There is genuine suspense in watching the actual growth of two persons who are extraordinarily alive. It is doubtful if more unusual characters have appeared in recent fiction, than these two central figures of Miss Dane's. The minor characters, too, are no less surely drawn.

THE MACMILLAN COMPANY
Publishers   64–66 Fifth Avenue   New York

Flood Tide

By DANIEL CHASE

With Frontispiece.

Decorated cloth, 12mo.

Mr. Chase's leading character is a man, essentially a student and dreamer, who is forced by circumstances into a business career. The story of his success, of the price which he pays for it and of the way in which he ultimately achieves the happiness which eluded him for so long, makes very interesting reading. The spirit of the sea broods over the entire narrative, adding much to its charm. The lad's boyhood in a New England coast town is most convincingly portrayed; later his poignant melancholy in the midst of material success in the city, and his loneliness of spirit are handled with vividness and insight. The tale is one not soon forgotten.

———

THE MACMILLAN COMPANY
Publishers   64–66 Fifth Avenue   New York

The Flying Teuton

By ALICE BROWN

Author of " The Prisoner," "Bromley Neighborhood,"
etc. With Frontispiece.

Cloth, 12mo.

Miss Brown has long been known as one of the fore-
most American writers of short stories. In this book
new proof is given of her skill and versatility. From
the initial tale — a truly remarkable work looking into
the future and picturing some of the after-effects of the
great war — to the last piece in the collection, it shows
the skilled literary workmanship, the thorough understanding of character and the sure dramatic instinct which
readers have come to expect of the author of " The
Prisoner " and " Bromley Neighborhood."

THE MACMILLAN COMPANY
Publishers   64–66 Fifth Avenue   New York